Sikh Spiritual Practice

The Sound Way to God

First published by O Books, 2010
O Books is an imprint of John Hunt Publishing Ltd., The Bothy, Deershot Lodge, Park Lane, Ropley,
Hants, SO24 0BE, UK
office1@o-books.net
www.o-books.net

Distribution in:

UK and Europe
Orca Book Services
orders@orcabookservices.co.uk
Tel: 01202 665432 Fax: 01202 666219
Int. code (44)

USA and Canada
NBN
custserv@nbnbooks.com
Tel: 1 800 462 6420 Fax: 1 800 338 4550

Australia and New Zealand
Brumby Books
sales@brumbybooks.com.au
Tel: 61 3 9761 5535 Fax: 61 3 9761 7095

Far East (offices in Singapore, Thailand,
Hong Kong, Taiwan)
Pansing Distribution Pte Ltd
kemal@pansing.com
Tel: 65 6319 9939 Fax: 65 6462 5761

South Africa
Stephan Phillips (pty) Ltd
Email: orders@stephanphillips.com
Tel: 27 21 4489839 Telefax: 27 21 4479879

Text copyright Siri Kirpal Kaur Khalsa 2008

Design: Stuart Davies

ISBN: 978 1 84694 289 1

A CIP catalogue record for this book is available
from the British Library.

Printed by Digital Book Print

O Books operates a distinctive and ethical publishing philosophy in
all areas of its business, from its global network of authors to
production and worldwide distribution.

Sikh Spiritual Practice

The Sound Way to God

Siri Kirpal Kaur Khalsa

BOOKS

Winchester, UK
Washington, USA

CONTENTS

Dedicated to the Spirit
of
Worldwide Religious Tolerance

A Note about Spelling

Gurmukhi (Sikh script) is nothing like English script, so spellings vary widely. For this book, I have commonly used spellings I'm most familiar with, except for the chants, where I have used specific transliterations. In some cases I use two spellings. The most obvious example of this is *Waheguru* and *Waa Hay Guroo*, two spellings for our most common and ecstatic Word for God. *Waheguru* is the more common spelling, and the one I use most. But since *Waa Hay Guroo* is a closer transliteration, I generally use it when describing Sikh chanting.

Part I

In the Beginning:

Introducing the Sikh Path

Walk even one step towards the Feet of the Guru,
And the True Guru will walk millions of steps to welcome you.
Bhai Gurdaas 1

Chapter 1

Introduction

What's a Sikh?

The Guru is an ocean filled with pearls.
Guru Nanak [1]

If you were with me when I'm out and about, you might notice complete strangers come up and ask me questions. They might ask me where I'm from or what religion I belong to. They ask me these things because I wear a turban and stand out in an average crowd. When people learn that I'm a *Sikh*, they may ask what a Sikh is or what Sikhs believe. Sometimes, when they learn that I wasn't born a Sikh (at least, not that my parents knew!), they ask how and why I became one. Even some people who were born Sikhs ask similar questions.

So this book is my extended answer to these questions, both to people who were born Sikhs and to people who have only just learned that Sikhs exist. But unlike most books on Sikhism that are primarily histories or translations or dry academic texts, this book is a highly personal, but thorough, look at Sikh spiritual practice, because the ultimate answer to *why* I became a Sikh lies in the superb value of the Sikh path (or *Sikh Dharma*) as a spiritual discipline.

But there are couple of caveats before we begin:

First, bear in mind that I am a Westerner, and most Sikhs even now hail originally from the Punjab, wherever they may currently live. I am writing about Sikhism as I know it. Therefore you will find very little about *Punjabi* culture in this book. So, if it didn't make the transition to the West, if Western Sikhs don't

2

practice it, you probably won't hear much about it in this book.

Second, some Sikhs, who have no problem with certain customs that have no place in Sikhism (like caste), may be shocked that a book on Sikhism contains so much yoga. Well, *yoga* means *union*—specifically union with the Infinite. As you'll see, yoga is the ultimate foundation of Sikh spiritual practice. (More on the relationship between Sikh Dharma and yoga in the next chapter.)

What's a Sikh?

So, for starters, what's a Sikh? The word *Sikh* literally means "student" or "disciple" in Punjabi and other Indian languages. *Sikhism* (the religion of these Sikhs or students) began as a group of followers of a series of ten human *Gurus*. The word *Guru*, which is often translated as "Teacher," actually means "one who provides the technology to get to light out of darkness."

The first of these Sikh Gurus was *Guru Nanak*, who was born in 1469 C.E. To put this year in context: Columbus had twenty-three years to wait for the trans-Atlantic voyage that he thought would take him to India; the official start of the Protestant Reformation was forty-eight years in the offing; the Renaissance in Italy was in full swing; and a boy named Leonardo from the town of Vinci was about to enter the apprenticeship that would give the world the Mona Lisa.

Guru Nanak was born in the *Punjab*, which occupies much of the northwest side of India and means "Land of Five Rivers," a description of the land's well-watered terrain. Despite centuries of use and political upheaval, the Punjab is still a fertile area, the breadbasket of India. Only... Well, to jump ahead of our story by several centuries, the Punjab was ripped violently in two when India and Pakistan parted company in 1947. The town in which Guru Nanak was born is some 35 miles southwest of Lahore and is now in Pakistan, but most other major Sikh sacred sites are in India.

As you might guess from its 1947 fate, the Punjab has been an intersection for the paths of Hinduism and Islam since at least the time of Guru Nanak. This intersection has wracked the Punjab with sectarian clashes, political infighting and military mayhem. But it has also provided for a cross-fertilization of spirit. When two paths are in opposition, you can choose to see the differences and the problems. And then you can moan in despair or go on a crusade. Or you can choose to see the Oneness of spirit indivisible in all things. The proving ground of the Punjab gave Guru Nanak this choice, and he chose the second path, the path of seeing God in All.

They say that the first words out of Guru Nanak's mouth when he became enlightened in 1496 were "There is no Hindu and no Muslim." That could mean several things.

Perhaps it meant that people really don't practice their religion; their minds are always elsewhere. This interpretation has some historic basis. Right after making the statement, Guru Nanak was invited to pray with a couple of high-ranking Muslims. He went with them to the mosque but didn't go through the usual motions of Islamic prayer. When asked why he hadn't joined them, Guru Nanak told the men that they weren't really praying, their minds were focused on horses. And the men confirmed that this was true.

Perhaps it meant that Guru Nanak had realized that the only Reality is God, so all differences of religion—or any differences that cause dissension—are false. We are all creations of the same Creator. This is certainly in line with what Guru Nanak would later teach.

Perhaps it meant that Guru Nanak had weighed the path of Hinduism and the path of Islam in the balance and decided he was neither. That too would fit with what Guru Nanak was about to teach.

Probably, Guru Nanak meant all these things, and perhaps others besides.

The divine path pioneered by Guru Nanak coincides on many levels—but not all of them—with modern thinking. Sikhs believe in One God, acknowledge the transcendental Oneness of spirit in all things, have no need to convert people, brand no one as "heretic," respect both genders, do not practice caste, live in the world (which we believe is a divine illusion created by God), are not required to fast, use the sword to *prevent* forcible conversion, believe in reincarnation and cremate our dead. We'll look at these items and many others in more detail later in this book.

Guru Nanak was followed by a succession of nine human Gurus: *Guru Angad, Guru Amar Das, Guru Ram Das, Guru Arjan Dev, Guru Hargobind, Guru Har Rai, Guru Harkrishan, Guru Teg Bahadur and Guru Gobind Singh.* All of these human Gurus embodied the *Shabad Guru*—the Guru of Enlightening Sound and Song (which we'll look at in detail a few chapters from now). In 1708, the dying Guru Gobind Singh formally turned the Guruship of all Sikhs over to the *Siri Guru Granth Sahib*, a compendium of songs and poems written by six of the Sikh Gurus as well as other holy people.

I would call the *Siri Guru Granth Sahib* the Sikh Holy Scriptures, except that it is really more a holy vibration in book form. When Shabads from the *Siri Guru Granth Sahib* are sung or recited with full devotion and intention, the singer becomes the song and eventually gains the consciousness of the Saints who wrote or sang the original words. So the *Siri Guru Granth Sahib* is the Sikh Guru, our path to God.

But note: the *Siri Guru Granth Sahib* contains no real articles of faith, no items a person *must* believe to be a Sikh. Sikhism is one of the least dogmatic faiths on Earth. It's main concern is with practice and experience. But there are some important Sikh concepts. So, to help you understand the upcoming chapters, I've included a quick guide to the more important concepts here.

Sikh Concepts

God: Sikhs believe in One God Who is both immanent and transcendent. That is to say, we believe that God is both totally Present in every atom of Creation and also totally beyond human comprehension. We often use the analogy of the ocean and its drops of water. The drop is totally part of the ocean, but has no comprehension of the ocean's limits (if a water drop had any comprehension of anything). So, there is nowhere God is not, and no one who can get outside of God to measure Him/Her/It.

Oh, yes, this is the Creator Who engenders all, but has no gender. So where you see the words "He" or "His" or "Himself," that is only because English requires a gender specific pronoun. Please feel free to substitute any pronoun your heart desires. It's all One with God.

Furthermore, one of our epithets for God is *Nirvair*, which means "without vengeance." God is non-vindictive and non-punitive, and would no more damn you to hellfire for making a mistake than He/She/It would set fire to His/Her/Its Big Toe (if God had a Big Toe).

God is benevolent, in the same sense that the Sun is benevolent: giving light to everyone equally without personal attachment. Because we believe God's Light permeates everything, we also believe in the sanctity of both genders, all religions, all people and all places.

Good and Evil: God is fully Present at all times, including in those actions and situations a human ordinarily considers "bad." Good and evil are human constructs. What is evil may lead to great good, and what is good may lead to great evil So we feel no need for a separate "evil" deity to explain the presence of evil in the world.

Sin: Since Sikhs believe that God creates everything and that good and bad are human constructs, we do not believe that particular actions are inherently sinful. Sikhs absolutely do not believe that any part of God's creation was "born in sin." We do acknowledge that some actions are less righteous than others and are best avoided. Mostly, we use the word "sin" to describe mental attachments and physical actions that cause us to forget the Presence of God in our lives. So when Sikhs use the word "sin," we are actually saying "disconnected from God."

The World: We see everything as God's Creation. We do not despise the world. But at the same time, we don't see it as "real." We see God as the only Reality, and Creation as a play or illusion staged by God. *Maya* is the illusion that we are separate from God, the illusion that we are little realities in our own right. We break Maya's hold on our minds by chanting God's Name.

Karma: This is the law of cause and effect. Newton's Third Law of Thermodynamics: For every action there is an equal and opposite reaction. What you do comes back to you. As you sow, so shall you reap A variation of that last line occurs in the *Siri Guru Granth Sahib* as *What's in the seed is what is eaten*.[2] As each embodied soul acts and reacts, it may accumulate karma over many lifetimes.

Afterlife: Sikhs have no belief in Heaven or Hell, except as states of mind. We do believe in *reincarnation*, the idea that each soul goes through multiple lives. However, once a soul attaches to the Vastness we call God, instead of to the petty interests of the world, that soul will NOT reincarnate but will return directly home to God upon "Death." In that case, the cycle of reincarnation ends. The realization that the soul is always united with God anyway is the usual precursor to this happy ending.

Sikhism Today

Since its beginnings five hundred years ago, Sikhism has become a religion with a global reach. There are currently (as of 2008) an estimated 23-25 million or more Sikhs in the world. To put those figures in context, there are now more Sikhs worldwide than there are Jews. According to census figures, about 18 million Sikhs still live in India. You can find large Sikh communities wherever the British went or places where English is spoken, like the United States and Canada. Most such Sikhs are ethnically Punjabi, but many non-Punjabi people have discovered that they are Sikhs at heart and formally stepped onto the Sikh Path. But wherever we may live and whatever our ethnic origins may be, ultimately all Sikhs—like all people—come from God.

Chapter 2

The Sun Shall Rise in the West[1]

Yogi Bhajan, 3HO & Sikh Dharma in the West

The Sikhs of the Guru are yogis of awareness;
In the midst of Maya, they practice detachment.
Bhai Gurdaas [2]

In the 1960s, a tall, bearded, turbaned Sikh named Harbhajan Singh Puri eyed with compassion the stream of hippies arriving in Delhi International Airport from the United States and Canada. Popular opinion both at home and abroad pegged them as a riotous, turbulent, disobedient bunch, prone to unbridled sex and drugs. Harbhajan Singh saw these things, but he also saw something else. He saw their spiritual hunger. For many of these hippies would come to India looking for spiritual masters and then depart with empty pockets and empty hopes. Because he worked as a Customs Officer, Harbhajan Singh would see them arrive and see them go. And because he had a job to do, because he was wearing a uniform of the Indian government, he was in no position to offer these hippies the immense spiritual legacy that was his. You see, Harbhajan Singh was a Master of Kundalini Yoga...and had been since the age of 16 1/2 years.

Eventually, a job teaching yoga was offered to him in Toronto. So Harbhajan Singh left his government position and flew into Toronto on September 13, 1968. He had just turned 39 years old, having been born on August 26, 1929. Some serious challenges confronted him. All his luggage, except one carry-on, was lost somewhere in transition. Then after waiting several hours at the

9

Toronto airport to be picked up, Harbhajan Singh discovered that the man who had arranged for the teaching job and planned to pick Harbhajan Singh up at the airport had died suddenly in an accident. Moreover, the promised job was gone. Despite these setbacks, Harbhajan Singh chose to trust in God, and he began teaching yoga in Canada anyway.

Harbhajan Singh was neither the first Indian, nor the first Sikh, nor even the first spiritual Master from India to set foot on the North American continent. People from India appear in the United States census of 1820. Sikhs were working in the lumber camps of the Pacific Northwest in both the United States and Canada by the 1890s. Swami Vivekananda spoke at the World Parliament of Religions in Chicago in 1893, and in 1920, Paramahansa Yogananda moved to the United States, becoming the first known spiritual master from India to actually live in the Western Hemisphere.

But compared to the foregoing lineup of East Indians, our Harbhajan Singh was unusual. Unlike those men in the lumber camps, he was not moving to the West due to financial hardships at home. His job with the Indian government had been well-paid, prestigious and secure. Nor was he a celibate Hindu monk like Paramahansa Yogananda; in keeping with Sikh customs, Harbhajan Singh worked in the world, was married and had children. (His wife and children stayed in India until they were able to join Harbhajan Singh in America in 1972.) And as far as anyone knows, no *Sikh* yoga masters had ever moved to the Western Hemisphere before. (We'll see the reason for that in a minute.)

This wasn't even the first major life move Harbhajan Singh had made. Like most Sikhs even today, Harbhajan Singh had been born in the *Punjab*, which, as you may recall from the last chapter, straddles the Indian/Pakistani border. When India and Pakistan parted company in 1947, millions of Sikhs on the Pakistani side of the Punjab were ousted from their homes and forced into exile. Harbhajan Singh and his family were among these exiles.

A few months after his arrival in Toronto, late in 1968, Harbhajan Singh traveled again, this time to Los Angeles. He went for a "short visit," and that visit turned into many years and a change in citizenship.

When he was granted US citizenship in 1974, his name became Harbhajan Singh Khalsa Yogiji. But his students usually called him *Yogi Bhajan* or the *Siri Singh Sahib*, from his title as head of Sikh Dharma for the Western Hemisphere. Sometimes we called him *Yogiji*. Hereafter, throughout this book, I will usually be calling him *Yogi Bhajan* or the *Siri Singh Sahib*. I might add that he never considered himself a *Guru*, and none of us ever called him that.

In Los Angeles, Yogi Bhajan gave a seminal lecture at the East West Cultural Center on January 5, 1969. That lecture marks the starting point of *3HO*—Healthy, Happy, Holy Organization—the organization that promotes Kundalini Yoga and the lifestyle that goes with it.

Yogi Bhajan didn't found 3HO to gather disciples. His stated mission was to train teachers, and he served that mission until his death on October 6, 2004. (And he may be serving it still!) He once said, "The purpose of my visit to America was to create teachers. A teacher is not a person. He is like a water pipe. A pipe brings water to you; pipe is not water, water is not pipe. They are just media. Teacher is a medium of teaching. It is the teaching which you live, not the teacher."[3]

Similarly, in line with Sikh teaching, Yogi Bhajan did not come to America to create Sikh converts. Sikhs consider the whole business of trying to convert people abhorrent. Yogi Bhajan often said that there is no such thing as a Sikh convert. "The Sikh way of life is not a conversion" is the way he once put it in response to a query about how one becomes a Sikh convert.[4]

Furthermore, many Sikhs believe that the practice of yoga is contraindicated for Sikhs. One reason is that yoga—which is at least 5000 years old—co-evolved with Hinduism. It does not originate in Sikhism. Starting in the late 1800s, a fervent reform movement sought to purge Sikhism of Hindu practices (like caste and idol worship) that had crept back into the religion. So some Sikhs, in their rush to release all ties to Hinduism, released all ties to yoga as well.

Another reason is that *Guru Nanak,* the father of Sikhism, had a few choice words to say about the more ridiculous yoga practices of his day. Here's one such passage:

Yoga is not a patched coat.
Yoga is not a walking staff.
Yoga is not smearing the body with ashes.
Yoga is not earrings, nor a shaven head.
Yoga is not blowing a horn.
Remain unstained in the midst of the world's mud,
In this way, you will find the way to Yoga.[5]

Some Sikhs take this and similar passages to mean that yoga is not on the agenda of a good Sikh.

Yet many of Yogi Bhajan's yoga students, including me, became Sikhs. As early as January of 1969, one of Yogi Bhajan's students wrapped his first turban. (You can find the story in the *Bana* chapter). Then in April of 1970, two students presented themselves to Yogi Bhajan and asked to be initiated as Sikhs. Since Yogi Bhajan never initiated anybody, he declined and sent these two students to the local *Gurdwara* (Sikh Temple) where a simple ceremony was devised for them. Over the ensuing years, many more of Yogi Bhajan's students made a formal commitment to the Sikh path.

Why? What was the attraction of this foreign faith to a bunch of Western kids? Is there some connection after all between Sikhism and Kundalini Yoga?

Well, as noted in the last chapter, much of the Sikh faith appeals to Western sensibilities. A religion that respects all religions will appeal to people who were raised with freedom of religion as an article of political faith. A religion that provides a method for experiencing the One God in all things while encouraging its members to live in the world will delight mystics with a practical Western bent. And a religion in which no hair is cut—as is true of Sikhism—was bound to attract a bunch of long-haired hippies.

It's also true that many students chose to emulate their beloved teacher. This was true of the man who wrapped that first 3HO turban. Desiring to become teachers themselves, many students made an effort to become as much like their own teacher as possible, including becoming Sikhs. Indeed, I recall one non-Sikh man sputtering with indignation when he saw a group of 3HO Sikhs, "What is this? A Yogi Bhajan look-alike contest?!"

But the real reason so many of Yogi Bhajan's students became Sikhs lies in Kundalini Yoga as Yogi Bhajan taught it. (There are other schools of Kundalini Yoga, but in this book, *Kundalini Yoga* refers to the version Yogi Bhajan taught.) Let's take a look at how Sikh practice and Kundalini Yoga practice interrelate.

For one thing, this form of Kundalini Yoga explains many Sikh practices. You can find such information sprinkled throughout this book—from why Sikhs don't cut their hair in the Bana chapter to why Sikhs cremate their dead in the Death chapter. Students who feel a resonance for Kundalini Yoga usually also feel a resonance for the yogic information on Sikh practice, and some may adapt their lives accordingly.

For another, many Sikh *mantras* appear in the Kundalini Yoga practices. A *mantra* is a repeated sound—usually a divine word or phrase—that alters the mind and consciousness. It's an important part of Kundalini Yoga. For instance, Yogi Bhajan taught us to silently chant *Sat* on the inhale and *Naam* on the exhale while practicing Kundalini Yoga exercises. *Sat Naam* (which rhymes with *But Mom* and means "Truth Name") appears regularly in the *Siri Guru Granth Sahib* (the Sikh Guru). Yogi Bhajan also taught us to greet everyone with these two words, to signal our awareness of the divine in every individual. Other Sikh-based mantras Yogi Bhajan taught include individual Sikh words, phrases or passages from *Shabads* (Sikh hymns), mantras based on Sikh inscriptions, mantras that combine Sikh words and phrases, Sikh words broken into their component parts, mantras honoring Sikh Gurus and whole Shabads. You can find examples that you can actually practice in the sidebars throughout this book. (See sidebars for how to practice the Kundalini Yoga material in this book.)

Kundalini Yoga
How to Practice the Kundalini Yoga in this Book I
Tuning In

Before any Kundalini Yoga practice, you MUST first tune in by chanting a mantra to align you with the past and present master teachers of this discipline, including Yogi Bhajan and *Guru Ram Das,* the Fourth Sikh Guru. Tuning in allows us to access the divine teacher within us and creates a flow between our finite selves and Infinite Consciousness. I cannot emphasize enough how important tuning in is. I know one man who neglected to tune in who began to see demons whenever he meditated. Yogi Bhajan assured him that they would go away if he tuned in. And it worked. I have never met anyone who tunes in before a Kundalini Yoga practice who has trouble like that. So, please do not neglect this practice!

How to Do It

Sit very straight and regally in a comfortable cross-legged position — or if this is difficult, in a chair with the feet flat on the ground — with the chin tucked in just a bit. Place the palms together as for prayer at the center of the chest with the thumbs pressed against the *sternum*. Close the eyes. Focus the attention at the *Third Eye* or *Brow Point*, which is centered between the eyebrows. You may inhale once or twice to center yourself. Then inhale deeply and chant *Ong Naamo Guroo Dayv Naamo* (literally: *I call upon the Creator. I call upon Divine Wisdom.*) on one breath. Chant this mantra at least three times. The entire sound should go out the nose. (I recommend taking a class with a KRI-certified Kundalini Yoga teacher or getting a CD with the mantra in order to learn its rhythm. See Resources.)

Extended Version

If you wish, immediately after chanting Ong Naamo, you may also chant *Aad Guray Nameh, Jugaad Guray Nameh, Sat Guray Nameh, Siree Guroo Dayvay Nameh* (literally: *I call upon the primal wisdom. I call upon the wisdom of the ages. I call upon the true wisdom. I call upon the infinitely great divine wisdom.*[6]) Chant this three times or more with one breath per repetition.

This mantra, which is from the writings of *Guru Arjan Dev*, the Fifth Guru, enhances wisdom and creates a protective field. It appears in other Kundalini Yoga practices and is also sometimes chanted in Sikh worship services.

Kundalini Yoga
How to Practice the Kundalini Yoga in this Book II
Other Basics

Your body will be happiest if your stomach is empty when you practice Kundalini Yoga. In the morning before breakfast is ideal. At other times, allow at least two hours after a meal before your practice.

Practice Kundalini Yoga barefoot.

Breathe through your nose unless otherwise specified.

To hold the breath, simply suspend your breathing. Keep your throat relaxed. Don't tighten up.

Unless another mantra is specified, maintain a good meditative focus by mentally chanting *Sat* on the inhale and *Naam* on the exhale. *Sat Naam* means "Truth Name" and rhymes with "But Mom."

Maintain the order of the exercises in the sets. Do not change the exercises and do not change the mantras. If you cannot do an exercise as stated, just do it as close to the directions as you can. You may cut down the times of the exercises in most cases, but do not leave exercises out.

Do not exceed the maximum times given except for relaxation times.

Do your best, strive for excellence, but if you experience nausea, dizziness or severe pain, STOP.

During meditation, keep your spine straight unless otherwise specified. That includes bringing the chin in a bit so that the neck is in line with the rest of the spine.

Unless otherwise specified, conclude an exercise or meditation by inhaling with the body centered, holding the breath briefly while mentally circulating the energy, then exhaling and relaxing the position. Relax briefly after each exercise unless told not to.

Drink plenty of water after your session to re-hydrate yourself and flush toxins out of your system.

Information on putting together your personal Kundalini Yoga practice is in the Sadhana chapter.

The pronunciation guide for the mantras is in Appendix B.

If you're a newcomer to Kundalini Yoga, it's a good idea to take classes with a KRI-certified Kundalini Yoga teacher in your area. (Contact information is in Resources.)

Chanting these Sikh mantras, including *Sat Naam*, in Kundalini Yoga is the same as the Sikh practice of *Naam Simran* or Remembrance of the Name, a practice which includes chanting God's Name out loud, remembering God's Name during meditation, and reciting God's Name silently with each breath. Any of several Names for God will do. Naam Simran is one of the very few things the *Siri Guru Granth Sahib* orders a Sikh to do. Chanting the Name, practicing Naam Simran, remind us that we are one with the One, that our identity lies in God, that God's Name is our name. This is true union and true yoga. It's also the path, the carriage and the true joy of the true Sikh.

And then, there's Guru Ram Das, the Fourth Sikh Guru. Yogi Bhajan had a special connection with Guru Ram Das, a connection embodied in the mantra *Guru Raam Daas Chant*. Yogi Bhajan received this mantra directly from Guru Ram Das who appeared in his astral body under miraculous circumstances in the winter of 1970-1. At that time, Yogi Bhajan was traveling in India with 84 students. The whole group was in dire straits. They were taking shelter in a mango grove from some murderous spiritual imposters, and each day their altar cloth would catch fire for no apparent reason. Yogi Bhajan began to meditate by chanting *Waa Hay Guroo,* the most ecstatic of the Sikh names for God. Suddenly, he realized that he was chanting completely different words—the words to the Guru Raam Daas Chant. As feelings of warmth and happiness engulfed him, he saw Guru Ram Das personified. At that time, Guru Ram Das stated, "At this time you need the protection of a mantra. The people who are following you are not yet ripe...You do not want to claim anything as your own achievement, and you don't want to take the blame either. Let the claim be mine, and let me also take the blame." [7] Yogi Bhajan had the whole group chant this mantra the following day. It helped; everyone survived the trip. Over the course of time, Yogi Bhajan taught a number of meditations using this mantra. (See sidebar for one such Guru Raam Daas chant meditation.)

Kundalini Yoga
Guru Raam Daas Chant Meditation[8]
Originally Taught on April 23, 1979

This powerful meditation is one of several Yogi Bhajan taught that uses the Guru Raam Daas Chant mantra. Yogi Bhajan specifically recommended teaching this meditation to children to invoke unbeatable values in them. I can testify that it is good for adults too. Practicing this meditation triggers a shield of protection and augments both our life force energy and our capacity to make decisions. I am awed by the creative solutions to difficult problems that come to me when I practice this one.

Guroo Guroo Waa Hay Guru, Guroo Raam Daas Guroo may be translated, *Great is the ecstasy and wisdom of serving God,* or *Wise, wise is the one who serves Infinity.*

How to Do It

Sitting in a meditative posture, relax your elbows by your sides. With your palms facing up, interlace your fingers with the fingers inside your palms. Then close your hands over the interlaced fingers. Press the sides of your thumbs together, and rest them on top of the index finger immediately beneath them. Raise your  hands so that they are in front of your heart. (Your hands will naturally turn towards your body.) Close your eyes briefly, then open them one-tenth and look downwards. Inhale very deeply and chant in a monotone *Guroo Guroo Waa Hay Guroo, Guroo Raam Daas Guroo* five times on one breath. (Author's comments: If you run out of air, just inhale deeply and start over again. Remember to touch your tongue to the upper palate just above the teeth to make the "r" sounds.) Continue for 31 minutes. (You may start with as little as 3 minutes.)

And finally, as indicated earlier, as more and more of Yogi Bhajan's students turned to Sikhism with all the enthusiasm of first love, Yogi Bhajan was granted the title of *Siri Singh Sahib* (literally "very great, respected lion") and so became the head Sikh minister for the Western Hemisphere. He received this title on March 3, 1971, in a large ceremony at the *Akal Takhat* (literally "Undying Throne"), the administrative seat of Sikh religious authority in *Amritsar*, the chief city of the Punjab.

Now, having seen some of the evidence—all the chanting of

Sikh mantras, a connection to a Sikh Guru, and all the yogic information that validates Sikh practice...not to mention the way elements of Sikhism mesh well with Western thought—you might think that most of Yogi Bhajan's students would end up as Sikhs. But that's not the way it works. Only those students destined to become Sikhs actually make the transition.

With the practice of Kundalini Yoga, destiny awakens. When destiny awakens, we blossom to become what God intended us to be. And as consciousness and destiny awaken, some Kundalini Yoga students discover that they always were Sikhs at heart.

Chapter 3

How I Became a Sikh

Siri Kirpal Kaur Khalsa's Story

After wandering and wandering, O God,
I have arrived and entered Your Sanctuary.
Guru Arjan Dev [1]

Once when I was an adolescent, perhaps 11 or 12 years old, I went with my family for an evening jaunt to the cliffs overlooking the ocean near our San Diego home. As I recall, the tide was up, and we stayed near the walkways at the top of the cliff. My brothers were soon digging in the dirt on some earnest young-boy project. My parents strolled off arm and arm. There were few other people except for occasional passersby. I looked at my brothers and knew they would resent the intrusion of their older (and only) sister. I looked at my parents and decided not to disturb their rare romantic moment. And I looked at myself and felt utterly alone. When my parents came back, I was sobbing like a fire hydrant, and no one knew why.

Even at the time, I knew the answer to my inner loneliness was God. But there had been a big hole in my life where God ought to be ever since my parents had a disagreement with the minister and pulled us out of church and Sunday school when I was eight. Thereafter, I began hiding my spiritual inclinations, reading the Bible the way some kids read pornography—behind the big chair in my room, where I could stuff it into the nearby bookcase if anyone entered unannounced. I avidly read saints' lives and snippets about saints in cookbooks (ever heard the legend about tea?), and pretended it was for other, more acceptable, cultural reasons. Only at Christmas did I let my spiritual inclinations run rampant. And to this day, I love Christmas, even though I am no longer even vaguely Christian, except by marriage.

The spiritual loneliness of my childhood is ironic given that I have deeply spiritual antecedents on both sides of my family. My mother's family tree has branches of religious reform. Through my mother's maternal grandmother, I am descended from the parents of John Knox, the founder of Presbyterianism. Closer to me both in time and intimacy was my maternal grandmother who helped found a little New Age sect called the Teaching of the Inner Christ. She was a "prayer therapist" and once told me that she would see a purple light when something especially good was about to happen.

My father's family tree has mystic branches. My father himself was "born with a veil," which means that a piece of placenta was attached to his head at birth. Among the Lebanese this is considered to indicate the gift of prophecy—a gift he was proud of. He also told me—after I had been a vowed Sikh nearly ten years—that he had had a profound and "palpable" experience of the Presence of God when he was in the Vale of Kashmir during World War II. His mother, an immigrant from Lebanon, was considered a saint by the people who knew her. Interestingly, she was born in the same hill town as Kahlil Gibran, the author of *The Prophet*. So religious reform and mysticism are both in my blood.

These spiritual lines are underscored by an unusual coincidence. By the Grace of God, I am the thirteenth grandchild on both sides. So when I was born, my parents chose to name me Katharyne Rose in honor of both grandmothers—the New Age mystic and the Lebanese saint. I sometimes wonder if my parents had any idea how strongly my name would link me to the spiritual branches of our family tree. Did they have any inkling that the name they gave me would instill in me the desire for sainthood?

But despite all these family connections, when people ask me what I was before I became a Sikh, I usually answer, "Good question!" My father's family was Lebanese Eastern Orthodox Christian, but I have never set foot inside any Orthodox Church. My mother's family was Protestant of various sorts, and I was baptized Methodist. After our family moved from Elmira, New York, where I was born, we attended Presbyterian and Congregational churches in San Diego until that fateful day when my parents decided church attendance was against their religion. I sometimes call my parents born-again intellectuals because they belonged to that generation that believed intelligence, higher education, and psychological health don't mix with religion or spirituality. Ultimately, they turned their backs on their spiritual heritage, although never completely because they still believed in God. My New Age grandmother provided a spiritual venue for me. In my teens, I often went to church with her and sometimes sang in the Teachings of the Inner Christ choir. We also had Jewish friends who invited us over for Passover each year, with the result that I attended five Passover Seders before I even saw Christian communion in a Protestant Church. So what was I??

One event of my childhood stands out for its interfaith intimations. The Jewish family that invited us over for Passover also invited us to a Hanukkah celebration at their home one year. Now, if you know the Hanukkah story, you know that the bad guys are Syrians. Did I mention that Lebanon used to belong to Syria? So, as the Hanukkah story was retold, my family and I formed a cheering squad for all the wrong parts of the story. Then, our hosts gave me a Hanukkah present: a recording of the Robert Shaw Chorale singing Christmas carols! When I commented to our hosts on the odd nature of this *Hanukkah* present, the husband said, "Oh, I never thought of that! I just knew you'd like it." And I did.

Another story stands out about my maternal grandmother,

the only grandparent I ever really knew, who lived a couple of miles from us in San Diego. When we went to visit her in her apartment overlooking San Diego Bay, we would drive by the Self-Realization Fellowship on First Avenue. I was intrigued by its Oriental architecture and mystique. So I asked my grandmother to take me there. But in my innocence, I actually asked her to take me to "that church you sometimes go to on First Avenue," since that's where I thought she went. (The Teaching of the Inner Christ had not yet been founded.) Instead, she took me to the Unity Church in the non-descript building across the street. Where, I must admit, I was thoroughly bored.

This divine misadventure presaged two others. The first of these occurred at the end of the second term of my freshman year at UC Santa Cruz, when everyone I knew was studying for a difficult chemistry final. I had no finals that term except for one at the end of finals week. I knew I could flip through my notes quickly before that exam, then go and ace the test, so I wasn't studying like mad the way everyone else was. Someone had given me a little card listing all the Zen missions in the Bay Area. I decided to use my time to go on an adventure and visit the Zen mission in the city I knew least about: Mill Valley. I boarded the Greyhound Bus without even knowing that Mill Valley was north of San Francisco. When the bus dropped me off on the side of the road, I walked across the street and approached a gardener—the only person I could see—and asked him where the Zen mission was. He answered, "Well, we meet in the community center in the morning, but we don't really have a place you can go to. You'll have to go to the Zen master's house." He proceeded to give me directions. To this day, I am convinced that he was one of God's angels looking out for me. I wended my way to the Zen master's house—a charming wood house filled with light, origami, and the fragrance of dinner cooking. When I arrived, the Zen master very kindly told me that they had no place to put me, but the Zen Center in San Francisco did. He had one of his students take me to the bus stop and wait with me to insure that I boarded the correct bus. On the bus back to San Francisco, I felt like a total babe in the woods.

The Mill Valley Zen master had very carefully drawn a map of the best route to walk once I got off the bus in San Francisco. It led me to the San Francisco Zen Center which was housed (and may still be housed) in a large Beaux-Arts building. Everyone was at dinner. After I had waited a lengthy, hungry time listening to the clink of other people eating, the San Francisco Zen master came out and asked about my circumstances. As it happened, the Zen Center required a minimum stay that was a couple of days more than I had available. I said I would find some other place to stay.

Since I hadn't noticed any hotels en route from the bus station, I decided to try a different direction. And I walked straight into the heart of one of San Francisco's worst areas. *Not* the sort of place for an innocent young woman wearing a red jacket to be walking! By this time it was dark. No hotels were visible. The streets were lined with formerly grand Victorians, now decayed and suitable for gothic novels. Many had stone lions guarding their front steps. These lions were the sort I loved to climb on as a child, and had it been daylight, I would have delighted in them. But in that evening gloom, they were eerie and scary.

I passed a few children and women—all with frightened faces. I saw no moving cars, no adult men and no other whites...until I saw a police car with two policemen. I stopped on the sidewalk and stared at them, and they stopped in the middle of the street and stared at me. Then I walked over to them and said, "I think I'm lost!" They whisked me to the nearby YWCA hotel.

The next morning I carefully examined the wall-sized map in the lobby before hunting for breakfast after an inadvertent 24-hour fast. (I was hungry in more ways than one on this trip!)

After breakfast and a short jaunt watching people practice Tai Chi in a little park in Chinatown, I boarded the bus back to Santa Cruz. That is the story of How I (nearly) Became a Zen Buddhist.

Shortly after this misadventure, I met the man who became my husband. At the time, we both believed in God, but neither of us believed in organized religion. After Jim graduated the following year, we married in a civil ceremony in front of the living room fireplace in my family's San Diego home. With my husband's blessing, I proceeded to study astrology, past-life regression, traditional folk music and such like, but as a dilettante. Something was missing. Although I loved (and still love) my husband, I felt restless.

We moved to Salem, Oregon. The cultural fun and games I was used to in California weren't available in Salem. It became obvious that being a dilettante wasn't going to be an option here. I worked in clerical jobs for awhile, then returned to college to complete my delayed degree. After graduating with a degree in Art from Marylhurst College (now Marylhurst University), I went through a spiritual crisis, which triggered both the final divine misadventure and my discovery of Sikhism.

The spiritual crisis occurred when a friend of mine, who had become a born-again Christian, began sending me rather offensively bigoted "Christian" literature. The intolerance of this literature was most unappealing, but it did reawaken my childhood desire to be a saint. Deciding that I would be just as bigoted as I perceived this literature to be if I didn't read the Bible all the way through (I had got stuck somewhere in the "begats" as a child and had never actually finished reading it), I began a complete door-to-door reading of the Bible that would take me two years. In the meantime, I decided to balance this reading with other spiritual literature.

One of these readings was *Yoga, Youth, and Reincarnation* by Jess Stearn. In addition to my spiritual longing, I had been thinking about doing something to bring my body, mind and soul into harmony, since they felt like separate entities. As I read *Yoga, Youth, and Reincarnation*, it occurred to me that yoga might prove the magic wand for both desires—the one for sainthood and the one for more harmony between my body, mind and soul—providing I could find yoga instruction that included meditation.

It also occurred to me that if I put my faith in a Christian context, I was probably a Quaker because Quakers depend, by in large, on the Inner Light for their answers. In those days, the Quaker Friends Meeting met at the YWCA. So I walked down to the YWCA and asked where I might find yoga with meditation and where exactly the Quaker Friends Meeting was held. After some consultation, the lady at the YWCA reception desk directed me to a local counseling center for suitable yoga classes and said that people from the Friends Meeting would be in the lobby Sunday morning.

The following Sunday I traipsed down to the YWCA to discover a lobby filled with people. I followed them all into the adjacent room, and inadvertently walked straight into a revival meeting! This was a Quaker Meeting!? But then, what did I know? So I joined in singing "Blessed be they which do hunger and thirst," and listened to a bunch of people say "Praise God!" Following the service, I mentioned to the person who seemed to be the minister (Quaker Meetings don't have ministers) that this was my first Friends service. He said, "That's interesting!" and walked away. Later that day, I learned that I had gone to the wrong room. That was my final misadventure and the story of How I (nearly) Became a Quaker.

So when I arrived for my first *Kundalini Yoga* class, on March 23, 1983, the day following my thirtieth birthday, I was prepared for commitment—providing God didn't send me to the wrong room, building or city! To be honest, I was already big on commitment. Even before I left high school, I had come to the conclusion that the only freedom any of us ever has is the freedom to choose how we will NOT be free. Even so, all these misadventures made me realize that I might only have one chance once God finally sent me to the correct room in the correct building in the correct city. I didn't want to miss it.

So on the appointed day, I drove in the leafy morning on one of the rural byways edging Salem, Oregon, to a former rural school building that now housed the counseling center. Nearly every Wednesday morning for more than a year I would drive this same leafy path. It was an idyllic route.

At first, I had some doubts about this yoga. I had expected *Hatha Yoga* with meditation. (When people think of yoga as human pretzels holding poses, they're usually thinking of Hatha Yoga.) But this Kundalini Yoga was manifestly different— involving more conscious breathing, more chanting, more movement, more use of the arms and fingers. And unlike Hatha Yoga, in which individual exercises are practiced with no prescribed pattern, Kundalini Yoga is practiced in prescribed series of exercises leading to specific results.

In the interim between class one and class two, I had a vision. I woke up in the middle of the night and, as I lay in bed, beheld the Trinity. God-the-Father appeared as a spiral-armed galaxy holding up a cross at the foot of which God-the-Holy-Spirit appeared as a line of golden electric light extending out into Infinity on both sides. God-the-Son was both crucified and trans-figured...and He looked like me. My doubts fled.

It didn't take long to acquire a couple of Kundalini Yoga manuals and begin practicing daily on my own. This daily practice, also known as *Sadhana*, lifted my spirits and stirred my soul. But it took awhile to make the connection between Kundalini Yoga and Sikh Dharma as my instructor was not a practicing Sikh. For the fullness of that connection, I had to meet *Yogi Bhajan*, the Kundalini Yoga master we met in the last chapter.

I first met Yogi Bhajan in October, 1984, at a *White Tantric Yoga* course in Seattle. White Tantric Yoga is a profoundly deep meditative experience which is practiced in groups at certain times and places under the strict guidance of the *Mahan Tantric* — who just happened to be Yogi Bhajan. I awaited his arrival eagerly as did all the other people clad in modest white cotton attire. Arriving with an entourage, Yogi Bhajan cheerfully bade us all sit down, made a few comments and surveyed the assembled group of 100-150 people. That he was reading our individual and collective *auras*, I already knew. When his eyes reached me, he stopped and stared, made a few comments and stared some more. He then gave a stirring talk during which he said, "Everything you want to know is in *Japji*." Hmm...

Japji, as *Japji Sahib* is popularly known, is the Sikh Morning Prayer. Devout Sikhs read it out loud every morning, preferably in *Gurmukhi*, the original language. I picked up a copy of the English translation that same day, but the question was: How was I going to learn it in Gurmukhi?

In the meantime, when the last meditation of the course drew to a close, my inner dam of pent-up longing burst. Yogi Bhajan had been talking about his upcoming death (he actually remained alive for another 20 years...almost exactly). I had been feeling like a homeless person who has just come home after several millennia of wandering, and I began sobbing uncontrollably at the thought of losing what I had just found. My instructor and his wife were holding me like a newborn babe, when all the assembled people rose in a single flourish, flowed past us, and followed Yogi Bhajan out the door. I felt surrounded by white angels and would have signed on the dotted line right then. Unfortunately, because Sikhs do not go out of their way to make converts, no dotted lines were visible.

I also had the mistaken idea that real Sikhs lived in *ashrams*. An ashram is usually a residential yoga center, similar to a commune. Since most of Yogi Bhajan's early students were hippies, ashrams were the natural next step. Sikhism is a religion for householders, but the Sikhs I knew either hadn't gotten there yet or they still *called* their houses *ashrams* — hence my confusion.

And since my husband and I were (and still are) homeowners, and Jim wasn't likely to become a Sikh himself, moving into an ashram wasn't an option.

In the month following the course, my consciousness opened up. I was in Seattle again—this time in the Pioneer Square area attempting to track down an art gallery that would carry my acrylics and colorpencil drawings. I received rejection after rejection after rejection. You might assume that the repeated rejections would catapult me into an abyss of depression. But that's not what happened. Instead, with each rejection, my spirits soared inexplicably higher and higher. And from that place of inner joy, I watched in awe as the tramps, the trees and the trash of this funky historic district turned luminous—shining with inner light. That light and that awe were still manifest both within me and outside me as I drove home to Salem...literally into the sunset.

My misunderstanding about Sikhs and ashrams cleared up a couple of months later. A visiting Sikh Dharma dignitary gave a talk on the importance of the *Naad* (sound current) at the Salem home of some friends of hers. I arrived for this talk somewhat early and introduced myself to two turbaned ladies standing in the entry hall. During the ensuing conversation, they mentioned the word *sangat*. I asked what *sangat* means, and one of the ladies said, "It means 'congregation.'" Suddenly I had an epiphany: real Sikhs do not necessarily live in ashrams, but instead live regular lives, and worship in congregations like everyone else. Being a homeowner would not bar me from becoming a Sikh. Indeed, it would be an asset.

On this occasion, God also blessed me with my Gurmukhi teacher. After her presentation, the lady who gave the talk on the Naad asked for questions. I raised my hand and inquired, "Where can I learn Gurmukhi?" A lady I had met through my Kundalini Yoga instructor and his wife piped up and said, "I can teach you."

And what a gift this teacher was! She taught me to pronounce Gurmukhi script with the help of flash cards. Near the end of our first class, she handed me a Gurmukhi-only *Nit Nem* (Sikh prayer book) and told me to practice what I had just learned by reading a specific section of Japji Sahib out loud in Gurmukhi on my own. As our class unfolded and I gained more expertise, she taught me how to read a *Hukam* (literally "command"), the random reading from the *Siri Guru Granth Sahib* (the scriptures all Sikhs revere as *Guru* or Enlightener) that is the pinnacle of every Sikh service. She also taught me how to recite the poetic songs called *Shabads* as a form of meditation. (You can learn to do this too, from the sidebar on *Shabad Yoga* in the Shabad Guru chapter.) And she invited me to my first *Gurdwara*, which is both the name of any building housing the *Siri Guru Granth Sahib* and the name Sikhs sometimes use for their worship service.

I'm the only Sikh I know who learned to read Gurmukhi before attending a Gurdwara service and arriving at the Guru's Feet. Believe me, it's not a requirement. At this first Gurdwara, I rejoiced watching the little kids toddle from one parent to another without shushing. We sang and sang, but no one preached. Heaven for a classically trained singer like me! And I was in humble awe when my Gurmukhi teacher invited me on the spur of the moment to watch over her shoulder while she read the Hukam, first in Gurmukhi, then in English. A religion without stuffiness! God be praised!

At my next Gurdwara, I read the Hukam. No, I wasn't expecting to. It was a total surprise. At every Sikh service, the *Siri Guru Granth Sahib* presides while someone sits behind it waving a flywhisk or *chauri sahib*. (More details on the chauri sahib and other aspects of a Sikh service are coming up in the chapter on the Guru's Court.) I had performed this *Seva* or service for the entire hour or two of that second Gurdwara. When my Gurmukhi teacher came up to me just before the Hukam, I assumed she was going to take over from me. Instead what she said was, "You're going to read the Hukam." So I did, by God's Grace...and only by God's Grace.

But I still wasn't quite a Sikh yet, at least not a fully practicing one. My hair had been mostly uncut since the late 1960s, except for a couple of times in the early 1980s when my husband had trimmed it a little after it got caught in equipment. Thanks to the Kundalini Yoga, my energy began to move so much I couldn't wear my hair down anymore. So, my Kundalini Yoga instructor's wife taught me how to put it up in a *Rishi knot*—something I had done for more than a year. But I wasn't yet wearing a turban, at least not regularly. I also didn't have my Sikh spiritual name.

Now that I love wearing a turban, it seems strange to me that I was ever concerned about it. But back then, I was afraid about how it would look, and how it would feel, and whether I would still be able to hear. None of those things has been a problem. In fact, when my Gurmukhi teacher helped me put on my first turban in October of 1985, I had no idea how useful it would be for hiding gray hair a couple of decades later.

Learning to wrap a turban well did take a bit of time. I was certainly no expert when an interesting test led to my wearing a turban every day. Through the Sikh community in Salem, I met a petite, but powerful lady who praised me to the heavens and involved me in her coterie of young people. Once I was firmly in her circle, she began a campaign, subtly urging me in her soft, breathy voice to remove my turban and cut my hair to "regain my power." I remembered screaming as a little child when my hair was cut, so hair cutting I nixed. But I did take the turban off and wear my hair down again. Although my energy felt slightly out of kilter, I continued this regime for about a month. Then on Valentines Day, 1986, it snowed, and I decided to don a turban just to keep my ears warm. Lo! my energy was happy and balanced, as it had not been the entire time my hair drooped down. No question: I would gratefully wear a turban every day for the rest of my life no matter what opposition I might face.

Less than a week before, on February 11, 1986, I had received my Sikh spiritual name. I had planned on asking Yogi Bhajan for my spiritual name when I saw him in November of 1985, but I couldn't bring myself to ask. Instead, he told us that we *are* God and to live to that understanding. I thought, "If I *am* God, then I ought to know my own name." No, I didn't pick a name, any name, for myself—that would have been an act of ego. I waited.

Three months later, I was reading in Paramahansa Yogananda's *Autobiography of a Yogi*. The chapter told of Master Mahasaya, a blissful, God-conscious teacher-saint, who corrected the young Yogananda instantly if he was in spiritual error, but always in such a kindly way that it would be impossible to take offense. With some cockiness, I thought, "I'd like to be like that, and I'm willing to do the work." The little voice of my heart said, "No, you're not!" I thought about going off to sulk, but hiding from one's own inner voice is a bit ridiculous, so I kept reading. As I read, I began to experience what it would be like to be so kindly and so divine. With much greater humility, I thought, "Oh, I *do* want to be like this, and I *am* willing to do the work." And the little voice said, "Yes, you are willing. Your name is *Siri Kirpal Kaur*." I've always been fond of *Kwan Yin* (the Chinese Goddess of Mercy), so I was thrilled to become a Princess of Incomprehensibly Great Compassion.

Later that year, I also discovered the invisible dotted line and signed on it. Sikh vows were created in 1970 for people like me who were not raised Sikhs.[2] Prior to that time, it was rare for any person unfamiliar with Punjabi language and culture to become a Sikh—which still seems strange to me as Sikhism is clearly global rather than tribal in scope and perspective.

I was literally high when I took formal Sikh vows in June of 1986—more than 7000 feet above sea level, in the Jemez Mountains of New Mexico. In the cool air of that high desert morning, I lay my head at the Guru's feet and vowed to:

1. Worship only the One Creator and to accept the *Siri Guru Granth Sahib* as my Guru.
2. Rise every morning and meditate on God's Name before sunrise...or remember God's Name upon awaking if circumstances made physical rising impossible.
3. Keep my body in its natural form, except for medical necessity, and especially never cut my hair.
4. Earn my living righteously and share what I have with others.
5. Never use drugs, alcohol or tobacco, except for medical necessity.
6. Never eat meat.
7. Never engage in sex outside a monogamous, legal marriage.

   Since that time, the vows have become a little more strict and a little more detailed. (See sidebar for the current Sikh Vows.) But in essence, these seven items are what all vowed Sikhs have promised. I've never regretted this commitment.

Sikh Vows [3]

The following is excerpted from the Sikh Vows as they appear in *Victory & Virtue* (a handbook for Sikh Dharma ministers), except for some definitions I have added in brackets.

A. *A Sikh believes in the Oneness of God who has created this creation. The Creator and the creation are one. God's essential name is Truth.*

B. *The* Siri Guru Granth Sahib *is the only Guru of a Sikh. A Sikh looks to the* Siri Guru Granth Sahib *as a Living Guru. A Sikh considers any Hukam or other message from* Siri Guru

---

Granth Sahib *as a direct communication from the Infinite.*

A Sikh bows to no person as Guru. A Sikh may accept a Spiritual Teacher, but knows that no Spiritual Teacher is a Guru.

A Sikh is encouraged to learn to read Gurmukhi, the language of Siri Guru Granth Sahib *and is encouraged to the Nitnem Banis (Japji Sahib, Shabad Hazare, Jaap Sahib, Tavprasad Swaye, Anand Sahib, Rehiras Sahib and Kirtan Sohila) daily, in any language.*

C. A Sikh keeps his or her form as God has created it, not removing or cutting hairs from any part of his or her body.

A Sikh also will not alter his or her body except for medical necessity. (This includes no tattoos and no circumcision.)

A Sikh shall tie his or her hair in a Rishi knot on the crown center at the top of the head and cover the head with a turban in public.

A Sikh shall wear a Kara (iron bangle) on the right wrist for males and on the left wrist for females. A Sikh is encouraged to wear the Bana of Guru Gobind Singh (chola/kurta, cumberband and churidars). [A "chola" is a tunic, as is a "kurta." "Churidars" are leggings.]

D. A Sikh shall rise to meditate upon God in the Amrit Vela (before the rising of the sun), and shall keep his or her mind centered upon the Name of God throughout the day. Minimally, the Amrit Vela meditations should include Ek Ong Kar Sat Nam Siri Wahe Guru [Long Ek Ongkars], *the Mool Mantra* [the opening section of Japji Sahib], *and the recitation of Japji Sahib (in any language).*

Whenever possible, a Sikh should join with the Sadh Sangat [Company of the Holy] *to meditate together and to do devotional singing (Kirtan) in the Amrit Vela.*

E. A Sikh shall earn his or her living by working in honest labor or service, to support himself or herself and his or her family. His or her dealings shall reflect the highest ethical and moral standards.

F. A Sikh shall share his or her wealth with the needy, and shall give to support the Dharma. He or she shall stand ready to protect the weak and shall serve the community and humanity.

G. The Guru's Sikh shall maintain the diet of the Guru's Langar [food of the Guru's kitchen]; this means a lacto-vegetarian diet, excluding meat, fish, poultry and eggs.

H. The Sikh shall abstain from the use of drugs, alcohol and tobacco, in any form except for medical necessities.

I. Sikhs shall be celibate if single, and monogamous if married. A Sikh shall have no sexual relations outside of a legal marriage. A Sikh man shall consider all women, except his wife, as his mother, his sisters or his daughters. A Sikh woman shall consider all men, except her husband, as her father, her brothers or her sons.

So—besides the minor detail that God finally sent me to the right room in the right building in the right city—why was I attracted to the Sikh path? Here's the list:

1. Sikhs do not proselytize. We network and we explain—as I am doing here—but we do not attempt to drag anyone onto our path.
2. The reason we don't proselytize is that we understand that God made all creation and that includes all religions.
3. In fact, Sikhs have the first martyr to give his life for members of *another* religion. (His name was *Guru Teg Bahadur*, and you'll hear more about him in the chapter titled "A Universal Path.")
4. Since God made all creation, we don't try to run away from

any part of life.

5. Therefore our lifestyle is very natural and wholesome.

6. Sikhs have a simple and effective technology for experiencing the Presence of God while maintaining these normal house-holding lives.

7. Sikhs have no belief in damnation. God doesn't set fire to His Own Toes.

8. Sikhs do believe in *reincarnation*. Since perfect strangers came up to me from the beginning of time to tell me I was an "old soul"—an exaggeration, but not by much—reincarnation has been an item on my spiritual agenda from day one.

9. Sikh services are mostly singing, and we place an enormous emphasis on using sound (the *Naad*) to experience Oneness with the One.

10. Sikhs look like saints and angels. What more could I ask for?

Chapter 4

Shabad Guru: The Sound Way to God

The disciple dwells on the Shabad and becomes one with God...
Dwelling on the Shabad and performing divine music, one merges in
the Holy Company.
Bhai Gurdaas[1]

Nanak was a twenty-seven-year-old, Hindu-raised man with serious symptoms of saintliness. One day in 1496, he went for a bath in the river near his home in a part of India that is so far North and West that it is now in Pakistan. He disappeared for three days.

In that three-day baptism, Nanak was immersed in a deep meditation on the *Naam*, the Name of God. When he emerged, there was light around his face. His speech had become song and poetry—song and poetry that lifted the hearts of all who heard it. He had become *Guru Nanak*, the founding father of Sikhism.

After his enlightenment, Guru Nanak traveled widely, to the far Eastern end of India, at least as far West as Mecca, as far South as Sri Lanka, and at least as far North as Tibet and parts of Russia. As he traveled, he sang his message, accompanied by *Mardana*, a *rebec* player of Muslim birth.

There's a charming story about Mardana and his *rebec*, a stringed instrument similar to a lute that is played with a bow. The story goes that when Mardana and Guru Nanak headed out on their first long journey, right after Guru Nanak's enlightenment, Mardana had no rebec and no idea how to play one.

Soon they came to a fork in the road. Guru Nanak said he would wait at this crossroads while Mardana took the narrower path to where his rebec was waiting for him. Mardana protested.

Where was he going to get this rebec? And what was he going to do with it if he got it? Guru Nanak smiled and essentially said, "Trust me." So off Mardana went. After walking a bit, he came across an old man who commented, "Few people ever take this path. What brings you this way?" Mardana said that he was looking for a rebec. To which the old man replied, "Ah! Nanak has sent you. I have your rebec ready."

When Mardana returned with the rebec, Guru Nanak ordered him to play it. Again, Mardana protested that he had never played a rebec in his life. To that Guru Nanak replied that Mardana had played the rebec in many previous lives and the knowledge would return to him as he played. Sure enough, Mardana picked up the rebec and began to play, and he played beautifully.

Now this story is almost certainly apocryphal. The earliest stories all claim that Mardana was born to a Muslim family of rebec players. Nonetheless, the story rings true in its depths. Mardana's talents blossomed when Guru Nanak touched him with divine song. This is what happens to anyone touched by the *Shabad Guru*.

You know how sound can shatter glass? Sound can also shatter the shell of ego and the hard spots in the mind. No, this isn't a non sequitur. The *Shabad Guru* is the sung word that shatters the glass of ego. It is the ultimate Teacher or *Guru* (which literally means one who provides the technology to get to light out of darkness) of all Sikhs, including Guru Nanak. You can call Sikhism the sound way to God, because Sikhs worship through the *Naad*, the divine sound current, by singing and reciting the hymns of the Shabad Guru.

Guru Nanak wrote down the *Shabads* or hymns that the Shabad Guru inspired him to sing in a special book. This book he gave to *Guru Angad*, the disciple who succeeded him to the Guruship. Guru Angad planned to share this treasure with everyone, but the script Guru Nanak had used to write the Shabads was a kind of shorthand, devoid of any vowels. Only those who really knew the Shabads could use the book to sing them. Fortunately Guru Angad knew all the Shabads well, and modified this script so that anyone could use it. This is *Gurmukhi*—which literally means "from the mouth of the Guru"—a script that can convey the pronunciation of any language. (I've actually seen the English word "Bathroom" written in Gurmukhi script on the necessary door in a Sikh house.) Having a holy script that anyone could use was a big departure because reading and writing Sanskrit were restricted to Brahmins in that time and place.

Guru Angad wrote some epigrammatic poems called *sloks*, but no long Shabads. *Guru Amar Das*, the disciple who became Guru after Guru Angad, was almost as prolific a poet/singer as Guru Nanak had been. In the chapter on *Banis*, we'll be hearing about *Anand Sahib*, the beautiful Shabad written by Guru Amar Das. The next Sikh Guru, *Guru Ram Das*, was also a noted poet/singer, famous for the *Lavaan*, the wedding song we'll be hearing about in the chapter on marriage. But it was *Guru Arjan Dev*, Guru Ram Das' son and disciple, who achieved the most prolific outpouring of Shabads.

In fact, Guru Arjan Dev received the mantle of the Guruship due to his capacity to allow the Shabad Guru to write poetry through him. The story goes that a relative of Guru Ram Das invited him to attend a wedding in Lahore. At the time, Guru Ram Das was deeply involved with work in *Amritsar*, which was to become the Sikh holy city. So he asked his two eldest sons to attend the wedding as his proxy. Both refused. When Guru Ram Das asked his youngest son to attend, Arjan agreed without hesitation. Guru Ram Das then requested Arjan to remain in Lahore until sent for and tend to the Guru's business there.

After two years or more with no word, Arjan became very homesick, longing to be in the company of the one who was both his father and his Guru. So he wrote the following poem and sent it to Guru Ram Das by way of a servant.

My soul longs for the blessed vision of the Guru.
It cries out like a pied-cuckoo.
My thirst is not quenched, and I find no peace
Without the vision of the Beloved Saint Guru.
I am a sacrifice, my soul is a sacrifice unto the vision of the Beloved
    Saint Guru.[2]

When the servant arrived in Amritsar with the poem/letter, he was intercepted by *Prithi Chand*, Arjan's oldest brother. Assuring the servant that he would deliver the message to the Guru, Prithi Chand took the message, read it and concealed it. After some months with no word from Guru Ram Das, Arjan wrote another poem/letter.

Your face is so beautiful, and the sound of Your words impart divine
    knowledge.
It is so long since this sparrowhawk has had a glimpse of water.
Blessed is the land where You live, O my friend and intimate Divine
    Guru.
I am a sacrifice, I am ever a sacrifice unto my friend and intimate
    Divine Guru.[3]

Prithi Chand intercepted this poem/letter also.
After more months had elapsed with no word, Arjan wrote yet another poem/letter.

When for one moment I could not be with You, the dark age dawned
    for me.
When shall I see You, O my Beloved Lord?
I cannot endure the night, and sleep does not come without the sight
    of the Beloved Guru's Court.
I am a sacrifice, my soul is a sacrifice unto the true court of the
    Beloved Guru.[4]

This time Arjan instructed his servant to deliver the poem/letter directly into the hands of Guru Ram Das and no one else. It was evident from the way Arjan had numbered it, that this poem/letter was the third of three. So, when Guru Ram Das received it, he inquired where the other two poem/letters were. The servant/messenger spoke of giving them to Prithi Chand, who disclaimed all knowledge. Guru Ram Das then told an attendant to go to Prithi Chand's room and retrieve the papers he would find in the pockets of a garment hanging on a particular peg. Sure enough, there were the missing poems. Guru Ram Das then summoned Arjan from Lahore with all honors.

Upon his arrival Arjan wrote one last poem/letter at the Guru's request.

By good fortune I met the saintly Guru.
The Immortal God I have found in my own home.
Now I will ever serve You and never for a moment will I be separate
    from You.
Servant Nanak is your slave, O Beloved Master.
I am a sacrifice, my soul is a sacrifice;
Servant Nanak is your slave, O God.[5]

The Shabad Guru rang so clearly in Arjan's words that Guru Ram Das ordained him as his successor, Guru Arjan Dev. Well over 2000 Shabads from Guru Arjan Dev's pen have come down to us.

Prithi Chand's sibling rivalry with his younger brother continued unabated when Arjan became Guru Arjan Dev. Indeed, we owe the very existence of the *Siri Guru Granth Sahib* (for the moment—but only for the moment—we'll call it the Sikh Holy Scriptures) to this rivalry. Word came to Guru Arjan Dev that Prithi Chand was writing poems and signing them with the name of Nanak, the signature of Guru Nanak and all his successors--a signature Prithi Chand had no right to use. These poems did not have the uplifting impact of the Shabads of the True Guru. Realizing the harm these spurious Shabads could do, Guru Arjan Dev decided to create a definitive canon of Shabads.

The most complete collection of Shabads composed by the first three human Gurus was in the hands of *Mohan*, the eldest son of Guru Amar Das. So Guru Arjan Dev dispatched his secretary, *Bhai Gurdaas,* to request this collection from Mohan. Bhai Gurdaas returned unsuccessful. *Baba Buddha,* a respected and elderly Sikh who had been one of Guru Nanak's followers and who had already installed four of Guru Nanak's successors (he would later install one more), then offered to go. He returned unsuccessful as well. So Guru Arjan Dev himself went from Amritsar to *Goindwal* to entreat Mohan to part with his collection. No one at Mohan's house answered his call. So Guru Arjan Dev began to sing sweetly.

O Mohan, lofty is your mansion and matchless is your palace.
O Mohan, saints adorn your temple doors.
In your temple, they ever sing the praises of the Infinite and
  Merciful God.
Where the company of the saints assemble, they meditate on you.
Show compassion and kindness, O Compassionate One, and be
  merciful to the poor.
Nanak says, I am thirsting for a sight of you, grant it to me, and all
  happiness will be mine.[6]

After this verse, Mohan opened the door. After two more verses in a similar vein, Mohan handed the collection of Shabads over to Guru Arjan Dev, who then sang one final verse.

O Mohan, may you be successful with your family.
O Mohan, you have saved your children, friends, brethren and
  family.
You have saved those, who having beheld you, have dispelled their

43

pride.

Death never approaches those who magnify you.

Endless are Your excellences; they cannot be described, O True Guru and Supreme God.

Says Nanak, You have preserved a prop clinging to which the world shall be saved.[7]

While this treasure trove of Shabads and his own Shabads formed the nucleus of the collection, Guru Arjan Dev received Shabads and poems from other people as well. He called for Shabads written by Hindu and Muslim/Sufi saints. He called for the exquisite poetry of his secretary Bhai Gurdaas, who declined the honor, but whose Shabads are still sung in Sikh *Gurdwaras* everywhere. (The header quote for this chapter is from one of Bhai Gurdaas's most popular Shabads.) Guru Arjan Dev did receive Shabads from other contemporary bards. With this wealth of material, he set to work to form his collection.

He didn't accept everything he received for this collection. He rejected anything that was too emotional or egotistical, anything that was idolatrous, anything that denigrated women, anything that promoted isolation from humanity as the path of salvation, anything that upheld the caste system or other forms of discrimination, and anything that wasn't in *Naad.*

Naad, which literally means sound current or inner sound, is the key to the value of the Shabad Guru. Shabads are designed to be sung and recited out loud. When Shabads are in Naad, the act of singing or reciting them types a code on the upper palate of the mouth that triggers the experience of God consciousness in the singer/reciter. Absolutely everything Guru Arjan Dev allowed into his magnum opus, which was to be called the *Adi Granth,* has this quality. *Adi Granth* literally means "Primal Knot"—that which ties a knot between the disciple and the Divine. Chanting those words, singing those words, raises the singer's consciousness to the level of the saints who originally wrote or sang the words.

To emphasize the need to sing and recite the Shabads, Guru Arjan Dev arranged the Adi Granth as a songbook. The Shabads do not appear in alphabetical order. They do not appear in chronological order. They are not organized by subject. The way Guru Arjan Dev placed them is according to the *Raag*, or melodic mode, they were originally written in. Within each Raag, Shabads are grouped by author and by length. Those few Shabads not originally written in any Raag appear in the Adi Granth and its successor, the *Siri Guru Granth Sahib*, either before or after the ones that are in Raag.

For approximately three years, Guru Arjan Dev selected the Shabads and dictated them to his secretary Bhai Gurdaas. They completed this labor of love on August 15, 1604. It took another 15 days to create an index and have the Adi Granth bound.

The Adi Granth was installed in *Amritsar* (which means Nectar Tank) at the *Hari Mander Sahib* (literally "Great Temple of God"—now known to us as the Golden Temple) in a gala ceremony on August 30, 1604. Baba Buddha, the elderly Sikh who in childhood had followed Guru Nanak, carried the Adi Granth on his head. Guru Arjan Dev walked behind carrying a *chauri sahib*, or flywhisk, so indicating that he was the Adi Granth's servant. Accompanying them were many, many Sikhs singing *kirtan* (Shabads set to music and sung). Baba Buddha reverently placed the Adi Granth on a decorated throne inside the Hari Mander Sahib—which is situated in the middle of the pool of water that gives Amritsar it's name. He then opened the Adi Granth at random and took the first *Hukam*—literally "command," a reading for Sikhs to ponder and follow. It began like this:

God has come to complete the tasks of His Saints. God has come to do their work.
In this beauteous land, in the beauteous pool, is contained the nectar

45

water.

Filled with this nectar water, tasks are completed and all desires are fulfilled.

Cheers of victory resound around the world, and all sorrows are ended.[8]

Guru Arjan Dev had appointed Baba Buddha to be the first *Granthi*, or caretaker of the Granth. So, when the ceremony ended, Baba Buddha asked Guru Arjan Dev where he should put the Adi Granth. Guru Arjan Dev told him to place it on his (Guru Arjan Dev's) bed. Thereafter, Guru Arjan Dev slept on the floor.

No Shabads have come down to us from Gurus Six, Seven and Eight—*Guru Hargobind*, *Guru Har Rai* and *Guru Harkrishan* respectively. But the Adi Granth was not yet a complete document. Certain pages had been left blank. When Bhai Gurdaas asked the reason for this, Guru Arjan Dev simply stated that those pages would be filled later. We now know that those blank pages were slated to receive the Shabads of *Guru Teg Bahadur*, the Ninth Guru.

There was one glitch. During the Guruship of Guru Teg Bahadur, the Adi Granth had fallen into the greedy hands of *Dhir Mal*, Guru Teg Bahadur's nephew. Nothing would induce Dhir Mal to give this volume up. Indeed, when Guru Teg Bahadur's son and heir, *Guru Gobind Singh*, the Tenth Guru, politely requested the return of the Adi Granth, Dhir Mal challenged him to produce his own *Granth Sahib* from memory if he really was Guru Nanak's heir and scion. (It couldn't be another *Adi* Granth, because it wouldn't be the *first* one.) So that's what Guru Gobind Singh did.

In 1705, Guru Gobind Singh dictated the entire 1430 pages of the Granth Sahib in its current form from memory to his secretary *Bhai Mani Singh*. He included the Shabads of his father Guru Teg Bahadur in all the correct places. With the exception of these added Shabads, the Adi Granth and the Granth Sahib of Guru

Gobind Singh differ by only one word: *khulasa* (freed man) in the Adi Granth became *Khalsa* (King's own) in the Granth Sahib.[9] (These two words are almost identical in Naad.) Although the Shabad Guru resounds through Guru Gobind Singh's own poetry, he did not include any of his own writings—with the possible exception of a *slok* (short verse) included with the sloks of Guru Teg Bahadur.[10]

Soon thereafter the Shabad Guru came full circle. In 1708, when Guru Gobind Singh was dying from wounds inflicted by an assassin, he ordained the *Granth Sahib* (the version he had dictated) as his successor, the *Siri Guru Granth Sahib*. Thus, the Shabad Guru—which had been Guru Nanak's one and only Guru—became the one and only Guru of all Sikhs. Whenever I say "the Guru" and am not obviously referring to a human being, I am nearly always referring to the Shabad Guru as it is embodied in the *Siri Guru Granth Sahib*.

Because Sikhs treat the *Siri Guru Granth Sahib* with all respect and honor, no one changes it. Oh yes, we do translate it, and yes, the translations vary according to the understanding and literary ability of the translator. But we don't change the original. Guru Arjan Dev chose to be tortured to death rather than change certain words in the Adi Granth at the whim of Hindu and Muslim powers-that-be. The Seventh Guru, Guru Har Rai, otherwise noted for his gentleness, disowned a son who purposefully changed a single word in the Adi Granth to please the Mughal Emperor. The script of early copies of the *Siri Guru Granth Sahib* linked all the words together—making it supremely difficult to read, but insuring that no one added or subtracted anything. Most modern copies are easier to read, but no one changes a word. The point has been made.

One way to understand the *Siri Guru Granth Sahib* is this: *if* Jesus had compiled 1430 pages of psalms, and said "Read these, sing these and you will become like Me," you would have the equivalent of the *Siri Guru Granth Sahib*. So calling the *Siri Guru*

Granth Sahib a book is no more appropriate than calling Jesus Christ a body. On the surface it seems accurate, but it totally misses the point.

Even to call it a Holy Scripture is a little disrespectful. How many Holy Scriptures were compiled by one of the saints who originally wrote the words? Just the *Siri Guru Granth Sahib.* How many Holy Scriptures are revered as a living Guru? Just the *Siri Guru Granth Sahib.* (Well, okay, maybe the Torah and the Koran also.) How many Holy Scriptures consist entirely of poems that may be sung or recited to elevate one's conscious to the level of the saints who wrote the original words? Just the *Siri Guru Granth Sahib.*

Reciting the words in the *Siri Guru Granth Sahib* is a privilege and a service. Those who listen to the words are uplifted. The vibration of the Shabad Guru can penetrate so deep, deep, deep that even people living several blocks away benefit. So, the *Siri Guru Granth Sahib* is no book. It's an elevator masquerading as a book.

Sikhs utilize the Shabad Guru as it manifests in the *Siri Guru Granth Sahib* in several ways. We read our daily *Banis* or prayers. You'll learn more about them in the next chapter. We hold worship services at which the Guru presides. You'll hear more about these in the chapter, "In the Guru's Court: How Sikhs Worship." We read the Guru out loud from beginning to end. You'll hear more about this practice in the chapter "The Path of *Paths."* We chant *mantras* (repeated sounds) and Shabads in the practice known as *Nam Simran* (Remembrance of the Name), which was discussed in Chapter 2. We chant to God in the early morning, a practice you'll hear more about in the chapter titled "Sadhana: Early in the Morning Our Song Shall Rise to Thee." And there is the practice I call *Shabad Yoga* —my terminology, not Yogi Bhajan's. (See sidebar for Shabad Yoga Basics.)

Shabad Yoga Basics

Shabad Yoga is a simple, easy and effective technique. Reciting Shabads in the original Gurmukhi types codes into the brain that produce a profound impact on consciousness, cutting through the negativity that lurks in the subconscious. So Shabads are most effective when sung or recited in the original Gurmukhi as meditations in their own right. The pronunciation guide is in Appendix B.

Shabads are usually practiced for 11 or 26 or 54 or 108 repetitions. I use a rosary bequeathed by an aunt when I'm reciting Shabads. At the end of the last repetition, I was taught to repeat the last two lines twice. It's great to pick a Shabad and practice it daily for 40 or 90 or 120 or 1000 or more days.

You really can recite a Shabad just about anywhere. I have seen people practice Shabads while walking, and I once had the opportunity to practice Shabads when I was in the hospital recovering from food poisoning.

But please treat this technique respectfully. Cover your head when chanting or reciting a Shabad. Chanting Shabads in the original Gurmukhi makes such a great impact on consciousness that the head needs be covered, preferably with white cotton, to provide insulation.

Although chanting Shabads is a Sikh technique, you do not need to be a Sikh to practice Shabad Yoga. Some of my non-Sikh students have reported success reciting certain Shabads as affirmations in English.

You will find several sidebars with Shabads that you may practice as Shabad Yoga in the next few chapters. All other Shabads in this book, including the protocol Shabads for a Gurdwara service and the complete Bayntee Chaupa-ee in Appendix C, may be recited in this way.

Shabad Yoga is the recitation of individual Shabads for eleven or more consecutive repetitions. It's like chanting an extended mantra. Reciting Shabads produces various effects according to the Shabad and the intent of the reciter. I know a lady who recited a Shabad for victory when she needed funds to travel. The funds obligingly appeared. I know a non-Sikh lady whose rather toxic relationship with her mother healed after she began to recite two Shabads in English translation for eleven repetitions each. My own favorite personal story with Shabad Yoga follows.

The lady who taught me to read Gurmukhi also introduced me to Shabad Yoga. Fired with enthusiasm for this blessed technology, I acquired a copy of *The Psyche of the Golden Shield*, a three-ring binder book with numerous Shabads for specific situations. As I pulled the book out of the box it arrived in, all the pages fell out of the binder except the one page with the Shabad *Moo Laalan Si-o Preet Banee*. I loaned the book to the lady who had taught me to read Gurmukhi, and when she returned the book, again every page fell out of the binder except for the page containing *Moo Laalan Si-o Preet Banee*. Figuring that God must be directing my attention to this one Shabad for a reason, I began chanting 11 repetitions of it daily. (See sidebar for the full text of *Moo Laalan Si-o Preet Banee* in both English translation and Gurmukhi transliteration.)

Shabad Yoga
Moo Laalan Si-o Preet Banee (I Have Fallen in Love with My Beloved)

This is the Shabad I practiced for 11 repetitions daily that opened my consciousness to a place where a sense of loss no longer existed. It increases the experience of devotion in relationships.

Remember to cover your head before reciting this or any other Shabad. The pronunciation guide is in Appendix B.

Moo laalan si-o preet banee. (Rahaa-o)
Toree na tootai chhoree na chhootai aisee maadho khinch tanee.
Dinas rain man maa-eh basat hai too kar kirpaa prabh apanee.
Bal bal jaa-o si-aam sundar kau akath kathaa kaa kee baat sunee.
Jan naanak daasan daas kehee-at hai mo-eh karaho kirpaa thaakur apunee.

Translation:

I have fallen in love with my Beloved. (Pause)
Such are the bonds of devotion which God has fastened me with:
Breaking, they are not broken.
Letting go, they are not let go.
Day and night, God abides within my mind.
Bless me with Your Mercy, O God.
I am a sacrifice, a sacrifice, unto my Beauteous Lord.
I have heard His Story and His Sublime Discourse.
Servant Nanak is said to be the slave of His Slaves.
O my Master, bestow Your Mercy upon me.[11]

During the time I was practicing this Shabad, someone I was most unhappily estranged from required surgery. I decided to hold the person in my heart surrounded with light for the day of the surgery. That felt good, so my soul and I decided to continue this practice indefinitely. One day as I was doing my daily repetitions of *Moo Laalan Si-o Preet Banee* in Gurmukhi, I looked over at the English translation and saw the words, *Breaking, they are not broken. Letting go, they are not let go.*[12]

The light went on! There wasn't any estrangement because the person was always in my heart. Furthermore, as I noticed this person in my heart, I saw God and anyone else in creation there too. The Infinite vastness was there within me! All creation was there within me! The loneliness I had carried from my childhood vanished. I have never been truly alone since. God and all creation are always there.

This is what the Shabad Guru does. It can uplift those who have fallen in a pit of depression and darkness. It inspires and heals and lightens the load. It is a vibration of joy. All that Sikhism is, is an outward manifestation of the Shabad Guru. It is the sound way to God.

Part II

Practicing the Sound Way to God

Sikh Devotions

Through songs of God, divine knowledge will come to you;
Through waves of melody, ecstasy will be produced.
Guru Gobind Singh [1]

Chapter 5

Banis: The Daily Word

Your Bani is nectar, O God, O God.
Hearing it again and again, I experience supreme bliss.
Guru Arjan Dev [1]

A number of years ago, a friend of mine was working as a music therapist in a hospital in British Columbia near the United States border in an area with a huge Sikh population. Residing in a long term care residential unit within this hospital was an elderly Sikh gentleman, probably in his 90s. "Bapu-ji" (not his real name) was disturbing other residents by muttering strange words audibly in the communal living areas, especially in the morning after he was bathed and dressed and in his wheelchair. When the muttering got too bad, the hospital staff would sedate him. (My friend assures me that sedation is no longer permitted for such "problems." Unfortunately, it was permitted then.) He was considered demented, and my friend the music therapist was called in to ameliorate the situation. And she did...but not by stopping his muttering.

My friend told me, "I had such a sense of sweetness from him...and when I really paid attention to the quality of the sounds he was making, I understood their inherent musicality—the sounds had pitch and had rhythm and pace." My friend wasn't a Sikh at the time, and she didn't understand the words at all. But she didn't think the man was demented—"just a very old man who couldn't hear very well and had severe cataracts." So my friend asked a Sikh colleague—an occupational therapist at the same hospital—to listen to Bapu-ji's mutterings and determine if the man was coherent or not.

Turned out, yes, he was. What the elderly Sikh man was doing, explained the occupational therapist, was reciting the prayers that devout Sikhs recite daily, "especially to prepare for death." My friend then learned from Bapu-ji's family that he had been devout all his life. And so my friend indeed ameliorated the situation: she shared the information she had acquired on the man with the rest of the hospital staff, and he was given the time and the space each morning to pray in privacy.

My friend ended this story by saying, "There were a few times that I came into his room in the late afternoon to hear him softly praying in his bed. I believe now with hindsight that he was preparing for his death as we are trained — to be uttering the name of God until our last breath."

The prayers Bapu-ji was reciting are called *Banis*. *Bani* (pronounced BAA-nee) literally means "word" and technically includes any words that come out of the mouth — anything we say, anything we recite, anything we sing. However, in practice, the word *Bani* refers to any of the set prayers a devout Sikh recites out loud daily. (Sikhs often speak of *reading* their Banis. Whenever you see — or hear — something along those lines, understand it to refer to reading Banis *out loud*.)

Reciting Banis is perhaps the most direct way individual Sikhs — and some people who consider themselves non-Sikhs — ordinarily connect with the vibration of the *Shabad Guru* (the Guru of enlightened sound that we learned about in the last chapter). Reciting Banis lifts the spirits and the consciousness of the reader and projects a positive vibration into the environment. We recite Banis to prepare for death as Bapu-ji's story illustrates, but we also recite them to prepare for life.

Reading Banis can have positive physical effects. For instance, I have Raynaud's syndrome, the condition of having more sympathetic nerve endings than parasympathetic nerve endings. What that causes, oddly enough, is a constriction to circulation in my extremities — it doesn't take much for my fingers to go blue, or even white, with cold. But when I recite my Banis, my fingers sometimes turn red hot, usually without the rest of my body overheating.

Reading Banis is much like meditating, impacting the mind in positive ways. When I read my Banis, the fogginess in my mind dissipates, I get creative ideas for dealing with sticky problems, I remember things I need to do, my spirits lift, and I understand things better. I feel much happier when I read all my Banis than when I don't. Other Sikhs (and a few non-Sikhs) have mentioned these things also.

Based on my experiences and the experiences of others, reciting Banis seems to stimulate the back part of the brain, which I once heard someone call the "Third Ear" — that ineffable part of us that hears inner vibrations. I often feel a band of vibrating energy across the back of my head when I read my Banis. Other people have mentioned this same phenomena.

Reciting Banis can have an amazing spiritual impact. I can personally attest to their spiritual power. Soon after I became a Sikh, there came a time when I would lie in bed and go into the most amazing state. I would dissolve and become a point of consciousness floating in the vast ocean of God's Light and Love. I was nothing, and in that nothingness, there was only God. It was the most humbling, ego-killing experience...and the most blissful. Boundless bliss! Gratitude unending! At that time, my spiritual practice consisted almost entirely of reading my daily Banis.

So, let's take a closer look at each of the Banis individually. They fall into three broad groupings. Three of them (*Japji Sahib, Anand Sahib* and *Sukhmani Sahib*) are longer individual works from the *Siri Guru Granth Sahib*. Another three (*Jaap Sahib, Tav Prasaad Swaiyay* and *Bayntee Chaupa-ee*) are from the writings of *Guru Gobind Singh*, the Tenth Guru. Yet another three (*Shabad Hazaaray, Rehiras Sahib* and *Kirtan Sohila*) are composites of several *Shabads* (hymns). All but *Shabad Hazaaray* and *Sukhmani*

Sahib are required reading for a "baptized" or Amritdari Sikh, a phenomenon we'll examine in the Amrit Ceremony chapter.

In the following pages, we'll be looking each Bani, not according to the above groupings, but by the order they appear in a *Nit Nem* (Sikh prayer book). We'll be looking at passages from each Bani, describing what each Bani does and explaining how some of them are featured in special spiritual practices.

Japji Sahib

Japji Sahib, which literally means "Respected Recitation for the Soul," is the first (and arguably, the foremost) of the Sikh daily Banis. Guru Nanak, the founder of Sikhism, wrote it right after his enlightenment in 1496. It sings with that experience. Reading Japji Sahib jumpstarts our souls, attunes us with the ethers, boldly awakens our humility and our creativity, and bestows vast tracts of wisdom upon us. It is one of the Banis recited during Sikh death ceremonies, one of the Banis recited during the Amrit Ceremony, and is the one Bani a devout Sikh would prefer to be reciting while dying. Condensed within this one Bani is the entire wisdom of the *Siri Guru Granth Sahib*.

The complete Japji Sahib begins a devout Sikh's day. Many Sikhs, including me, read it before breakfast every morning. Because Japji Sahib starts the *Aquarian Sadhana* of Kundalini Yoga practitioners, it is the one Bani most frequently recited by people who consider themselves non-Sikhs. (More details on the Aquarian Sadhana are in Chapter 8.)

Japji Sahib opens with *Mool Mantra*, literally "Root Mantra," a verbal package of soul wisdom. When I took *Amrit*, the people who administered it told us that 110 Mool Mantras could replace one whole Bani. It's also one of the mantras used in Kundalini Yoga. (See sidebar for translation and transliteration of Mool Mantra, plus a Kundalini Yoga exercise using it.)

Kundalini Yoga
Mool Mantra Kriya [2]
Originally Taught on July 23, 1977

I love this kriya; I soar with happiness when I do it. It's good for body, mind and soul. The physical position enhances flexibility, energizes the body and puts tremendous pressure on the liver and navel point, causing the glands to secrete and become balanced. According to Yogi Bhajan, if you perfect this kriya, you cannot think wrong thoughts, as it enables you to control the flight of your mind.

Here's a fairly literal translation of Mool Mantra:

One Creator Creation. Truth Name.
Being of Action. Without fear. Without vengeance.
Undying. Unborn. Self-illumined.
By Guru's Gift. RECITE!
True in the beginning.
True through all time.
True even now.
Nanak: Truth shall always be. [3]

Be sure to tune in before practicing this—or any other—Kundalini Yoga kriya. See the information on Kundalini Yoga Basics in Chapter 2. For information on how to end the deep relaxation at the end, please see the sidebar in the Sadhana chapter. Pronunciation guide is in Appendix B. Please note that *Jap* sounds more like *Jup*.

How to Do It
Sit with your spine erect and your legs spread as wide as

possible, straight on the ground. Bring your arms up to shoulder level, parallel to the ground, directly over the legs. Palms face up. (See figure 1.) Chant:

Ek Ong Kaar, Sat Naam
Kartaa Purakh, Nirbhao, Nirvair
Akaal Moorat, Ajoonee, Saibhang,
Gurprasaad,
Jap!
Aad Sach
Jugaad Sach
Hai Bhee Sach
Naanak Hosee Bhee Sach.

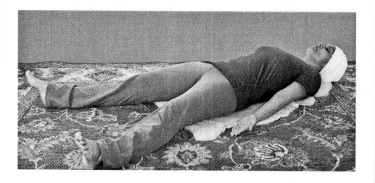

As you chant, begin leaning backward, so that you are flat on your back with your arms relaxed by your sides by the time you complete one repetition of the mantra. (See figure 2.) Relax in this position for 5 seconds. Then inhale and chant another repetition of the mantra as you slowly raise yourself—keeping your arms stretched out—as you return to the original erect position. Then inhale and chant

another repetition of mantra as you slowly bend forward, bringing your forehead to the ground (or as far as it will go) with your hands resting on top of your feet. (See figure 3.) Throughout the movement, keep your back as straight as you can.

Once you get the hang of this process, continue the same movement, but chant more slowly, so that you reach the word *Jap!* by the time you are in the original position both on the forward motion and the backward motion. Continue for 11 minutes. (You may eventually increase the time up to 108 rounds of mantra.)

Relax on your back for 5-10 minutes.

Japji Sahib closes with the following *slok* (short verse) that figures in every Sikh service:

> *The breath of air is the Guru; water is the Father; And the earth is the Great Mother of all.*
> *Day and night are the two nurses in whose lap all the world plays.*
> *Good deeds and bad deeds — The record is read in the Presence of the Lord of Dharma.*
> *By our own actions, we are drawn closer or pushed farther away.*
> *Those who have meditated on the Name And departed after toiling by the sweat of the brow,*
> *O Nanak, their faces shine, and many are liberated with them.*[4]

(Transliteration of the slok of Japji Sahib is in the sidebar.)

Protocol Shabad
Slok of Japji Sahib

According to The Psyche of the Soul, the ending slok of
Japji Sahib by Guru Nanak may be recited for eleven or
more continuous repetitions as a form of Shabad Yoga for
elevation and respect. My music therapist friend enjoys
chanting it on its own for 31 minutes. A single repetition of
this slok immediately follows the first five pauris of Anand
Sahib towards the end of every Gurdwara service.

Remember to cover your head when practicing this or
any other Shabad. Pronunciation guide is in Appendix B.
Please note that the word "door" in the transliteration
actually rhymes with "pure."

Pavan guroo paanee pitaa maataa dharat mehat.
Divas raat du-i daa-ee daa-i-aa khaylai sagal jagat.
Changi-aa-ee-aa buri-aa-ee-aa vaachai dharam hadoor.
Karmee aapo aapanee kay nayrai kay door.
Jinee naam dhi-aa-i-aa ga-ay masakat ghaal.
Naanak tay mukh ujalay kaytee chhutee naal.

In between Mool Mantra and the slok are 38 pauris of unequal
length. A *pauri* is literally a rung of a ladder. Sikhs use the word
to mean a stanza in a longer poetic composition. Each pauri in
Japji Sahib is a rung in the ladder leading to spiritual heights.
And each pauri may be practiced as a form of *Shabad Yoga* (see
the last chapter).

For eleven and a half years, I recited eleven daily repetitions
of the 24th Pauri of Japji in *Gurmukhi* (the original language), in
addition to reading my daily Banis. My consciousness expanded
vastly. For the first few years I experienced the bliss of floating in

God's Light and Love as described earlier in this chapter. I still have this experience, but no longer need to be lying down to have it...usually. Later, by the end of the eleven and a half years, I had dropped a huge dump truck load of limiting beliefs about what I could do and what I couldn't do...or more accurately, what God could and couldn't do through me. Here's the translation for this pauri:

> *Unlimited are the Praises, and Unlimited those who speak them.*
> *Unlimited are the Actions; Unlimited are the Gifts.*
> *Unlimited is the Vision; Unlimited are the Sounds resounding.*
> *The limits cannot be perceived. What is the mystery of the mind?*
> *The limits of the created universe cannot be perceived.*
> *Its limits here and beyond cannot be perceived.*
> *Many struggle to know the limits.*
> *But those limits cannot be found.*
> *No one can know these limits.*
> *The more one says about them, the more remains to be said.*
> *Great is the Master Whose Abode is High.*
> *Highest of the High, above all is the Name.*
> *Only one as Great and High as God*
> *Can know the Lofty and Exalted State.*
> *Only the Great One knows that Greatness.*
> *O Nanak, by the Glance of Grace, blessings are bestowed.* [5]

(See the sidebar for how to recite the 24th Pauri of Japji Sahib as a form of Shabad Yoga.)

Shabad Yoga
The 24th Pauri of Japji Sahib (Unlimited Are the Praises)

I recited 11 repetitions of this pauri every single day for eleven and a half years. According to The Psyche of the Soul, reciting it destroys limitations and misfortunes. I highly recommend it for experiencing divine vastness.

Use the pronunciation guide in Appendix B. The word *Ant* in the following transliteration is not pronounced like the English word for a small insect, but is closer to *Unt*. Remember to cover your head when reciting this or any other Shabad. More tips on reciting Shabads are in the chapter on the Shabad Guru.

Ant na sifatee kehn na ant.
Ant na karnai dayn na ant.
Ant na vaykhan sunan na ant.
Ant na jaapai ki-aa man mant.
Ant na jaapai keetaa aakaar.
Ant na jaapai paaraavaar.
Ant na kaaran kaytay bilalaa-eh.
Taa kay ant na paa-ay jaa-eh.
Ayho ant na jaanai ko-i.
Bahutaa kehee-ai bahutaa ho-i.
Vadaa sahib oochaa thaa-o.
Oochay upar oochaa naa-o.
Ayvad oochaa hovai ko-i.
Tis oochay kau jaanai so-i.
Jayvad aap jaanai aap aap.
Naanak nadareee karmee daat.

In addition to reciting the pauris of Japji Sahib as a form of

Shabad Yoga, there are a couple of other special spiritual practices connected with this Bani.

One of these is the recitation of eleven consecutive, complete Japji Sahibs daily—a practice engaged in by my friend Ravitej Singh Khalsa, a successful advertising designer—who incidentally does not read *Gurmukhi* script. (He uses a transliteration.) Reading Japji Sahib for him is like the most exciting entertaining ride in an amusement park. He says, "Doing this has been a quantum shift in consciousness." Ravitej further commented that eleven Japji Sahibs per day shifts time and space, which makes everything different—and easier—from that point forward on a daily basis. When I asked Ravitej what had specifically shifted in his life since beginning the eleven consecutive Japji Sahibs per day, he replied, "The axis of the Earth!" Most notably, Ravitej, who was born in December of 1944, enjoys superlative health. At one physical exam, his doctor was astounded that a sixty-year-old man was in better shape than he had been at his previous physical, which had occurred before Ravitej began reciting those eleven Japji Sahibs per day. Ravitej has also noticed an extraordinary increase in wisdom, insight and knowledge.

Another special practice requires a trip to the Punjabi city of *Goindwal*, the home of a Nectar Tank, a sacred pool of water, built by *Guru Amar Das*, the Third Guru. Eighty-four steps lead down into this Nectar Tank. Guru Amar Das is said to have promised that the accumulated *karma* of 8.4 lifetimes will be washed away and the cycle of *reincarnation* will end for the person who recites Japji Sahib on each of these eighty-four steps—starting with the lowest step and ending with the top step. This procedure is challenging because the person must dunk his/her body into the Nectar Tank after each repetition of the complete Japji Sahib before ascending to the next step. It's not a dry process! But those who have had the discipline and courage to complete this practice have commented on the vastness they have experienced...and sometimes, even the healing.

One non-Sikh lady started the practice with pneumonia and ended it cured. This same lady, who had begun the process with a huge fear of the germs she might pick up, remarked, "No longer was I a separate entity, recoiling from the people, shrinking from the mosquitoes, and protecting myself from hidden germs." By the eighty-fourth step, she felt, "Greater than the greatest and smaller than the smallest." [6]

Shabad Hazaaray

Unlike Japji Sahib, *Shabad Hazaaray* (literally "a thousand Shabads") is a composite. No, it doesn't actually contain a thousand Shabads. Its name is a graceful compliment to its effectiveness—as great as a thousand Shabads.

It opens with *Mayraa Man Lochai*, the four poetic letters that turned *Arjan* into *Guru Arjan Dev*, the Fifth Guru, (the story's in the chapter on the *Shabad Guru*). Following that are six more Shabads, all by Guru Nanak. Each of these Shabads express the longing of the soul for God. So, this is a Bani for devotion, for merging with the Infinite, for ending separations, and God willing, even for preventing divorce. (But we make no guarantees.) The Shabad that ends Shabad Hazaaray expresses this fulfillment of longing. Here's the translation:

My mind is the temple, and my body the course gown of a wandering seeker;
I bathe in the shrine of my heart.
The One Song lives in my breath; I shall not be born again.
My mind is pierced by the Merciful One, O my mother.
Who can know the pain of another?
I care for nothing other than God. (Pause.)
O Unfathomable, Invisible, Infinite, Unknowable One, take care of me!
You pervade the water, land and sky; Your Light is in every heart.
All teachings, instructions and understandings are Yours;

All mansions and sanctuaries belong to You as well.
I know of nothing without You, O Master, so I sing ever Your Praise.
All creatures seek Your Refuge for the care of all is in Your Hands.
That which pleases You is good; so Nanak prays to You alone.[7]

Although many Sikhs, including me, recite Shabad Hazaaray daily, it's not required reading for an Amritdari Sikh.

Jaap Sahib

Guru Gobind Singh, the Tenth Guru, wrote *Jaap Sahib*, the longest required daily Bani. Jaap Sahib means "Great Recitation." If you want to learn what Sikhs really think about God, this is the Bani to read. Its 199 short pauris are a poetic catalog about God...and a goldmine of mantras. Mantras from Jaap Sahib—and Kundalini Yoga practices containing them—appear in both the *Path* chapter and the Sadhana chapter. Here's another mantra taken from Jaap Sahib:

Invincible. Indestructible. Fearless. Unchanging.
Unformed. Unborn. Immortal. Universally Pervasive.
Unbreakable. Impenetrable. Invisible. Needing no food.
Undying. Merciful. Indescribable. Un-costumed.
Nameless. Beyond desire. Unfathomable. Incorruptible.
The One above all. Ultimate Annihilator. Beyond birth. Beyond
*   silence.*
Without attachment. Without color. Without form. Without feature.
Unbound by actions. Beyond delusion. Unvanquished. Beyond
*   depiction.* [8]

(See sidebar for the transliteration and for a meditation using this mantra.)

Kundalini Yoga
Ajai Alai Meditation [9]
Originally Taught on August 1, 2001

The Ajai Alai mantra from Guru Gobind Singh's Jaap Sahib helps us receive what we need from the Hand of God. It may also be practiced on its own as a form of Shabad Yoga. Information on Shabad Yoga is in the Shabad Guru Chapter.

Yogi Bhajan used this mantra in several meditations. He recommended this meditation as a practice for taking ourselves in hand so that we can take any situation in hand, to pull ourselves together so that we can pull through anything. Practicing it can free us from tension, depression and other problems.

Be sure to tune in before beginning any Kundalini Yoga practice. For more information, see the sidebars on tuning in and other Kundalini Yoga in Chapter 2. CDs with this mantra are available (see Resources). Pronunciation guide is in Appendix B.

How to Do It

Sitting in a cross-legged position with your chin in and your chest out, cross your arms over your chest and hold your shoulders, hugging yourself tight. Focus your eyes on the tip of your nose. Sing the Ajai Alai Shabad using the tip of your tongue to pronounce the words precisely. Chant the following words rhythmically:

Ajai. Alai. Abhai. Abai.
Abhoo. Ajoo. Anaas. Akaas.
Aganj. Abhanj. Alakh. Abhakh.
Akaal. Dayaal. Alaykh. Abhaykh.
Anaam. Akaam. Agaaha. Adhaaha.
Anaathay. Pramaathay. Ajonee. Amonee.
Naraagay. Narangay. Naroopay. Naraykhay.
Akaramang. Abharamang. Aganjay. Alaykhay.

Continue for 3-11 minutes. Then inhale deeply, hold the breath, and stretch your spine while hugging yourself tight with every bit of energy. Relax.

Once you get into it, reading Jaap Sahib out loud in Gurmukhi is like listening to horses galloping. It has that rhythm. Reading Jaap Sahib stimulates courage, opens the heart, grants grace and greatness, promotes radiance and prosperity, magnifies the power of the word, and grants deep understanding of people's words and actions.

Tav Prasaad Swaiyay

Like Jaap Sahib and all other works by Guru Gobind Singh, *Tav Prasaad Swaiyay* appears in the *Dasam Granth* (Writings of the Tenth Guru) rather than in the *Siri Guru Granth Sahib*. Like Japji Sahib and Jaap Sahib, Tav Prasaad Swaiyay (which means "Measures by Thy Grace") is one of the Banis used in the Amrit Ceremony.

A *swaiyay* is a short verse, usually four lines long, generally used in songs of praise. So Tav Prasaad Swaiyay is a song in praise of God. The version of this Bani in my *Nit Nem* (prayer book) has three groups of ten swaiyays. Some Nit Nems have just one or two of these groups.

Tav Prasaad Swaiyay is a heart-warming Bani, good for releasing dissatisfaction. Here's a translation of one of the swaiyays.

> *God always cherishes the meek and helpless, saving the honor of the*
> *Saints and obliterating their enemies.*
> *Birds, beasts, mountains, snakes, and kings: God cherishes them all.*
> *God cherishes all living beings in the sea or on the land, and does*
> *not hold their bad actions against them.*
> *The Ocean of Mercy is kind to the poor, and continually gives gifts,*
> *even though seeing the unworthiness of those who receive.* [10]

Bayntee Chaupa-ee

Bayntee Chaupa-ee is also by Guru Gobind Singh, also used in the Amrit Ceremony, and also appears in the *Dasam Granth* rather than in the *Siri Guru Granth Sahib*. Bayntee Chaupa-ee is a Bani in its own right to be recited in the morning as a prayer for protection, but it also appears in its entirety as a section of the evening Bani *Rehiras Sahib*. It is sometimes recited during *Sukhasan*, the ceremony of closing the *Siri Guru Granth Sahib* for the day, a procedure we'll learn more about in the next chapter.

Most unfortunately, Bayntee Chaupa-ee is truncated in most *Nit Nems* I have seen, where it is often missing its last two pauris and the *Arill* (short verse). Right after I took Amrit, I had the pleasure of sitting next to the *Siri Singh Sahib* during a meal at which he spoke in Punjabi to the *Panj Pi-aaray* (literally "Five Beloveds") who had administered the Amrit. He was speaking with emphasis, and the Panj, between bites of food, looked very intent and nodded earnestly at regular intervals. When I asked them afterwards what the Siri Singh Sahib had been saying, they told me that he been speaking seriously of the damage caused by reciting the incomplete Bayntee Chaupa-ee during the Amrit Ceremony. To correct that situation—and because it's too long to include the whole thing here—I have placed the complete text of

Bayntee Chaupa-ee in both translation and transliteration in Appendix C.

Anand Sahib

The last of the morning Banis is *Anand Sahib* (Song of Bliss) by Guru Amar Das. Its full forty pauris provide a scenic highway to bliss, happiness and good fortune. My heart sings with happiness when I recite it.

The creation of Anand Sahib has a special story. One day an aged Yogi appeared in Guru Amar Das' court. With great reverence, the Yogi stated that he had found no lasting happiness on his path, and requested as a special boon that he might be born into the Guru's family where he hoped to find happiness at last. The Guru gracefully acquiesced to this request. The Yogi then departed to meditate by a river and passed away soon after. Less than a year later, the wife of the second son of Guru Amar Das gave birth to a son. Upon hearing the news, Guru Amar Das sent for the infant, who was, of course, the reincarnated Yogi. Guru Amar Das took the infant Yogi on his lap, named him *Anand* (Bliss), and sang to him Anand Sahib, which Guru Amar Das composed on the spot.

Sikhs have been singing Anand Sahib ever since. We recite the entire Anand Sahib daily—literally for the joy of it. We sing the first five pauris near the end of every Gurdwara service and at the end of every Akhand Path. We sing the first five pauris at every wedding. The complete Anand Sahib (never just part) is one of the Banis used in the Amrit Ceremony. And we also recite the first five pauris of Anand Sahib as part of *Rehiras Sahib*, the evening Bani. Here is a translation of the first five pauris:

O my mother, I am in ecstasy for I have found my True Guru.
I have found the True Guru effortlessly,
 And my mind resounds with the music of bliss.
With jeweled music, the celestial fairies sing the Word.

They sing God's Word, which they enshrine in the mind.

Says Nanak, "I am in ecstasy for I have found my True Guru."

O my mind, dwell always on God.

Dwell always on God, O my mind, and all sufferings will be forgotten.

The One shall accept you and arrange all your affairs.

God does everything! Why forget this?

Says Nanak, "O my mind, dwell forever on God."

O True Master, what is not in Your Home?

Within Your Home are all things; as You give, so we receive.

Constantly singing Your Praises, Your Name is enshrined in the mind.

When the Name abides in the mind, the Shabad resounds within.

Says Nanak, "O True Master, what is not in Your Home?"

The True Name is my support.

The True Name is my support and satisfies all my hunger.

It has brought peace and tranquility to my mind and fulfilled all my desires.

I am ever a sacrifice unto my Guru who possesses such greatness!

Says Nanak, "Listen, O Saints, enshrine the Shabad with love.

The True Name is my only support."

The five primal sounds resound in that most fortunate home.

In that most fortunate home where the Shabad resounds, God has infused Great Power.

Through You, we subdue the five demons, and slay death, the torturer.

Those who have such a high destiny remain attached to God's Name.

Says Nanak, "They are at peace in whose homes the unstruck sound current resounds." [11]

(Transliteration for the first five pauris of Anand Sahib is in the sidebar.)

Protocol Shabad
Song of Bliss (First Five Pauris of Anand Sahib)

The first five pauris of Anand Sahib (Song of Bliss) by Guru Amar Das, the Third Guru, begin the ceremonial finale to nearly all Gurdwara services. In that case, they are always followed without a break by the ending slok of Japji Sahib, which appears in an earlier sidebar in this chapter. These five pauris also appear in Rehiras Sahib, the evening Bani. They may be practiced for eleven or more continuous repetitions as a form of Shabad Yoga for bliss.

Remember to cover your head when reciting these pauris. Pronunciation guide is in Appendix B.

Anand bha-i-aa mayree maa-ay satiguroo mai paa-i-aa.
Satigur ta paa-i-aa sehj saytee man vajee-aa vaadhaa-ee-aa.
Raag ratan parvaar paree-aa shabad gaavan aa-ee-aa.
Shabado ta gaavaho haree kayraa man jinee vasaa-i-aa.
Kahai naanak anand ho-aa satiguroo mai paa-i-aa.
Ay man mayri-aa too sadaa reho har naalay.
Har naal reho too man mayray dookh sabh visaarnaa.
Angeekaar oho karay tayraa kaaraj sabh savaarnaa.
Sabhanaa galaa samarath su-aamee so ki-o manaho visaaray.
Kahai naanak mann mayray sadaa reho har naalay.
Saachay saahibaa ki-aa naahee ghar tayrai.
Ghar ta tayrai sabh kichh hai jis day-eh so paava-ay.
Sadaa sifiti salaah tayree naam man vasaava-ay.
Naam jin kai man vasi-aa vaajay shabad ghanayray.
Kahai naanak sachay saahib ki-aa naahee ghar tayrai.
Saachaa naam mayraa aadhaaro.
Saach naam adhaar mayraa jin bhukhaa sabh gavaa-ee-aa.
Kar shaanti sukh man aa-i vasi-aa jin ichhaa sabh pujaa-ee-

aa.

Sadaa kurbaan keetaa guroo vitaho jis dee-aa ay-eh vadi-aa-
ee-aa.

Kahai naanak sunaho santaho shabad dharaho pi-aaro.

Saachaa naam mayraa aadhaaro.

Vaajay panch shabad tit ghar sabhaagai.

Ghar sabhaagai shabad vaajay kalaa jit ghar dhaaree-aa.

Panch doot tudh vas keetay kaal kantak maari-aa.

Dhur karam paa-i-aa tudh jin kau si naam har kai laagay.

Kahai naanak teh sukh ho-aa tit ghar anahad vaajay.

Rehiras Sahib

All the Banis we've talked about so far—Japji Sahib, Shabad
Hazaaray, Jaap Sahib, Tav Prasaad Swaiyay, Bayntee Chaupa-ee,
and Anand Sahib—are morning Banis. That is to say, they are
most effective when recited in the morning, preferably before
breakfast. But *Rehiras Sahib* is most effective recited at twilight or
in the evening.

Rehiras Sahib is an intricate and sophisticated mosaic of some
twenty items by Guru Nanak, Guru Amar Das, Guru Ram Das,
Guru Arjan Dev, and Guru Gobind Singh. It includes the
complete Bayntee Chaupa-ee with Arill and the first five pauris
of Anand Sahib and concludes with Guru Arjan Dev's *Rakhay
Rakhanahaar*, which we'll meet in the Sadhana chapter.
Unfortunately, the opening slok of Rehiras Sahib, which is by
Guru Nanak, appears in very few Nit Nems. (None of mine
contain it.) In some Nit Nems, some of the ending sloks by Guru
Arjan Dev also turn up missing. But it's much more effective
with the whole thing.

The word "Rehiras" is derived from words for energy, life and
commodity and means something like the Flow of Life, Energy
and Goods. So Rehiras Sahib is a rejuvenating Bani—both for

health and energy and for one's pocketbook. Here's a sample
Shabad from Rehiras Sahib:

> *O my mind, why suffer anxiety?*
> *God provides for your sustenance,*
> *God created beings in slabs and stones and provided sustenance for
> them.*
> *O God, whoever joins the holy company shall be released.*
> *By Guru's Grace, the Supreme State is obtained.*
> *The shriveled wood has blossomed. (Pause.)*
> *Mother, father, the world, children, wife: no one is the support of
> anyone else.*
> *For everyone God provides sustenance.*
> *O my mind, why be apprehensive?*
> *The crane that flies hundreds of miles away leaving her brood
> behind.*
> *Who is there to feed and provide for them?*
> *Consider this in your mind.*
> *All treasures and 18 spiritual powers lie in God's Hands.*
> *Nanak, God's servant, is ever a sacrifice unto the One Whose Extent
> is immeasurable.* [12]

(See sidebar for transliteration of this Shabad from Rehiras
Sahib.)

Shabad Yoga
Kaahay Ray Man Chitveh Udam (O My Mind, Why Suffer Anxiety?)

This Shabad from Rehiras Sahib is by Guru Arjan Dev, the
Fifth Guru. For prosperity, recite it for 11, 26, 54 or 108
consecutive repetitions for 40, 90, 120 or 1000 days or

more.[13] Remember to cover your head when reciting this Shabad—or any other Shabad. Pronunciation guide is in Appendix B.

Kaahay ray man chitveh udam jaa aahar har jee-o pari-aa.
Sail pathar meh jant upaa-ay taa kaa rijak aagai kar dhari-aa.
Mayray maadhau jee sat sangat milay su tari-aa.
Gurprasaad param pad paa-i-aa sookay kaasat hari-aa.
  (Rahaa-o.)
Janan pitaa lok sut banitaa ko-i kisakee dhari-aa.
Sir sir rijak sambhaahay thaakur kaahay man bhau kari-aa.
Ooday ood aavai sai kosaa tis paachhai bacharay chhari-aa.
Tin kavan khalaavai kavan chugaavai man meh simran kari-aa.
Sabh nidhaan das ast sidhaan thaakur kar tal dhari-aa.
Jan Naanak bal bal sad bal jaa-ee-ai tayraa ant na paaraavaari-aa.

Kirtan Sohila

Kirtan Sohila (Song of Praise) is the last of the Banis that are required reading for an Amritdari Sikh. Like Rehiras Sahib, Kirtan Sohila is a composite, albeit a much shorter one. It contains a total of five Shabads: three by Guru Nanak (one of which appears in the *Path* chapter) and one each by Guru Ram Das and Guru Arjan Dev. Here's the translation for the opening Shabad:

In that house where the Praises of the Creator are spoken and contemplated,
In that house, sing the Songs of Praise, meditate and remember the Creator.
Sing the Praises of my Fearless One.

I am a sacrifice to that Song of Praise which brings lasting peace.
(Pause.)
Day after day, the Great Giver cares for and watches over all beings.
Your Gifts cannot be appraised. How can one appraise the Giver?
The day of my wedding is pre-ordained.
Come, let us join together and pour oil on the threshold.
Give me your blessings, O my friends, that I may attain union with
my Master.
In every home, in every heart, this summons is sent out and the call
comes every day.
So meditate and remember the One Who summons you, O Nanak,
for the day is drawing near.[14]

A Sikh's day and a Sikh's life both end with Kirtan Sohila. We recite it at bedtime, surrounding ourselves with harmony and neutralizing negativity for miles around us. We recite it during *Sukhasan*, the ceremony of closing the *Siri Guru Granth Sahib,* especially when we perform it in the evening. And we also recite Kirtan Sohila when a Sikh (or anyone we wish to honor) dies. It's a calming, quieting practice.

Sukhmani Sahib

Another Bani we recite after a death is *Sukhmani Sahib*—which refers to a state of mind and heart that is happy, peaceful and comforted. That peace and comfort also make Sukhmani Sahib a favorite Bani with the dying Sikh. In fact, the music therapist we met earlier in this chapter played tapes of Sukhmani Sahib for all of her moribund and elderly Sikh patients—including "Bapu-ji"—as a way of easing their upcoming transitions.

Although Sukhmani Sahib, which is by Guru Arjan Dev, the Fifth Guru, is not required reading for an Amritdari Sikh, many Sikhs recite it for many reasons. It's supremely fulfilling as I found out when I tried forty days of it many years ago. Childless couples may recite it in hopes of having children. Many people recite it for the fulfillment of their loved ones. I know a *sangat* (congregation) where the ladies met once a month to chant Sukhmani Sahib together, and during the years they did this, the sangat grew tremendously in size and was also comparatively peaceful and happy. Several short passages from Sukhmani Sahib are popular Kundalini Yoga mantras. We've already met one of these in the Tuning In sidebar in Chapter 2. Also, a small section of it is chanted at every Gurdwara service. (See Chapter 6.)

The one drawback to reciting Sukhmani Sahib daily is its length. It's the longest single composition in the *Siri Guru Granth Sahib*, and is composed of 24 *astapadis* (poems of eight *pauris* or stanzas) each of which has a slok (short verse) preamble. Fortunately, it can be read in small doses. These days, I read one astapadi, including its slok, every day. Here's the translation for one pauri from the 14th astapadi:

By Guru's Grace, one understands the Self.
With this understanding, one's thirst is quenched.
In the Company of the Holy, one chants to God, to God.
Such a servant of God is free of all disease.
Night and day, sing the songs of God.
In the midst of your household remain balanced and unattached.
One whose Mainstay is the One alone
Is freed from the noose of death.
One whose mind hungers for the Supreme God,
O Nanak, shall suffer no pain.[15]

There are other Banis, but these are the main ones. Each Bani is an exquisite jewel. The whole collection is a treasure trove, a bountiful blessing, a sublime gateway to endless bliss.

Chapter 6

In the Guru's Court: How Sikhs Worship

Blessed, blessed is the Sat Sangat, the True Congregation,
where God's Sublime Essence is received.
Guru Ram Das [1]

The sky is a parade of clouds applauded by the sun when Jim and I arrive in Eugene. We will be taking part in a *Gurdwara*, literally "Guru's Door"—the name for a Sikh service as well as a Sikh temple. Jim is as welcome here as I am. At any Gurdwara worthy of the name, non-Sikhs are welcome as members of God's great human family...not as possible converts.

Just outside the building, after walking past some shady trees and a patch of fragrant flowers, I help Jim tie a bandana on his head. My head is already covered due to my turban. Wearing a headcovering will help us focus our minds for the service.

We remove our shoes on the threshold of the building. I also remove my socks, but Jim chooses to leave his on. Removing shoes is a cleanly custom—essential for people about to sit on the floor and good for all 72,000 nerve endings in the feet. Here in Eugene, the shoe removal area is currently outside the Gurdwara building, but in many places it's indoors in a special entry. Once inside the entry, for further cleanliness, we wash our hands—and I wash my feet—in basins of water that today are strewn with rose petals, a pleasant and fragrant (but not essential) variation.

Only a few people are here. Sikh services start, *then* the congregation begins arriving, not the other way around. (See sidebar for Gurdwara protocol.)

Gurdwara Protocol
What To Do If You Attend Gurdwara

* Dress for sitting on the floor.
* Wear a headcovering.
* Remove your shoes.
* Sit on the floor. Do not point the soles of your feet towards the Guru.

As we proceed, bear in mind that all duties in a regular Gurdwara service can be performed by either men or women. (Unfortunately, this isn't true in those few Gurdwaras where the Guru's words concerning the holiness of women seem to be forgotten.)

Prakaash

We are about to begin *prakaash* (literally "brightening"), the process of opening the *Siri Guru Granth Sahib*, the Sikh Guru, for the day. In most Gurdwaras, prakaash occurs in the early morning, well before the service. People who live in homes with a formal set up for the Guru—like me—do prakaash early in the morning in their homes too. But where the main sanctuary of the Gurdwara must serve several functions—as is true in Eugene—we do prakaash just before the service begins.

One of the things I love about Sikh services is their informality. It's not uncommon for a Sikh to show up for a service and be asked to participate in some special way. That happens today when someone hands me a long sword (called a *Siri Sahib*) as prakaash is about to start. The lady who does so then opens the doors to the upper cupboard where the *Siri Guru Granth Sahib* rests between appearances. And we begin.

We all proclaim *Waheguru ji ka Khalsa! Waheguru ji ki Fateh!*

Translation: "The Pure Ones belong to God! Victory belongs to
God!" We are acknowledging that everything that has happened
or will happen is done by God...and only by God. We make this
proclamation before and after nearly everything we do in
Gurdwara. For simplicity's sake, I will indicate this proclamation
with words like "We make our proclamation..." throughout this
chapter.

We bow our foreheads to the ground, which is tricky for me
because of the sword. Then we stand with our hands folded as
best we can while the lady who opened the cupboard recites a
short version of the *Ardas*, the supplication or prayer we'll look at
in more detail later in this chapter. We recite the last two lines of
the prayer together, then bow our heads to the ground again. As
we all rise, we make our proclamation.

The lady who recited the Ardas then places a *ramala* (cloth of
honor) on top of her head, lifts the ramala-covered Guru from the
cupboard, and places it on her head. I walk in front of the Guru
as a sort of honor guard carrying the unsheathed Siri Sahib.
Walking behind the Guru is a young man waving a fancy
flywhisk. As we walk, we chant *Sat Naam, Sat Naam, Sat Naam Jee,
Waa Hay Guroo, Waa Hay Guroo, Waa Hay Guroo Jee.* There are
many chants we could use while carrying the Guru. The one we
chant today is essentially untranslatable, but praises Truth,
praises God's ecstatic wisdom and grace, and praises God's
Name.

Our little procession wends its way into the large room across
the hall. Under a ceiling-hung, gold and white canopy (it could
be any color) sits the *palki sahib*, the Guru's resting place—a cross
between a throne, an altar, a bed and a palanquin. Indeed, in the
Guru's room is a palki sahib resembling a miniature four-poster
brass bed, complete with its own little canopy. The palki sahib we
are heading for is more open—a low table with a miniature
mattress, covered first with a clean white sheet that drapes down
onto the floor. Completely covering this sheet are *ramalas*—a

cross between altar cloths and robes of honor—always of the finest fabrics, of any color. Today's ramalas are brilliant green satin with gold fringes and Sikh symbols appliquéd in gold. One of the large ramalas drapes gracefully down from the palki sahib onto the sheet-covered floor. There are other ramalas around the edges of the palki sahib. The entire ensemble rests on carpeted floors covered with clean white sheets.

To the side of the palki sahib are two small tables. The small wooden table to the left as we come bearing the Guru into the room will receive the *Gurprashaad*—literally "Gift of the Guru"— the sweet you could call Sikh communion food. The one to the right looks like part of a brass bed ensemble and contains a translation of the *Siri Guru Granth Sahib*. As a mark of respect, this is covered with a ramala also—the one today has a subtle pattern in gold.

Vases filled with greenery, pink roses and some white flowers I don't identify sit on coasters flanking the palki sahib. On the large floor-touching ramala are a large *Adi Shakti* symbol (often called a *Khanda* for the double-edged sword in the center of the symbol), three artistically arranged *chakras* (large steel rings that warriors used to wear on their heads for protection), and a couple of other Siri Sahibs. Pictures of several human Sikh Gurus adorn the walls. These decorations—and any others we might use—are all optional, but help create a rich and respectful atmosphere.

The lady carrying the Guru walks behind the palki sahib where no ramalas cascade to the floor. She lays the Guru on the palki and then sits cross-legged in front of the Guru. I lay the sword down with the other Siri Sahibs. The young man stands behind the Guru and waves the flywhisk as we proceed.

While the lady removes the gold ramala covering the Guru and unwraps the white cotton wrapping cloths one by one, we begin singing the *Shabad* (Sikh hymn) *Mayraa Man Lochai*. (This is the series of poetic letters that turned young Arjan into *Guru*

Arjan Dev, the Fifth Guru, as we saw in the chapter on the Shabad Guru.) We could sing any Shabad or Sikh mantra. Placing a small ramala on top of the Guru, the lady lifts the Guru up on her own ramala-covered head again. The young man and I help her fold up the wrapping cloths. Then she sets out three small pillows in the center of the palki sahib in a C-shape, with the opening of the C facing her. These will prop up the Guru for reading. Laying the spine of the *Siri Guru Granth Sahib* carefully in the center of the central pillow, the lady opens first the front cover, inserting a small ramala between the cover and the pages with the help of the young man. She repeats the process with the back cover with my help.

It's now time to take our first *Hukam*. Hukam literally means "command." It's a random reading from the *Siri Guru Granth Sahib* and is the Guru's message for the occasion—in this case, the Gurdwara worship service about to begin. The Guru's word is law for any devout Sikh. So we listen carefully to the Hukam and do our best to follow what it says. Sometimes that's very clear. I recall the time our house was burglarized. Seeing the burglars as God testing us, I had no further problems with it (I thought), except for the hassle of police and wailing neighbors. So when the police held a meeting in our neighborhood, I decided not to go...until I got a Hukam the morning of the meeting that said something like, "I consort with thieves, but avoid the righteous." I went to the meeting!

Both of today's Hukams will be more subtle. The lady opens the *Siri Guru Granth Sahib* randomly, then reads a complete Shabad in Gurmukhi. When she finishes, she makes the proclamation and we all join in.

Then I read the English translation:

Gauree Reverend Kabir:
Why mourn when one dies?
Mourn if one remains forever alive.

I shall not die as the world dies.
For I have now met the Life-giving God. (Pause.)
One perfumes the body with sandalwood,
And in that pleasure forgets supreme bliss.
There is one well and five water carriers.
Even with a broken rope the foolish ones continue trying to draw
 water.
Says Kabir, through deliberation I have gained understanding:
For me there are no more wells and no more water carriers. [2]

At the end, I make the proclamation and everyone present joins in.

Clearly, this Hukam is about releasing undue attachment to physical life and paying more attention to the life of the soul. But as the Guru's words ring through the corridors of my consciousness, I hear the Guru telling me to drop certain expectations I have for the day and enjoy what is given instead. That proves to be excellent advice.

We have now completed prakaash. A great many Sikhs, including me, have miniature Gurdwaras inside our homes. Inside those miniature Gurdwaras, we perform prakaash nearly every morning, and *Sukhasan*—which we'll look at later in this chapter—nearly every evening. Usually in our homes, the *Siri Guru Granth Sahib* stays on its palki sahib, so there is no procession in or out. But for prakaash, we always recite an Ardas, open the *Siri Guru Granth Sahib*, and take a Hukam for the day.

While we perform prakaash, a young man dressed in clean blue jeans and t-shirt enters the Gurdwara, bows to the Guru and gives an offering as soon as the *Siri Guru Granth Sahib* is unwrapped. He listens respectfully to the Hukam, then bows his forehead to the ground, puts his hands together and quietly leaves the Gurdwara. He's on his way to work at the local Indian restaurant. It's fairly common for Sikhs to stop by an open

Gurdwara for a few minutes to receive the Guru's *Darshan*—the experience or vision one has when one is in the company of someone or something deeply holy.

Now it's my turn to bow at the Guru's Feet, my turn to receive the Guru's Darshan and align myself with the Guru's understanding. I do that by bringing my forehead to the ground in front of the Guru. As I bow, I place a monetary offering on top of the large, floor-touching ramala. Although money is the usual offering, other gifts are welcome. There was one occasion when I ran out of money while traveling and gave the Guru the only thing I had to give—an unopened box of graham crackers. Monetary offerings keep the lights on and pay other bills. The graham crackers were probably served to the *sangat* (congregation) during *langar* (the communal meal) after the next Gurdwara service. Giving paves the way to receive. Giving upfront turns the offering into an act of honest devotion without strings.

Bringing the forehead to the ground is a spiritual technology in its own right. I am bringing blood to my brain and activating my pituitary and pineal glands—thereby awakening my intuition and higher consciousness. I am not bowing to a book, a thing of paper, ink and binding. I am bowing to the embodied *Shabad Guru*—the Teacher through divine sound and song of Infinite wisdom, knowledge and ecstasy, whose story we looked at in an earlier chapter. Symbolically, I am giving my head to the Guru and stating that the Guru's wisdom rules me. In addition, I am picking up the dust of the feet of the Saints (their understanding), and joining the Company of the Holy by granting the dust of my feet to someone else. It's an act of humility and an act of utmost self-exaltation.

Kirtan

While I bow to the Guru, the young man with the flywhisk replaces the lady sitting behind the Guru. She and another person then set up their instruments for the *kirtan* (sacred singing) program which is the main spiritual muscle of most Gurdwara services. As I finish bowing, the musicians make the proclamation and begin singing. Today we have a violin as well as the usual *harmonium* and *tablas* accompanying the kirtan. Although the *rebec* (a bowed lute-like instrument) provided the original instrumentation for Sikh songs, *harmoniums* (portable hand organs, originally brought to India by Christian missionaries) are now the instrumental stars in Gurdwaras. Generally, *tablas* drum up musical energy by beating out contrapuntal rhythms to the melodies. Tablas are a pair of drums of unequal size, vaguely similar in shape to bongos, but larger, much more musical and capable of subtle rhythmic patterns. They're steadied on the floor with cloth rings. Other instruments are welcome. Notably, we accompany contemporary Sikh songs with acoustic guitars.

Sometimes we improvise. One Gurdwara improvisation etches my memory. It was one of those days when everyone expected everyone else to bring instruments. As a result, no instruments were present, except for one lone acoustic guitar — an instrument few people ever use for classic Indian-style kirtan. Most of the kirtan players, other than the owner of the guitar, were flummoxed. But one talented young lady, who is now a recording artist, picked up that guitar and struck up with an extraordinarily moving classic rendition of *Lakh Khusee-aa Paatishaahee-aa*. It's a Shabad with a refrain line that translates, *One enjoys the pleasures of tens of thousands of royal empires through the Guru's Grace*.[3] As I sang along with the refrain, one of the puzzles cluttering my mind suddenly resolved and I felt a huge surge of energy flooding up my spine.

That surge of energy was the *kundalini* rising. The *kundalini* is a coil of energy that normally drowses at the base of the spine, but which awakens and rises from its torpor through spiritual discipline. (Yes, awakening the kundalini is what Kundalini Yoga is all about.) The Guru says, *The kundalini rises in the Sat Sangat, the True Congregation.*[4] That's exactly what happened to me.

Quietly, reverently listening to kirtan as a meditation has its place. But singing is even better. Singing the songs of the Shabad Guru specifically awakens the kundalini. It does this by tapping codes on the roof of the mouth that trigger an opening parachute of God realization in the brain. For that reason, all Gurdwara programs are sing-a-longs. Sometimes the kirtan player will recite the refrain lines first and ask everyone to sing with them. Some Gurdwaras facilitate singing with *Amrit Kirtan* books, which are books of popular Shabads compact enough to sit on a harmonium. These books are fine if you read Gurmukhi script and know which page the Shabad is on, but completely useless if you don't. Here in the West, we usually provide Shabad sheets-- sheets of paper with individual Shabads printed in Gurmukhi, transliteration, and English translation. As the Gurdwara program progresses, people pass around Shabad sheets for most of the Shabads we sing today.

After we've sung a Shabad or two, I bow my forehead to the ground, then get up and replace the young man sitting with the Guru. He places his forehead to the flywhisk (called a *chauri sahib*) and hands it to me. I replicate his gesture and sit down in his vacated spot.

Someone always sits behind the Guru during a Gurdwara worship service. That person protects the Guru and performs *chauri seva*, waving the chauri sahib behind the Guru. Remember that Sikhism comes from India—a hot, insect-pestered land. Rulers in early India always had someone standing behind them, waving a chauri sahib to keep off insects and create a pleasant breeze. By installing someone behind the Guru with a chauri sahib during worship services, Sikhs are clearly stating that the Guru's word rules us. We are also symbolically whisking away negativity of all kinds from the Guru's Court.

We began with a few people, but by the time the service is over, the room will be packed. As I sit with the Guru, I watch the *sangat* (congregation) trickle in. Nearly everyone is dressed in his or her Sunday best.

Sometimes devotion cloaks the whole group like a robe of honor. But always certain actions move me close to tears. It's particularly touching to watch a mother tenderly touch her infant's head to the ground so the infant will receive the full measure of the Guru's blessings. It's even more moving to watch the crippled and the elderly hobble up to the Guru on crutches, lay their crutches down, bow to the Guru, then get up and hobble away—all without assistance.

Sometimes the crippled or the infirm sit in chairs—which are always placed to the very back of the room. But other than that, everyone sits on the floor. We can sit any way we like as long as the bottoms of our feet do not point directly to the Guru. Since lots of energy shoots out from the bottoms of people's feet, this custom is merely to insure that we don't punch the Guru's blessings away from ourselves.

The men sit on one side, and the women sit on the other—much the way basses and sopranos usually sit on opposite sides of a choir. The Guru, who is neither male nor female, presides in the middle. Little children may wander from parent to parent without regard to gender. And no one raises an eyebrow if someone goes to the opposite side to whisper a message or pass out Shabad sheets, etc.

After I've been on *chauri seva* for about half an hour, someone comes to relieve me. I touch my head to the chauri sahib and hand it to my successor, who repeats the gesture. Then I get up and sit on the women's side of the Gurdwara. We've now been singing kirtan for about an hour. Time spans for Gurdwara services vary widely depending on the number of Shabads sung. Some Gurdwara programs go on all night: these are called *Rainsabhai Kirtans*. Some programs—especially at the end of morning spiritual practice—are very short with only one Shabad.

Today's Gurdwara will go a bit longer than average because

we have a guest kirtan player. Some of our musicians today are recording artists, and some are deep-dyed amateurs. Our guest today is technically a *Ragi,* someone who plays classic Indian *Raags* (classic Indian melodic modes). As he sings, the casements of my heart open wide. It reminds me of records of Arabic music my father used to play when I was little. Northern Indian music strongly reflects its *Mughal* and Arabic influences. My parents used to call this style of singing "wailing." Actually the singing is extremely intricate, as richly embroidered as a Kashmir shawl — and supremely uplifting. I've never heard any genuine wailing that made me feel tiptop with happiness the way this music makes me feel.

A few people get up and lay some money in front of our young Ragi. Ragis in India make their living as singers and teachers of this musical tradition, so monetary offerings are necessary to maintain them. However, the money is being offered not so much to the person, as to the spirit of the Guru that flows through the singer. Truthfully, the Guru is only the Guru when its Words are recited or sung. As we sing or recite the Guru's Words, we become the Guru. The monetary offering acknowledges that.

Most of the Shabads today have been ones I don't know. But the second Shabad the young Ragi plays is very popular and one I know well: *Mihravaan Saahib Mihravaan* — literally *Merciful Lord Merciful.* As I sing along in Gurmukhi, I'm reminded of the time I attended a Gurdwara that was held in a new restaurant as a blessing ceremony. An older wandering Ragi sang *Mihravaan Sahib Mihravaan,* which he interwove with a spoken story of how *Guru Nanak,* the First Sikh Guru, redeemed a thief.

Although sermons are not a big item on the Sikh agenda, a talk (*katha*) may be part of the service. Often an accomplished Ragi will interweave a story with a Shabad as happened at the restaurant Gurdwara. On *Gurpurbs* (Sikh holy days), someone will usually tell a story that goes with that holy day. Sometimes visiting dignitaries give talks. It's good to hear the stories, especially on Gurpurbs. And sometimes we learn interesting tidbits of information or gain some greater understanding.

But talks can be a problem. Many Gurdwaras in the West are multi-lingual, and talks are worthless if you don't know the language. Talks are also the one place in a Sikh service where politics can rear its cobra head. Singing the Guru's Word merges us with the Guru's consciousness, so having someone talk to us about the Guru's Word (even if that person is very holy) can lead to false notions of separation. So, in most Western-style Gurdwaras, talks are kept to a minimum. Better to do without, except for the occasional story.

There's one place though where short talks are welcome, and this is the children's program. Children's programs are a Western innovation; you won't find them in every Gurdwara. The idea behind children's programs is to give Sikh youngsters a safe place to practice being in the public eye—something every turban-wearing person in the West has to deal with. Usually the children sing some simple songs in English with the hand motions that we call *Celestial Communications*, (a form of meditative dance in which only the upper body, arms and hands move). This is the only place in a Gurdwara program with anything that evenly vaguely resembles dancing, although we certainly allow dancing outside the Gurdwara. We may sing songs like the following with hand gestures to match.

We are the Khalsa,
Mighty, mighty Khalsa.
Everywhere we go
People want to know
Who we are
So we tell them:
We Are the Khalsa! [5]

The children lead us in these songs—with an adult leading the children. Sometimes one of the older children will regale us with a short Sikh story. All of these things are about teaching the youngsters to be comfortable with who they are.

Today, there is no children's program, which is in its summer hibernation. So after the young Ragi sings a final Shabad and we make our proclamation, a middle-aged man picks up his guitar and leads us in a rousing version of *Song of the Khalsa*. (See sidebar for the song.)

Protocol Song
Song of the Khalsa

Verse: *Many speak of courage; speaking cannot give it.*
It's in the face of death we must live it.
When things are down and darkest, that's when we stand tallest.
Until the last star falls, we won't give an inch at all.
Chorus 1: *Stand as the Khalsa, strong as steel, steady as stone.*
Give our lives to God and Guru, mind and soul, breath and bone.
Verse: *Guru Arjun gave his life to stand for what was right.*
He was burned and tortured for five long days and nights.
He could have stopped it any time just by giving in.
His strength a solid wall, he never gave an inch at all.
Chorus 2: *Sons of the Khalsa, remember those who died,*
Stood their ground until their last breath so we who live now might live free lives.
Verse: *A princess is not royal by her birth or blood inside,*
But if her family's home is Anandpur Sahib,
She'll walk with such a grace and strength the world will bow in awe.

Until the mountains fall, she'll never give an inch at all.

Chorus 3: *Daughters of the Khalsa, in your strength our future lies.*

Give our children fearless minds to see the world through the Guru's eyes.

Verse: *Baisakhi Day we were thousands, but only five had the courage for dying.*

Then one brave man, one flashing sword, turned us all to Lions.

And now we live his legacy: to die before we fall.

And like the five who answered his call, we can't turn back at all.

Chorus 1: *Stand as the Khalsa, strong as steel, steady as stone.*

Give our lives to God and Guru, mind and soul, breath and bone.

Verse: *The tenth Guru gave even his sons to give the Khalsa life,*

And his words stand like mountains against the winds of time.

That Khalsa will rule the world; all will be safe in its fold.

But if the Khalsa falls there won't be a world at all.

Chorus 1: *Stand as the Khalsa, strong as steel, steady as stone.*

Give our lives to God and Guru, mind and soul, breath and bone.

Verse: *Many speak of courage; speaking cannot give it.*

It's in the face of death we must live it.

When things are down and darkest, that's when we stand tallest.

Until the last star falls, we won't give an inch at all.

Chorus 1: *Stand as the Khalsa, strong as steel, steady as*

> *stone.*
>
> *Give our lives to God and Guru, mind and soul, breath and bone.*
>
> Then the women sing Chorus 2:
>
> *Sons of the Khalsa, remember those who died,*
>
> *Stood their ground until their last breath so we who live now might live free lives.*
>
> Then the men sing Chorus 3:
>
> *Daughters of the Khalsa, in your strength our future lies.*
>
> *Give our children fearless minds to see the world through the Guru's eyes.*
>
> Then we all sing together Chorus 1:
>
> *Stand as the Khalsa, strong as steel, steady as stone.*
>
> *Give our lives to God and Guru, mind and soul, breath and bone...*
>
> *Mind and Soul are His Alone....*[6]

Written in 1975 by Livtar Singh Khalsa, *Song of the Khalsa* is another Western innovation. There are other contemporary Sikh songs, but this song is special to *3HO* Sikhs (Sikhs who practice Kundalini Yoga) because we sing this one at every Gurdwara service just before *Anand Sahib*. *Song of the Khalsa* expresses the courage everyone on this path must have to stay the course. It alludes to many stories in Sikh history—the martyrdom of Guru Gobind Singh's four sons, the martyrdom of Guru Arjan Dev, and the birth of the Khalsa, which is a story we'll hear in the chapter on the Amrit Ceremony. It also alludes to the Sikh prophecy that the world will end if seven years pass without the sun shining on the Golden Temple (*Hari Mander Sahib*), the foremost Sikh Temple.

In the reverberating silence that follows the *Song of the Khalsa*, I notice the young Ragi and the lady who was scheduled to play

Anand Sahib quietly conferring. The Ragi nods, moves his harmonium into position, makes the proclamation and leads us in the first five *pauris* (stanzas) of *Anand Sahib*, the *Bani* by *Guru Amar Das*, the Third Guru.

We sing Anand Sahib at every Gurdwara service where *Gurprasaad* will be served—which is nearly every service. To be honest, I've attended Gurdwara services where we sang Anand Sahib even when Gurprasaad wasn't served. Anand Sahib is always followed instantly by the *slok* (short verse) that ends *Japji Sahib*, the morning Bani by *Guru Nanak*, the founder of Sikhism. (The translation and transliteration for the first five pauris Anand Sahib and the Slok of Japji Sahib are in the Bani chapter.)

Theoretically, we could sing the entire 40 pauris of Anand Sahib, although I don't recall ever attending a Gurdwara where that was done. Many sangats sing the first five pauris, then the last pauri of Anand Sahib, before singing the slok of Japji Sahib. But here's the problem. *Pauri* literally means the rung of a ladder. The first five pauris create a sturdy little stepping stool to elevation. But if you take the first five pauris and the last pauri with nothing in between, what you end up with is an extension ladder with most of its rungs missing—hardly useful for rising to any occasion.

After we sing the last two lines of the Slok twice, we make our proclamation, then bow our foreheads to the ground, rise to our feet, and begin singing in Gurmukhi the Shabad *Too Thaakur Tum Peh Ardaas*, a short section from *Sukhmani Sahib* by *Guru Arjan Dev*, the Fifth Guru. Here's the translation:

You are our Master; to You I pray.
This soul and body are all Your Property.
You are our Mother and Father; we are Your children.
Your Grace brings so many joys!
No one knows Your limits,
Highest of the High, Most Generous God.

All creation is strung on Your Thread.
All that comes from You is under Your Command.
You alone know Your State and Extent.
Nanak, Your slave, is forever a sacrifice. [9]

(Transliteration is in the sidebar.)

Protocol Shabad
Too Thaakur Tum Peh Ardas (You, O Master, to You I Pray)

We sing this section of Guru Arjan Dev's *Sukhmani Sahib* as an invocation before the *Ardas,* the formal prayer or supplication, and sometimes as a Shabad in its own right.

We are using the pronunciation guide in Appendix B. So *ant* and *ham* in transliteration are actually pronounced like *unt* and *hum* are in English.

Too thaakur tum peh ardaas.
Jee-o pind sabh tayree raas.
Tum maat pitaa ham baarik tayray.
Tumaree kirpaa meh sukh ghanayray.
Ko-i na jaanai tumaraa ant.
Oochay tay oochaa bhagavant.
Sagal samagree tumarai sootr dhaaree.
Tum tay ho-i so aagi-aa kaaree.
Tumaree gat mit tum hee jaanee.
Naanak daas sadaa kurbaanee.

As we sing, we all clasp our hands together or bring our palms together as for prayer. I wend my way singing through the narrow straits between people until I am standing in front of the

English translation. After washing her hands, the lady who will read the Hukam arrives at the palki sahib a few moments later. The young mother who will recite the Ardas is already standing directly in front of the Guru.

As we end *Too Thaakur Tum Peh Ardaas*, the young mother takes a deep breath and begins the *Ardas* (literally, "servant with folded hands," a supplication or prayer included in every Sikh worship service). We listen intently. She is representing all of us and focusing our longing and devotion.

She begins in Gurmukhi with the following invocation from Guru Gobind Singh's epic poem *Chandi ki Vaar*:

> *There is one Creator of Creation. All victory belongs to God.*
> *May God's sword be our protection.*
> *This is the Ballad of the Supreme Sword of the Divine composed by the Tenth Master.*
> *After worshipping the Primal Power, meditate on Guru Nanak,*
> *Then pray to Guru Angad, Guru Amar Das and Guru Ram Das for protection.*
> *Remember Guru Arjan, Guru Hargobind and Siri Har Rai.*
> *Meditate on Siri Harkrishan, seeing whom all sufferings depart.*
> *Meditate on Guru Teg Bahadur and the nine treasures shall run to you.*
> *May the Gurus help us everywhere.*
> *Great is Guru Gobind Singh, the Tenth Master: may he help us everywhere.*
> *Meditate on the Divine Message and Divine Light of all Ten Masters, the Great Guru, the Siri Guru Granth Sahib.*
> *Call on God, O Pure Ones: Satinaam. Siree Waheguru!* [10]

And all of us join in calling out *Waheguru!*

Without stopping, the young mother reciting the Ardas continues in Gurmukhi, although some people switch to the language of the sangat at this point, since the rest of the Ardas was not written by Guru Gobind Singh. The Ardas has a set pattern, but we may leave whole sections out—as happened at the beginning of Prakash today. Even if we are reciting the full Ardas, many people extemporize at this point, although we always do our best to include references to Sikhism's many martyrs, who include the following:

The Five Beloved Ones, the Guru's Four Martyred Sons,
The Forty Liberated Ones, all those devotees absorbed in the Guru
    Teachings,
Those who were true to the Guru, who recited the Naam,
Who shared their earnings, who sacrificed for Truth,
Who saw the faults of others and overlooked them.
Reflect on their deeds, O Khalsa ji, and call out Waheguru!
And all of us join in calling out *Waheguru!*
Those who were broken by the wheel, cut up limb by limb,
Who gave their scalps, but not their hair,
Who were flayed alive,
Those ladies whose children were slaughtered before their eyes,
But who never gave up their faith and determination
To live as Sikhs with all their hair to their last breath:
Reflect on their sacrifice, O Khalsa ji, and call out Waheguru!
And all of us join in calling out *Waheguru!*
Now let the whole Khalsa offer its prayer.
May the first prayer of the Khalsa always be
Waheguru! Waheguru! Waheguru!

We all sing out Waheguru three times with the lady reciting the Ardas. She continues with a series of verses asking for the blessing of protection. Then she continues:

Bless us to ever live in the righteousness of true disciples.
May we live to the living principle of the Guru's Teaching.
Grant us the gift of reading and understanding the Guru's Divine

Word.
Grant us faith, insight, trust in You,
And the blessing of blessings, the Name.
Grant us the sight and bath in the Nectar Tank in Amritsar.
May our choirs, banners and mansions abide through all time.
May our flags, seats of religious authority, forts, houses, ashrams
*   and Gurdwaras ever stand.*
Then call on God, O Khalsa ji, Waheguru!
And all of us join in calling out *Waheguru!* Without stopping, the
lady leading the Ardas switches to English.
O God, save us from the five obstacles of lust, pride, greed, anger
*   and attachment.*
Keep us always attached to Your Lotus Feet.
O Honor of the honorless, Home of the homeless,
Strength of the weak, Hope of the hopeless,
O True Guru, Shelter of the poor,
We stand before You and offer our prayer.

At this point, the lady's speech comes to a brief halt as she
thinks of what special prayers the sangat may need. Before she
moved directly in front of the Guru, I saw her checking the
places where people might leave notes about trials for which
they are requesting prayers or about births, birthdays and
anniversaries. But today there are no special notes. The young
mother adds some requests for the spiritual guidance and
upliftment of all Sikh children. She prays for peace on earth. She
asks that we remember and follow the example of the *Siri Singh
Sahib*, whose birthday and first death anniversary are fast
approaching. She asks that we always rise early for *Sadhana*
(spiritual practice). Then she says:

Please bless this Gurprasaad which has been placed before You.
May its sweetness remind us of the sweetness of Your Name, and
*   the sword that cuts it remind us to be strong.*

As she says these words, the young man who brought in the Gurprasaad takes a clean kirpan (short sword) and draws it through the Gurprasaad.

She then adds some words of blessing for the *Gur Ka Langar*, the food of the Guru's Kitchen. And the young man—after first wiping the kirpan—draws the blade of the kirpan through a sample of each dish we will enjoy when we sit down for *langar*— the communal meal that follows a Sikh service. The Ardas-blessed food will return to the pots and dishes it came from to infuse the Guru's blessing into the rest of the food.

The lady reciting the Ardas switches back into Gurmukhi and concludes:

> *O True King, by Your Grace we have sung Your sweet hymns,*
> *Heard Your life-giving Word and experienced Your Manifold*
> *   Blessings.*
> *May these things find a loving place in our hearts and serve to draw*
> *   our souls to You.*
> *Forgive us our sins. Help us that we may keep ourselves pure.*
> *If we've made any errors or omissions, please fill in for us.*
> *May we always be in the company of men and women of love that we*
> *   may remember Your Name in their presence.*
> *Through Nanak, may Your Name forever increase.*
> *May the spirit be exalted, and may all people prosper by Your Grace.*

As the lady reciting the Ardas, chants the last two lines in Gurmukhi, we all join in. Then we all bow our foreheads to the ground.

We all stand again, make the proclamation and sing *Aagi-aa Bha-ee Akaal Kee* in Gurmukhi. (See sidebar for translation, transliteration and other information about this Shabad.)

Protocol Shabad: Aagi-aa Bha-ee Akaal Kee (The Order Has Come from the Undying One)

Aagi-aa Bha-ee Akaal Kee is actually a composite. The first two couplets appear in Giani Gian Singh's history of Sikhism in verse. Unfortunately in Gurdwaras today, we invariably misquote the fourth line. Because this is current practice, I let the misquote stand in the transliteration and translation below. The original text actually reads, *Jaa kaa hiradaa sudh hay khoj Shabad meh layh*, which translates: *Those who wish to purify their hearts should turn to the Shabad.* The remaining two lines are by *Bhai Nand Laal*, one of Guru Gobind Singh's disciples.

Two things: The Order given to Sikhs to accept the *Siri Guru Granth Sahib* as Guru does not mean that we expect non-Sikhs to follow this ruling. And when we say the Pure Ones will rule, we are not talking about a petty theocracy of Khalsa Sikhs. We are either saying that Khalsa Sikhs will always keep their inner sovereignty intact no matter what (the usual explanation)—or we are saying that the time will come when the purity within us will rule all our actions, that our invincibility resides in our purity.

Aagi-aa bha-ee akaal kee tabee chalaayo panth.
Sabh sikhan ko hukam hai guroo maanee-o granth.
Guroo granth jee maani-o pragat guraa(n) kee dayh.
Jo prabh ko milabo chahai khoj shabad mai layh.
Raaj karaygaa khaalsaa aakee rehai na ko-i.
Khwaar ho-i sabh milaingay bachai sharan jo ho-i.

Translation:
The Order has come from the Undying One to follow the

> *spiritual path.*
>
> *The Order given to all Sikhs is to accept the Siri Guru Granth Sahib as Guru.*
>
> *Accept the Siri Guru Granth Sahib, and Guru's Blessings will manifest.*
>
> *Whoever wishes to meet God should turn to the Shabad.*
>
> *The Pure Ones will rule, and none shall stand against them.*
>
> *All those who meet together in humility will be in the protection of God's Sanctuary.* [11]

As we end this song, the lady leading the Ardas calls out, *Bolay So Nihaal!* (*Speak and be joyful!*) Then we all chorus at the top of our lungs *Sat Siri Akaal!* (*Truth is Great and Undying!*) In Eugene and some (but not all) other gurdwaras, this *jaikara* ("victory cry") is accompanied by a huge Sikh kettle drum. Then we make our proclamation and sit back down to listen quietly to the Hukam.

Although the *jaikara* is the loudest part of any Sikh service, the actual climax is the Hukam. Everything we have done today is designed to focus us so that we understand and receive the full blessing of this message and command from the Guru. Listening to the Hukam and following its directions can provide invaluable help.

The lady who will read the Hukam today begins singing a short Shabad I don't happen to know — one of several we can use while taking a Hukam. Many people in the sangat know this Shabad well, however, and sing it along with her. As she sings, she picks up all the pages of the *Siri Guru Granth Sahib*, brings them together reverently, then opens them at random near the center as is usual. After she reads the Hukam in Gurmukhi and we all make the proclamation, I read the English translation.

O righteous one, speak up. Why are you silent?

You have seen with your eyes the treacherous ways of Maya.

Nothing in the world goes along with one except God's Name.

Neither one's lands, nor fine clothes, nor gold, nor silver are of any avail.

One's spouse, children, worldly glory, elephants and horses and all luxury leave one in the end.

Nanak prays, "Except for the Society of Saints, the whole world is false."

O kingly being, why are you asleep and not awake?

To wail for worldly valuables brings no peace, although many hanker for wealth.

Many wail for Maya, the bewitcher, but receive no peace without God's Name.

Thousands of clever devices do not work, and one goes here or there, according to God's Will.

God pervades the beginning, the middle and the end, and fills all hearts.

Nanak prays, "Keeping the Company of the Saints, one goes with honor to God's Abode."

O king, all your palaces and all your wise courtiers are of no avail to you.

Let them go, for leaning on them only brings you pain.

You are deceived by a mirage. How can you find peace?

If you involve yourself in anything other than God's Name, you waste the human birth.

Your thirst is not quenched by ego, nor are you fulfilled, nor do you attain Wisdom thus.

Nanak prays, "Without God's Name, many grieve in the end."

Showering blessings, God has mercifully owned me.

Catching me by the arm, God has pulled me out of the mire and blessed me with the Society of the Holy.

Meditating on God in the Holy Congregation, my sins and miseries are burned.

This is the highest religion and act of merit, for it goes with me to the end.

My tongue recites God's Name, and my body and mind are drenched with it.

Says Nanak, "Whomsoever God unites with Himself becomes full of all virtues." [12]

After the proclamation, I hand the translation over to the lady who will read the translation in Punjabi. It came as a huge surprise to me, many years ago, to discover that Punjabi speakers often do not understand Gurmukhi. I've attended a couple of Gurdwaras where no translations were read. So I would ask my Punjabi friends—or the people sitting near me—what the Guru actually said, and generally they couldn't tell me. It's rather like the Canterbury Tales: no living English speakers understand the original Middle English words—unless they happen to be English teachers, English majors, or the child of an English teacher, like me. Gurmukhi is the same way. It encompasses a great many languages, including archaic Punjabi, but that doesn't mean a Punjabi speaker can understand it. So, we read the Punjabi translation as well as the English whenever we have enough Punjabi speakers present to warrant it.

Following the Punjabi translation and the proclamation, we all sing words that more or less translate as "All Sikhs are ordered to consider the *Siri Guru Granth Sahib* as their Guru."

Gurprashaad

And now, young children toddle or skip or saunter up to the table with the Gurprashaad and grab a handful of napkins, which they enthusiastically pass around to everyone present. It's time for the sweetest part of a Gurdwara service: Gurprashaad (familiarly called *prashaad*), a sort of pudding made from flour, water, *ghee* (clarified butter), and either raw sugar or honey. It tastes something like warm cookie dough and represents the abundant sweetness of the Guru's Blessings. (Recipe is in sidebar.) Children love it! Indeed, if a service goes longer than usual, it's not uncommon for some toddler to start passing around napkins in the middle of the service!

Recipe for Gurprashaad

This is the classic recipe for *Gurprashaad* as given by *Guru Gobind Singh*, the Tenth Guru. Many Sikhs make it with honey instead of sugar, in which case the proportions change to about 2/3 parts honey and somewhat less than 3 parts water.

Ghee (clarified butter) may be purchased in ethnic and natural food stores. It can also be made ahead of time at home by melting butter. Skim off the curds that rise to the top. The clear liquid underneath is *ghee*.

Note: I recommend wearing an apron while making Gurprashaad.

1 part flour (preferably whole wheat)

1 part *ghee* (clarified butter)

1 part raw sugar

3 parts water

Brown the flour slowly in the ghee. Be sure that the vessel you are using is large enough for the completed Gurprashaad. You will need to stir the flour nearly contin-uously to prevent sticking and scorching. Chant *Mool Mantra* (see below) or other mantra or Bani as you stir the flour. In a separate pot, dissolve the sugar in the water and bring to a low simmer. Keep stirring the flour. The slower it browns the better the prashaad will taste. The browned flour will have a nut-like fragrance when it is ready. When the flour is sufficiently browned, pour the hot sugar-water

---

slowly but consistently into the browned flour. The mixture will erupt. Stir very thoroughly as you keep chanting. A small amount of additional water may be stirred in at the end to help the Gurprashaad coagulate.

Traditionally one recites *Japji Sahib* throughout the entire process of making Gurprashaad. Other Sikh mantras are acceptable substitutes for Japji Sahib. The most popular of these is *Mool Mantra*, which I include here.

Mool Mantra: *Ek Ong Kaar, Sat Naam, Kartaa Purakh, Nirbhao, Nirvair, Akaal Moorat, Ajoonee, Saibhang, Gurprasaad, Jap, Aad Sach, Jugaad Sach, Hai Bhee Sach, Naanak Hosee Bhee Sach.* (Pronunciation guide is in Appendix B.)

Translation: *One Creator Creation. Truth Name. Active Being. Without fear. Without vengeance. Undying. Unborn. Self-illumined. By Guru's Gift. RECITE! True in the beginning. True through time. True even now. Nanak: Truth shall always be.* [13]

While the children pass around the napkins, the couple who brought the Gurprashaad are busy. Just before the Ardas started, they scrubbed their hands thoroughly. What they are about to do requires good hygiene, so no one with open sores or communicable diseases prepares or serves Gurprashaad.

After the Hukam and all its translations, they scoop up five small handfuls of Gurprashaad, and place them on a separate plate or napkin—all while remembering the *Panj Pi-aaray* (the Five Beloved Ones, whom we will learn about in the Amrit Ceremony chapter). These handfuls they mix thoroughly with their hands back into the bowl of Gurprashaad. The couple serving Gurprashaad also set aside a handful for the Granthi—in this case, the person who performs *Sukhasan* (the procedure of putting the Guru to bed).

Next they take the bowl (or bowls) around to every person present and give each person a handful, the size of which depends on the number of people present and the amount of Gurprashaad. That includes babies too small to actually eat the Gurprashaad as the Guru's Blessings must go to everyone. In the case of babies, a tiny extra handful is given to the mother—or whoever is holding the child. People with allergies to wheat or dairy or who are diabetic may request small amounts, which they sometimes hand to other people. As the couple distributing the Gurprashaad take the bowl around, I see people lifting their cupped hands with the palms side by side to receive the Gurprashaad.

Sukhasan

I am not yet one of the number receiving Gurprashaad because I am helping with *Sukhasan*—which literally means "easy pose" or position of rest. Basically, we are putting the Guru to bed. In my in-house Gurdwara, I perform Sukhasan every evening, providing I have performed Prakash that morning. In large Gurdwaras, where the Guru will remain on the palki sahib after a Gurdwara service, Sukhasan is also performed in the evening, not as part of the service. But this Gurdwara building has no separate *langar* hall—no separate place where we can eat after a service. That means the Guru must return to its room to make way for *langar* (the communal meal). So, we must perform Sukhasan now.

Sukhasan begins just before the Gurprashaad is distributed when a lady opens her *Nit Nem* (Sikh prayer book) and leads us all in reciting *Kirtan Sohila*, the Sikh evening prayer. (Sometimes instead, we recite *Bayntee Chaupa-ee*, which you can find in full in Appendix C.)

The lady who read the Gurmukhi Hukam had set the chauri sahib to one side before she read. Right after the translations, she hands the chauri sahib to me. I stand and wave it over the

Guru—and of necessity, also over her—as she quickly reads a short Hukam in Gurmukhi only. As she does this, two or three young boys pick up Siri Sahibs and long kirpans and stand at attention behind the palki sahib near the Guru.

As we continue reciting Kirtan Sohila, the lady behind the Guru removes the small ramalas and closes the *Siri Guru Granth Sahib*. She places one small ramala on top of the Guru and the other one on top of her head. Then she lifts the Guru on top of her head. With the help of another sangat member, she unfolds all the white cotton wrapping cloths, then lowers the *Siri Guru Granth Sahib* onto the open cloths on the palki sahib. One by one, she carefully, lovingly, but quickly, wraps the cloths around the Guru. She completes this task by placing a ramala on top of the Guru.

We finish reciting Kirtan Sohila a moment later. Then we all stand and begin singing *Kaal Akaal, Siree Akaal, Maahaa Akaal, Akaal Moorat, Waa Hay Guroo,* a mantra we commonly use in religious processions—although others may be used. (Translation: *Undying Death, Infinitely Great Deathlessness, Greatest Deathlessness, Undying Image, Wow! How great is this Indescribable Understanding.*) The lady performing Sukhasan stands and lifts the Guru onto her ramala-covered head. With the young boys carrying swords leading the way, we process out of the room. I wave the chauri sahib as I follow the Guru. Everyone in the sangat bows to the ground as the Guru passes by. And we return the Guru to its resting place in the little room across the hall.

The lady who is carrying the *Siri Guru Granth Sahib* lifts it off her head and places it in its cupboard, which is hung with a miniature canopy. Then she put her hands together—as does everyone in the room who isn't holding a sword or chauri sahib— and begins an Ardas, a short one giving thanks for the blessings of the Gurdwara. If we were taking the Guru a long distance, we would give an Ardas before moving the Guru. But since this is just across the hall, we give the Ardas as it reaches its final resting place. As she ends the Ardas, we all bow and the music in the other room ends. Then she cries out *Bolay So Nihaal!* And we all cry out *Sat Siri Akaal!* Sukhasan is now complete.

I place the chauri sahib on the palki sahib in the Guru's room. The young boys place the swords in the Guru's cupboard. Turning around, I spot the young man holding the bowl of Gurprashaad. Now, I bow my head and receive the handful he places in my cupped hands. It tastes good. Very good. It distills the sweet strength of the service.

Several friends accost me as I cross the entry hall back into the main room where glad bedlam now reigns as people lower the canopy, remove the Guru's paraphernalia, and bring in the serving table for *langar* (the communal meal). All around me, people are greeting old friends and making new ones. My husband and I congratulate a newly engaged couple.

Langar
Once the Guru's paraphernalia is out of the room, a man rolls out butcher paper "tablecloths," and we all start sitting down on the floor. Several servers—some of the older youngsters and some middle-aged men—come by with laden plates of food and with napkins and spoons. In some Gurdwaras, people stand in line in get their langar. In other places, people are handed plates or bowls, and the servers go through the lines with buckets of food. But here we receive filled individual plates. Today we are having Indian food, as is most common. There's rice, *dal* (any dish made from legumes), a curried vegetable dish and *raita* (a yogurt/vegetable dish). But we could be having lasagna with bread and salad or any other food.

Well, *almost* any other food. The food of the Guru's langar is always lacto-vegetarian. We do use milk products, especially ghee and yogurt, but we don't eat any animals when we sit down to enjoy each other's company.

And enjoy each other's company we do. Langar is very grounding after the elevated heights of a couple of hours of near non-stop singing and chanting. It's also very leveling. We're all sitting on the floor together, eating the same food.

From the beginning, Sikhism has been against caste and all other distinctions that create walls between people. Guru Amar Das, the Third Guru, established a 24-hour langar and insisted that anyone who wished to see him had to eat a communal meal first. Kings might be sitting next to beggars, and thieves next to saints. That tradition continues in langar to this day. In a very real way, langar is our clearest statement of equality and fraternity with everyone. I recall the time in Portland when a homeless man chanced to wander into the building as we were serving langar. We fed him.

And so we end the service. Jim and I are exhilarated and grounded as we head back to Salem. It's been a good day.

Chapter 7

The Path of *Paths*

The Granth Sahib was completed perfectly.
Reading it, the mind's desires are fulfilled.
Guru Gobind Singh [1]

Just before 11pm, I look out the window and see a young man with a growing beard and an informal turban sprinting toward the Gurdwara. He removes his sandals, opens the door, takes a couple of gasping breaths, checks the clock, washes his hands, enters the Guru's room, and bows his head at the Guru's feet. The lady sitting behind the Guru glances up only briefly while she continues reading out loud. She subtly moves over as the young man rises and quietly goes to her side. They read a couple of words together as the lady rises and the young man shifts into her place. Then the lady bows her head at the Guru's feet and quietly leaves the room. The *Akhand Path* continues.

The Sikh word *Path* (which is pronounced closer to the English word "pot") literally means "recitation" and technically may refer to any reading from the *Siri Guru Granth Sahib*. Often, Punjabi speakers will ask me if I "do *Path*," by which they mean, "Do you read your *Banis*?"—the prayers we looked at in an earlier chapter. But in common Sikh parlance, a *Path* is an out loud, beginning-to-end recitation of the entire *Siri Guru Granth Sahib*.

Using this second definition, there are two main types of *Path*, which differ primarily in the speed with which they are read. In an *Akhand Path* (literally "unbroken recitation"), the *Siri Guru Granth Sahib* is read non-stop, which requires a team of readers. This type of *Path* resembles a spiritual relay race. A *Sahaj Path* (literally "natural" or "effortless recitation") is a slower complete recitation of the *Siri Guru Granth Sahib*. We'll look at both of these in this chapter. Both are ways to let the vibration of the *Shabad Guru* seep into the fiber of a building or a business or a community.

Sikhs often hold Akhand Paths or Sahaj Paths to celebrate weddings, anniversaries, new homes and businesses, or to commemorate deaths. But special occasions aren't a requirement for Akhand Paths and Sahaj Paths. They also are a way to immerse ourselves in the Guru's Word and receive the full measure of the Guru's Blessings on all aspects of our lives.

Guru Gobind Singh, the Tenth Sikh Guru, was responsible for the first Akhand Path. After dictating the complete text of the *Siri Guru Granth Sahib* from memory, Guru Gobind Singh had five members of the *sangat* (congregation) read the complete text to him while he listened to the entire thing without a break. Another five readers read in the Akhand Path held in 1708, just before Guru Gobind Singh turned the Guruship over to the *Siri Guru Granth Sahib*. Then in 1742, as a lady warrior named *Bibi Sundari* lay dying of battle wounds, she asked as her dying wish to hear the entire *Siri Guru Granth Sahib* one last time. To accommodate her request, an Akhand Path was completed rapidly, within 48 hours.

Due to this history, a tradition arose of five readers completing an Akhand Path within 48 hours—in the original *Gurmukhi*, of course. In places sustaining huge Punjabi-speaking populations, there are now professional *Panthis*—people who read Akhand Paths for a living.

But Sikhs in the West have not always had this luxury. We have had to improvise. Few of us here can read Gurmukhi quickly, and many cannot read Gurmukhi at all. In the early days, five of us could no more have completed an Akhand Path in the original Gurmukhi in 48 hours than we could have danced jigs on the rings of Saturn. So, just as those 18th Century Sikhs created the 48-hour Akhand Path as an innovation to meet the needs of the times, so too we have innovated to meet the needs of our situation. We let everyone read in our Akhand Paths, whether they are officially Sikhs or not and whether they can read Gurmukhi or not. In an average Akhand Path, we might have 40 to 70 readers. We take 72 hours to complete our Akhand Paths. (To be honest, it's occasionally longer than that.) We allow our readers to recite the Guru's words in their own native tongue — English, Spanish, Portuguese or whatever — as well as in Gurmukhi. And God and Guru have blessed us.

Reading in Akhand Paths has provided an easy way for neophytes to learn about the *Siri Guru Granth Sahib*. Several people have stepped onto the Sikh Path by reading in Akhand Paths. You'll hear one such story in the chapter titled "A Universal Path." Listening to professional Panthis read an Akhand Path can be as passive as watching TV. But there's nothing passive about our community Akhand Paths. Everyone gets involved, and that has bonded our communities together. What was our great weakness has become our great strength.

Every Akhand Path, whether read by Panthis or by neophytes, starts and ends with a *Gurdwara* service. After first reading a *Hukam* (the random reading), the *Granthi* turns to the first page of the *Siri Guru Granth Sahib* and starts the Akhand Path by reading *Japji Sahib*. Underlining the sweetness of the Guru's word, we distribute *Gurprashaad* (the sweet treat common to all Gurdwara services — see recipe in the last chapter) after listening to the first five *pauris* (stanzas) of Japji Sahib. The Granthi continues reading out loud for an hour or two, then another reader replaces him or her without any break in the recitation. This process will continue the whole time the Akhand Path is in session.

As the Akhand Path nears completion, the sangat gathers for the *Bhog* (Ending) Ceremony — the reading of the last few pages of the *Siri Guru Granth Sahib*, beginning with the *Sloks* of *Guru Teg Bahadur*, the Ninth Guru. These begin with the *slok* (short verse) whose translation follows:

Without singing God's Praises, life is rendered useless.
Says Nanak, "Immerse your mind in meditation on God as a fish is
immersed in water." [2]

Many people have attended so many Bhog Ceremonies that they chant along while the Granthi reads the words in Gurmukhi. After the sloks come a couple of short verses by *Guru Arjan Dev*, the Fifth Guru. Then the Granthi completes the reading of the *Siri Guru Granth Sahib* with the recitation of the *Raag Mala* (the Rosary of Raags).

Of all the Shabads in the *Siri Guru Granth Sahib*, the Raag Mala is the most controversial. It appears to be inoffensive, and there's nothing scandalous about it on the surface, but many people consider it spurious and unfit for inclusion in the *Siri Guru Granth Sahib*.

For one thing, the Raag Mala is a poetic catalogue of *Raags* (Indian melodic modes), but the Raags are not always the ones in the *Siri Guru Granth Sahib*, nor are they in the same order. So it can't be a sort of poetic index. Furthermore, we know from historical documents that Guru Arjan Dev utterly rejected the system that separates the Raags into dominant *Raags* and subordinate *Raaginis*. But from its opening line to its last, the Raag Mala clearly embraces this system. No other Shabad in the *Siri Guru Granth Sahib* does so. Many people claim that the Raag Mala is apocryphal. I would think so too, if it weren't for the minor detail that it does appear in the original copy of the *Adi Granth*—which is still extant—and in the same handwriting that the other Shabads are written in. So, what the Raag Mala is doing in the *Siri Guru Granth Sahib* is a puzzle.

Anyway, the reading of the Raag Mala completes the reading of the *Siri Guru Granth Sahib*. After it, the Granthi reads both *Anand Sahib* and *Japji Sahib* again—either the whole thing or the

first five pauris in both cases. If the sangat is going to sing Anand
Sahib later in the service, the Granthi may skip it and go directly
to Japji Sahib. The Bhog Ceremony may end here after an *Ardas*
(the standing prayer) and Hukam—or it may continue with a
larger Gurdwara service.

Often we sing a lovely medley of Gurmukhi Shabads known
as the *Aartee* (which means "Worship Service") to conclude the
Bhog Ceremony. The Aartee begins with my favorite Shabad (in
translation) in the entire *Siri Guru Granth Sahib*. Here's the translation:

> In the salver of the sky, the sun and moon are lamps;
> The stars and their orbs are studded pearls.
> The fragrance of sandalwood is the incense, and the breeze is the fan.
> All plants are flowers offered to You, O Luminous One.
> What a beautiful worship service this is!
> O Destroyer of dread: this is Your worship service.
> The unstruck sound of the inner song resounds like temple drums.
>   (Pause.)
> Thousands are Your eyes, and yet You have no eyes.
> Thousands are Your forms, and yet You have no form.
> Thousands are Your Lotus Feet, and yet You have not even one foot.
> Without any nose, thousands are Your noses.
> These plays of Yours entrance me.
> Amongst all there is Light; You are that Light.
> By the Illuminating One, that Light is within all.
> By the Guru's Teachings, the Divine Light is revealed.
> That which pleases God is the true worship.
> My soul is enticed by the honey of God's Lotus Feet.
> Night and day, I thirst for them.
> Bestow the water of Your Mercy upon Nanak, the thirsty songbird,
> That he may have a home in Your Name. [3]

(Transliteration is in the sidebar.)

Shabad Yoga
Gagan Mai Thaal (In the Salver of the Sky)

This beautiful Shabad appears in *Kirtan Sohila*, the bedtime *Bani*, and also at the beginning of the *Aartee*, the medley of Shabads often sung at the end of an *Akhand Path*. According to *The Psyche of the Golden Shield*, practicing 11 or more repetitions daily opens us up to receive God's blessings. Remember to cover your head before practice. Pronunciation guide is in Appendix B. Other information on Shabad Yoga is in a sidebar in Chapter 4.

> Gagan mai thaal rav chand deepak banay taarika mandal
>   janak motee.
> Dhoop mala-aanlo pavan chavaro karay sagal banaraa-i
>   foolant jotee.
> Kaisee aartee ho-i.
> Bhav khandanaa tayree aartee.
> Anahataa shabad vaajant bhayree. (Rahaa-o.)
> Sehs tav nain nan nain hai to-eh kau sehs moorat nanaa ayk
>   tohee.
> Sehs pad bimal nan ayk pad gandh bin sehs tav gandh iv
>   chalat mohee.
> Sabh mah jot jot hai so-i.
> Tis kai chaanan sabh meh chaanan ho-i.
> Gur saakhee jot pragat ho-i.
> Jo tis bhaavai so aartee ho-i.
> Har charan kamal makarand lobhit mano anadino mo-eh
>   aahee pi-aasaa.
> Kirpaa jal day-eh Naanak saaring kau ho-i jaa tay tayrai naa-
>   i vaasaa.

The Aartee continues with four other short Shabads by Hindu and Sufi saints and five quatrains by Guru Gobind Singh, then ends with these lines that also end Guru Gobind Singh's Bani *Jaap Sahib*:

In all four directions, pervading. In all four directions, enjoying.
Self-existent. Self-illumined. United with all beings everywhere.
Destroyer of the pain of reincarnation. Embodiment of compassion.
Always with us. Life and limb. Glorious Grandeur Everlasting. [4]

(See sidebars for the transliteration and a Kundalini Yoga set using this mantra.)

Shabad Yoga
Chattar Chakkar Vartee (In All Four Directions, Pervading)

This Shabad consists of the last four lines of *Jaap Sahib* by Guru Gobind Singh, the Tenth Guru. It's also the last four lines of the *Aartee*, the Shabad medley that often ends an *Akhand Path*. According to *The Psyche of the Golden Shield*, reciting these words for 11 or more consecutive repetitions daily can erase fear, anxiety, depression and phobias. Recite them for victory, courage and fearlessness. Remember to cover the head during practice. Pronunciation guide is in Appendix B. Several musical versions are available through the Resources listed in the back of the book.

Chattar Chakkar Vartee, Chattar Chakkar Bhagatay
Suyambhav Subhang, Sarab Daa Sarab Jugatay
Dukaalang Pranaasee, Dayaalang Saroopay
Sadaa Ang Sangay, Abhangang Bibhootay.

Kundalini Yoga
Set to Release Stored Pain [5]
Originally Taught on February 27, 1985

Practicing this fairly short and fairly easy set releases stored pain and refreshes us.

The last exercise (#6b) may be done as a meditation in its own right. It uses the last four lines of Jaap Sahib by Guru Gobind Singh as a mantra for removing fear, anxiety, depression and phobias, for instilling courage and fearlessness into the fiber of our beings, and for granting victory and self-command.

Remember to tune in before you practice this set. See the sidebars in Chapter 2 for more information. See the sidebar in the Sadhana chapter for coming out of the meditation that concludes this set.

How to Do It

1. Lying on your back with your arms by your sides, bend your knees and kick your buttocks alternately with left and right heels. Continue for 4 1/2 minutes at a moderate speed.

Keep the motion going and move as fast as possible. Continue 1 more minute.

Move directly into the next exercise.

2. Continue kicking your buttocks with alternate heels. Bend your arms, make fists of your hands, and hit your shoulders with alternate fists. Coordinate the rhythm of arms and legs, moving quickly.

Do not let your hands hit the ground. Continue for 2 minutes.

3. Cat Stretch: Lying on your back and leaving both shoulders on the ground, raise one knee and bend it over the extended leg until it reaches the ground on the opposite side. Both arms are stretched out to the side on the  ground. Move quickly alternating legs from side to side. Continue for 2 1/2 minutes.

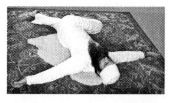 4. Sitting in a cross-legged position, place your hands lightly on top of your head. Quickly and forcefully, twist your torso alternately left and right. Continue for 2 minutes.

5. Sitting in a cross-legged position, place your hands on your knees and rotate your head in a figure eight, moving quickly and powerfully, but also carefully.

Continue for 30 seconds.

6a. Corpse Pose Variation: Relax on the back with the arms by the sides, palms facing up. Concentrate on the pituitary gland at the Brow Point. Breathe slowly and deeply through the nose. Continue for 7-8 minutes.

6b. Remain in Corpse Pose. Immediately move your concentration to the Navel Center.

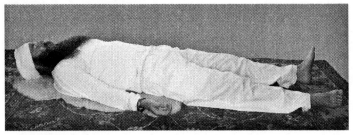

Mentally chant

Chattar Chakkar Vartee, Chattar Chakkar Bhagatay
Suyambhav Subhang, Sarab Daa Sarab Jugatay
Dukaalang Pranaasee, Dayaalang Saroopay
Sadaa Ang Sangay, Abhangang Bibhootay.

Pull in your navel in a steady heartbeat rhythm with the chant. (Use the tape/CD of Jaap Sahib, Last Four Lines by Healing Sounds of the Ancients if possible. See Resources.) Continue for 9 minutes.

Akhand Paths often induce profound experiences that defy description. But sometimes the experiences are both profound and astonishingly practical as the following story illustrates.

During World War II, an Englishman whose last name was

David was commanding a Sikh Regiment that had suffered severe losses. Only a few soldiers survived, and they were completely surrounded. In this desperate situation, David suggested that the soldiers attempt to escape individually to save their lives. This idea didn't set well. Running away from a battlefield is not a Sikh trait. Instead one of the officers suggested that they seek guidance by reading an Akhand Path. This they did. Fortunately, they were able to complete this Akhand Path without interruption.

The Hukam following the Akhand Path basically said not to abandon the field of battle, that victory was theirs. This was hopeful, but there was further guidance. During the *Ardas* (prayer), while David was standing with his eyes closed, he had seen "a fully armed Sikh on horseback, with a unique grandeur," who had commanded, "Follow me." The Sikhs present felt sure that this must be Guru Gobind Singh come to guide them. David accordingly pointed out the direction the Guru had taken. They launched an attack in this direction, broke through the enemy encirclement, and by God's Grace, were saved. After the War, David reflected on this incident. He took *Amrit* (Sikh baptism), changed his name to Devinder Singh, and chose to follow the Guru the rest of his life. [6]

Sahaj Paths also can produce profound effects. In keeping with the word *Sahaj*, which means something like "easy flow," a Sahaj Path is a much simpler, more leisurely, go-at-your-own-pace, door-to-door reading of the *Siri Guru Granth Sahib*. Although some Sahaj Paths end with fancy Bhog Ceremonies, perhaps the majority do not. Sometimes communities will get together for a Sahaj Path. But usually individuals read them on their own.

So far, I've completed three personal Sahaj Paths. I can vouch for their spiritual effectiveness and power. As I read my first Sahaj Path, my consciousness awakened. I experienced the height, the vastness and the refreshing quality of a vast mountain meadow in spring. I developed a deeper understanding of some deep subjects. That's the best I can explain it. Most deep spiritual experiences don't translate well into ordinary language. But in addition to touching unfathomable spiritual depths, Sahaj Paths—like Akhand Paths—can have a practical side, as the case of Sat Pavan Kaur Khalsa illustrates.

Sat Pavan, who was born into a Sikh family on October 25, 1974, has loved the Guru all her life. She can remember crawling up the stairs of her family home to get to the Guru's room—her favorite place in the whole house to be, even as a toddler. That love of the Guru proved to be her saving grace...literally.

While she was a teenager attending Guru Nanak Fifth Centenary School in India, she began having seizures in the early morning. Unfortunately, the seizures occurred around exam time, and weren't visibly noticeable, being petit mal, rather than grand mal. So the school medical staff assumed she was making it up to get out of the tests.

But three days after she came home for the holidays, grand mal seizures made a grand entrance. Her mother (the only parent home at the time) whisked her off to the hospital, which performed lots of tests, one of which revealed an ominous spot in her brain. But the exact cause of that spot remained a mystery. The doctors prescribed dilantin to control the seizures, which helped some, but did nothing for Sat Pavan's sinking spirits. Given the circumstances, her parents understandably refused to send her back to school in India. But from the beginning, Sat Pavan insisted that she would someday go back.

Soon after the seizures started, Sat Pavan and her parents went to consult with the *Siri Singh Sahib* (Yogi Bhajan) about her situation. He suggested in an offhand kind of way that 62 minutes of *Sat Kriya* (see the sidebar) every morning and evening would take care of it. The teenage Sat Pavan did the full 62 minutes twice daily for 40 days. Although practicing Sat Kriya lifted her spirits and opened her to future wonders, by the end of the 40 days, Sat Pavan was not yet healed.

Kundalini Yoga
Sat Kriya

Sat Kriya is a basic Kundalini Yoga practice. It is outstanding for health maintenance and emotional stability. Practicing it gently massages all the inner organs, strengthens the heart and the glandular system, improves sexual function and channels excess sexual energy towards self healing. It can help release depression and other negative emotional states. In addition, Sat Kriya is good for stimulating and channeling the *kundalini*, which means that its practice can awaken all our potentials.

Sat Naam rhymes with "But Mom!" It's a basic mantra for Sikhs and a basic mantra for Kundalini Yogis. It means that Truth is our Identity and the only Reality of anything.

Caution #1: Earlier in this chapter, you heard how Sat Pavan Kaur Khalsa practiced Sat Kriya for 62 minutes twice daily. But please, start your practice slowly. Do NOT jump directly into 62 minutes of practice! Start with 3 minutes and gradually increase your time.

Caution #2: Sat Kriya is not recommended for pregnant and menstruating women, nor for prepubescent children.

Caution #3: Tune in first, if you have not already done so. See sidebars in Chapter 2.

How to Do It

Sitting on your heels, stretch your arms overhead with your arms hugging your ears. Interlace your fingers except for the index fingers which point straight up. Men cross the right thumb over the left thumb; women cross the left thumb over the right thumb. Close your eyes and focus at the *Brow Point*, (also known as the *Third Eye*) the point centered over the nose just above the eyes. Chant *Sat* and pull in on your navel as far as it will go, then chant *Naam* and release it. Continue for 3 minutes.

Then inhale, hold the breath, and apply *Root Lock* (*Moolbandh*) by pulling up on the anal sphincter muscle and sex organ and pulling in on the navel. Squeeze the muscles all the way up from the buttocks to the top of your head. Exhale, hold the breath out and apply *Mahabandh*, by applying Root Lock (as on the inhale), Neck Lock (by pulling your chin in a bit so your neck is in line with the rest of your spine), and Diaphragm Lock (by lifting your chest and pulling your diaphragm and upper abdominal area in and up).

Inhale and relax on your back in *Corpse Pose*, with your arms by your sides with the palms facing up. Don't cross your legs. Relax for at least the amount of time you did Sat Kriya and preferably twice the amount of time. (See sidebar in the Sadhana chapter for how to end the deep relaxation.)

Sat Pavan hated the medical tests and the medication, but as time went by, she found she hated being cut off from the spiritual connection she had had with her friends in India even more—a connection she did not have with the friends she made after returning to America. So, in July 1989, she began a Sahaj Path specifically with the intention to return to India and walk again in the Guru's footsteps. Her parents confronted her with being in denial. There was no way she could go back! Through tears, Sat Pavan kept insisting that she would indeed go back. And indeed she did.

And then the miracles began to happen. Shortly after Sat Pavan's meeting with the Siri Singh Sahib, some friends of her parents recommended a certain homeopathic doctor, who discovered that Sat Pavan was infested with parasites. He prescribed a month-long course of homeopathic medicine to expel these parasites from her system. He also told her to keep up her prayers and spiritual work as this also would help heal her.

Before Sat Pavan started her Sahaj Path, she was slapdash in taking these homeopathic remedies, so at the end of the month, she was not healed. But after starting the Sahaj Path, as her spirits grew stronger, she also took the homeopathic remedies religiously. So at the end of the next month, the homeopathic doctor suggested that Sat Pavan go back to the hospital for a retest. Sure enough, the spot on Sat Pavan's brain was gone, and the hospital doctor claimed it was a medical miracle. As a result, both her parents and the doctors were completely willing to allow her to return to India...providing she stayed on the dilantin.

Sat Pavan returned to India right around the time the Punjab was reopened to foreigners. (It had been closed for several years due to political problems, which hadn't affected her school in *Mussoorie*, north of the Punjab in the Himalayan foothills.) One weekend shortly after the Punjab reopened, the school nurse and her husband took Sat Pavan with them to the Golden Temple (*Hari Mandir Sahib*) in Amritsar. Specifically, they took her to the Nectar Tank surrounding the Golden Temple that has soaked up the vibration of years of continuous *kirtan* (Shabads set to music). It's a reservoir of the Guru's vibration—a sort of watery Akhand Path or Sahaj Path in its own right.

There, in a secluded area where the women dunk themselves,

Sat Pavan dipped her whole body, including her head, in the waters of the Nectar Tank. Wearing a bathing suit and turban, she laughed and prayed and chanted out loud for her own recovery...and also for Nelson Mandela, who was released from prison soon after. She returned to school cured. To be on the safe side, she tapered off her medication. But she has never had to use it since.

Often after the completion of an Akhand Path or Sahaj Path, we sing the following Shabad, which refers to this Nectar Tank:

> *I have seen all places, and none compare with you.*
> *God, Who established you, embellishes and exalts you.*
> *Multitudes of devotees dwell in the unparalleled beauty of the township of God's Servant.*
> *Says Nanak, "All sins and errors are washed away by bathing in the Nectar Tank of Guru Ram Das."* [7]

Sat Pavan's story is a living embodiment of what this Shabad is about. She turned to the Guru's Word, and it lifted her up. That's why we read Akhand Paths and Sahaj Paths. We take the Guru's Word into ourselves, and, in ways both subtle and obvious, it elevates us.

Chapter 8

Sadhana: Early in the Morning Our Song Shall Rise to Thee

God's Name is the jewel, the pearl, the ruby one attains
In the ambrosial hours before dawn when attuned to God with
utter devotion.
Sowing God's Name at this perfect time,
The devotee reaps an inexhaustible harvest.
Guru Ram Das [1]

It's a bit after three o'clock in the morning in our high desert camp in the Jemez Mountains of New Mexico. Accompanied by someone carrying a flashlight, Guru Singh Khalsa is striding through the holy, star-spangled darkness, playing the guitar and singing.

Rise up, rise up, sweet family dear,
Time of the Lord and remembering love is here.
"Love, love" is all you'll say,
If you'll awake and rise up right, right away. [2]

The song penetrates my consciousness. I hear the words—and often an accompanying flute obbligato. I silently chant *Waheguru* (the most ecstatic Sikh Name for God) as I stretch. Grabbing my flashlight, toilet bag, water bottle (in this climate I don't go anywhere without a water bottle) and clothes that I set out the evening before, I exit my tent and head down the pinon-scented path. It's time to prepare for *Sadhana* (spiritual practice).

Holy, Holy, Holy! resounds the wonderful old Protestant hymn, *Lord God Almighty! Early in the morning our song shall rise to Thee.*[3] I loved this hymn in the Sunday schools of my childhood, and wondered why we weren't getting up *early in the morning* to sing God's praises like the hymn said we would. Worship services at ten or eleven in the morning on Sundays only just didn't seem to meet the case. I sometimes credit this one song with making me a Sikh because Sikhs rise and shine before the sun does to sing God's praise. Indeed, I've been in several Sikh houses where the residents have urged me to make lots of noise when I get up early so they will get up too. That never happens in any non-Sikh residence I've ever been in!

Wielding my flashlight, I head down the rocky dirt path. The high desert air is chill and filled with life. I enter the ladies' shower area and place my clothes on a nearby table. Extracting a toothbrush from my toilet bag, I proceed to gag myself. Well, actually, I'm brushing the base of the tongue to release and spit out the mucous that collected in my throat during the night. After a hefty swig from my water bottle, I wash the grit of sleep out of my eyes with water. Around me, I can hear ladies chanting *Waheguru* and other Sikh mantras as they take a cold shower. Because God blessed me with Raynaud's syndrome, which causes my extremities to turn blue and white with cold even in mild weather, I do not take the cold shower, but take the alternate method of rubbing myself down with water really thoroughly instead. After dressing in white cotton clothing, I comb out my hair with a wooden comb or *kangha*, one of the five "k"s a Sikh carries on his or her person. (You'll hear more about each of these "k"s and other items of Sikh garb in the chapter on Bana.) My hair is so long I can sit on it, and lots of static collects in it in the desert dryness, so combing out my hair takes some time. Then, I coil my hair up and crown myself with a turban.

I return to my tent to drop off my toiletries and last night's clothes. Up in the shelter at the top of the hill, I can hear hundreds of voices begin *Japji Sahib*—the Sikh morning prayer and my favorite *Bani*. I never miss Japji Sahib. So I stay in my tent and recite it in the original *Gurmukhi* (the Sikh holy language), using my flashlight to illuminate my *Nit Nem* (Sikh Prayer Book). Reciting Japji Sahib takes me about 20 minutes. For native Punjabi speakers and some fluent Westerners, it takes 10 minutes or less. I know that up in the shelter the men and women are reciting the lines alternately, a procedure that enhances the capacity to listen.

After completing Japji Sahib, I exit my tent again—this time with a blanket and exercise mat as well as the water bottle and flashlight—and trudge up the hill to enjoy group Sadhana. By the time I reach the covered, but mostly open-air shelter, perhaps eight hundred people are already there. Although many of the people around me are Sikhs, not all of them are.

Sadhana has the unique distinction of being the Sikh practice hardest for most people to maintain and the one Sikh practice non-Sikhs are most likely to engage in on a regular basis. The answer to that conundrum is *Kundalini Yoga*. Most Sikhs who are not ethnically of Punjabi descent, like me, began as Kundalini Yoga students. But not all students and practitioners of Kundalini Yoga become Sikhs. Indeed, Kundalini Yoga predates Sikhism by thousands of years.

Getting up this early may be difficult, but the *Amrit Vela* (literally Nectar Hours—the time before dawn) is the most potent time for Kundalini Yoga Sadhana. It is not, I hasten to add, the only time for Sadhana. Technically any spiritual discipline of any spiritual or faith tradition practiced at any time of the day or night is Sadhana. But the Amrit Vela is the most effective time, because this is when the pituitary is most active. Everyone who ventures onto this mountain does so for spiritual elevation. We're all up early to experience the excellence of our spirits. All around me, the chill, dry, pre-dawn air is charged with spiritual expectancy and vibrancy.

I locate a vacant patch of concrete near the stage, put down my mat, and wrap myself in the blanket. As the group has already tuned in, I quickly *tune in* on my own. I put my hands together at my heart and chant *Ong Naamo Guroo Dayv Naamo* three times. (*I call upon the Creator; I call upon the Divine Guru.*) I follow this by chanting *Aad Guray Nameh, Jugaad Guray Nameh, Sat Guray Nameh, Siree Guru Dayvay Nameh* three times. (*I call upon the respected Primal Guru. I call upon the respected Guru of the Ages. I call upon the respected True Guru. I call upon the Vast and Divine Guru.*) Now I'm ready to begin. (See the sidebar in Chapter 2 for how to tune in.)

Tuning in with the first chant aligned me with Yogi Bhajan and the whole lineage of Kundalini Yoga masters before him—including *Guru Ram Das*, the Fourth Sikh Guru. The second chant was written by *Guru Arjan Dev*, the Fifth Sikh Guru; it creates a field of protection and connects me with all the Sikh Gurus, human and divine.

Up on the stage, a young-looking woman is leading us in warm-up exercises. Kundalini Yoga is done in prescribed sets of exercises, but in the early morning especially, we often warm up the spine first with assorted exercises. As I stretch my spine, I am grateful for the enhanced flow of spinal fluid to my brain, and I am grateful for the opportunity to stay limber. (See sidebar for sample warm-up exercises.)

Kundalini Yoga Basics
Warm-Up Exercises

Here are a couple of good warm-up exercises. Please be sure to begin any Kundalini Yoga practice by tuning in (see sidebar in Chapter 2).

How to Do Them
Spinal Flexes: Sitting cross-legged, grab your ankles with

both hands. Inhale and stretch your spine forward so that your chest lifts up. (See figure 1.) Exhale and stretch your spine backwards. Keep your head level—no flopping up and down. (See figure 2.) Gradually increase the pace as your spine warms up. Continue for 1-3 minutes.

Then inhale with your spine straight, hold the position briefly, then relax.

Life Nerve Stretch: Sit with both legs stretched straight out in front, bend from your hips and grab your toes by wrapping your index and middle fingers around your big toes and pressing the nails of the big toes with your thumbs. Leave your legs straight on the ground. (If that is not possible for you, grab your ankles or calves. It is more important for your legs to remain straight than it is to touch your toes.) Inhale and stretch up from your waist. (See figure 1.)

Exhale, bend forward from your waist and bring your head to your knees (or as far down as it will go). (See figure 2.) Continue for 1-3 minutes.

Inhale in the up position, hold briefly, then relax.

As I follow along with the exercises, I silently chant *Sat* on the inhale and *Naam* on the exhale. I am inhaling God's Truth and exhaling that Truth is my Identity, the only Reality of anything. This is a Kundalini Yoga practice; it's also a Sikh practice. Many Sikhs, including me, silently chant either *Sat Naam* or *Waa Hay Guroo* on the breath nearly all the time. This inward remembrance of God's Name on the breath is called *Simran*, which literally means remembrance. It's one of the pillars of the Sikh path.

Now we begin a special set of exercises, called a *kriya*. There are many, many kriyas—short kriyas and long kriyas, easy kriyas and difficult kriyas, sedentary kriyas and active kriyas, kriyas for general health and kriyas that work on specific areas of the body. The kriyas differ, but all raise the *kundalini* in those who practice them. The kundalini is a coil of energy that usually lies dormant at the base of the spine. When the kundalini is activated through Kundalini Yoga practice, numerous dormant talents and poten-tialities awaken in the practitioner. So practicing this yoga is deeply fulfilling. It is also good exercise, especially excellent for the glands and the nervous system in addition to whatever the kriya is specifically for. As a Sikh, I practice Kundalini Yoga to respect my Creator by keeping my body temple in the best possible shape. As the instructor on the stage leads us through the exercises, I continue inhaling *Sat* and exhaling *Naam*, except where the exercise calls for a different mantra. (See sidebar for a sample kriya.)

Kundalini Yoga
Sample Kriya (Set for the Nervous System) [4]

Here is a sample Kundalini Yoga physical kriya. Practicing this set is good for the nervous system, the message system of the brain, the neck, the knees and the sex organs. According to yogic tradition, it helps prevent senility. In addition, practicing the first exercise opens the lungs, enhances alertness and clarity of mind, and helps remove anger, grief and insecurities.

Har is the most frequent word for God in the *Siri Guru Granth Sahib*.

Remember to tune in before practicing this set. See both sidebars in Chapter 2. Pronunciation guide is in Appendix B. Please see the sidebar in this chapter for how to come out of the deep relaxation at the end.

How to Do It

1. Sitting cross-legged, place your hands by your sides with your knuckles and forefingers on the ground. Breathing powerfully, inhale through your mouth and arch your spine forward, lifting your neck up and pushing your chin and chest out. (See figure 1.) Then exhale powerfully through

---

your mouth and arch your spine back, bringing your chin to your chest. (See figure 2.) Continue for 3-4 minutes.

2. Throughout this exercise, move rapidly and powerfully in the following sequence keeping your fingers stiff and the movements tight and precise. Sitting cross-legged, on the count of 1, place your hands in front of your neck with your fingers pointing up and your palms facing each other about 4-6 inches apart. (See figure 3.) On the count of 2, move your hands towards your shoulders with your palms diagonal to your torso and the fingers still pointing up. (See figure 4.) On the count of 3, straighten your arms out to the sides parallel to the ground with the palms

facing down. (See
figure 5.) On the
count of 4, return your
hands towards your
shoulders with the
palms diagonal to your
torso. (See figure 4.)

Continue this rhythm for 3-11 minutes.

3. Sitting cross-legged, extend your arms straight out to
the sides with the palms facing up. (See figure 6.) Keeping
your hands and arms straight, lift your arms lightly
straight up overhead without
touching your palms together.
(See figure 7.) Lower your
arms as if a ton of weight were
falling. (See figure 6.) Move
rapidly and breathe powerfully. Your chin and neck
should come up about one
and a half inches as you move.
Continue for 3-4 minutes.

4. Cobra Pose Variation:
Lying on your stomach, place
your palms flat on the
ground under your shoulders.
Leaving your legs and pelvis
on the ground with the heels
together, inhale and arch your
upper body off the ground
until your arms are straight

and your elbows are locked. Your head is arched back.
Kick your buttocks with alternate heels quickly and

powerfully. (See figure 8.) Continue for 6 minutes or less.

5. Crow Pose Variation: Squat down with your feet flat on the ground. (It helps to splay your feet somewhat.) Interlace your fingers in *Venus Lock* behind your neck. (Venus Lock: Women interlace the fingers with the right little finger on the bottom. The right thumb goes on webbing between the left thumb and index finger. The left thumb is on top and presses the fleshy mound at the base of the right thumb. Men reverse the direction of all fingers so that the right thumb is on top and the left little finger is on the bottom. See figure 9.) Spread your elbows, open your chest wide and bounce up and down into a squatting position (called Crow Pose) for 3 counts. (See figure 10 for standing position.) Stand up on the count of 4, then lower yourself back into Crow Pose for the count of 1 without breaking the rhythm. (See figure 11 for Crow Pose position.) Continue for 4 minutes

or less.

6. Stand up and stretch your arms straight overhead with your arms hugging your ears and your palms together with the thumbs crossed. Stretch up and chant *Har* continuously with the tip of your tongue touching the upper palate just above your teeth to make the "r" sounds. (See figure 12.) Continue for 2 minutes.

Then inhale and stretch your whole body powerfully. Exhale.

Relax down on your back with your arms by your sides and your arms stretched out straight. Deeply relax for 5-10 minutes.

At the end of the kriya, we relax on our backs with our legs out straight and our arms by our sides with the palms facing up. All of us are wrapped in blankets and coats in an attempt to stay warm as the pre-dawn chill intensifies. Just before we lie down for this relaxation, I feel a whoosh of air as the stage door opens and the musicians troop in carrying an assortment of instruments—flute, viola, *harmonium* (small portable organ), guitar, *tablas* (small Indian drums). After we relax for a few minutes, the lady on the stage guides us back from the relaxation. All of us rotate our ankles and wrists, stretch from side to side, rub the bottoms of our feet and the palms of our hands together, rock on our spines a couple of times, and roll up. (See sidebar for how to end a Kundalini Yoga deep relaxation.)

Kundalini Yoga Basics
How to End a Deep Relaxation

Bring yourself back from the deep relaxation at the end of any set in the following way:

1. Inhale and exhale deeply. Consciously bring yourself back.

2. Still lying on your back, wiggle your fingers and toes. Then rotate your ankles and wrists in small circles a few

times. Then reverse the direction and rotate your ankles and wrists in small circles in the other direction a few times. (See figure 1.)

3. Cat Stretch: Leaving both shoulders on the ground, stretch one knee over the other extended leg, first on one side and then on the other. Both arms may be stretched out to the side on the ground, or the arm on the side with the moving leg may be stretched overhead on the ground. (See figure 2.)

4. Lying on your back, rub your palms together and the bottoms of your feet together briefly. (See figure 3.)

5. Bring your knees to your chest and wrap your hands around your legs. Roll back and forth on your spine several times. Then roll up into a sitting position and prepare to meditate or conclude your practice. (See figures 4 and 5.)

By this time, the musicians are mostly set up and tuning their instruments. The sound tech is adjusting the mikes. It's time for the Kundalini Yoga Aquarian Sadhana chants, one version of the Sikh practice of *Naam Simran*. As mentioned earlier, remembering the Name of God on the breath is one way Sikhs practice *Simran*. Remembering the Name of God by chanting is the other form. It's a meditative discipline we maintain so the little whips of the mind do not flay us. Like reciting Shabads, chanting types codes on the roof of the mouth that stimulate the experience of God consciousness and simultaneously clear the subconscious of gunk. We are about to wash the windows of our minds so that the Light of God shines through.

We begin our 62 minutes of en-chanting meditation with seven minutes of *Long Ek Ongkars*. The words of this mantra appear in inscriptions on two buildings erected by Sikh Gurus: one over a doorway into the Gurdwara built by *Guru Amar Das*, the Third Guru, at *Goindwal* and the other over the main gateway into the *Hari Mander Sahib* (literally "God's Great Temple," better known as the Golden Temple) built by *Guru Ram Das* and *Guru Arjan Dev*, the Fourth and Fifth Gurus, at *Amritsar*.

I rarely experience much emotion while chanting Long Ek Ongkars, but Snatam Kaur Khalsa, who often plays the accompanying music says, "I learned that every fear, every emotion, every physical discomfort could be channeled into Long Ek Ongkars."[5] As we chant, we're opening and polishing our *chakras*—the eight vortices of energy we all have—awakening our intuition and other latent abilities in the process. (See sidebar for how to chant Long Ek Ongkars.)

Kundalini Yoga Aquarian Chants
Long Ek Ongkars

Chanting Long Ek Ongkars (also known as Morning Call, Long Chant or the *Adi Shakti Mantra*) is an outstanding practice for awakening all the chakras—our vortices of latent potential—and increasing intuition. You may chant this mantra as part of the Aquarian Sadhana or on its own. Here's a fairly literal translation: *One Creator-Creation, Truth Name, Great is the Ecstasy of the Enlightener.*

If you have not already tuned in, be sure to do so before your practice. See the sidebars in Chapter 2. Pronunciation guide is in Appendix B.

How to Chant It

Sitting cross-legged with a straight spine, place your hands palms up on your knees keeping your elbows straight. Be sure to keep your chin in so that your neck is in line with the rest of your spine.

Create *Gyan Mudra* by touching the tips of your index fingers to the tips of your thumbs, leaving your other fingers straight. Focus at the *Brow Point*, the point between the eyes and a bit above them. Chant *Ek Ong Kaar Sat Naam Siri Waa Hay Guroo* a cappella in the following manner:

Inhale deeply and chant *Ek Ong Kaar* on one breath, pulling your navel slightly on *Ek*, which is very brief. Make *Ong* and *Kaar* longer and equal in length. Inhale deeply and chant *Sat Naam Siri* on one breath, pulling your navel on *Sat*, which is very short. Extend *Naam* as long as possible, then chant *Siri* with the last little bit of breath. Take a half breath and chant *Waa Hay Guroo*. *Waa* and *Hay* are short with a short break between them, and *Guroo* is somewhat extended. Continue for 7 minutes as part of the Aquarian Sadhana. You may chant this for up to two and one half hours as a separate meditation. (I recommend getting a CD with this chant, so you can learn the accurate pitch and rhythm.)

As soon as our seven minutes of Long Ek Ongkars are over, the musicians strike up with the tune for *Waa Yantee*, our next Sadhana chant, an ancient prayerful mantra attributed to *Patanjali*, the author of the *Yoga Sutras*. All the other mantras are Sikh-based, but *Waa Yantee* is much older since Patanjali lived in India sometime between 400 BCE and 400 CE. You wouldn't know that from the tune however. Today's tune is somewhat jazzy, but the tunes of all the Sadhana chants other than Long Ek Ongkars can vary. They may be in classical Indian *Raag* or hard rock or sweet and lyric or any other music. (See sidebar for how to chant Waa Yantee.)

Kundalini Yoga Aquarian Chants
Waa Yantee

This mantra attributed to Patanjali is a prayer to the Macroself, beyond time and space. Translation: *Great Macroself. Creative Self. All that is creative through time. All that is the Great One. Three aspects of God: Brahma, Vishnu, Shiva. That is Waheguru.*

Pronunciation guide is in Appendix B.

How to Chant It
Chant *Waa Yantee, Kar Yantee, Jag Doot Patee, Aadak It Waahaa, Brahmaadeh Trayshaa Guroo, It Waa Hay Guroo* in any melody. No particular *mudra* or position was specified. Continue for 7 minutes immediately after Long Ek Ongkars as part of the Aquarian Sadhana.

For Snatam—a recording artist whose Celebrate Peace concerts reach out to people worldwide with the spirit of Sikh music—*Waa Yantee* is "the mantra of creativity and renewal."[6] She rhapsodizes over how she can tap into a pipeline of creativity that chanting this mantra provides her. For me, however, it's time for *sob-na*—my special term for sobbing during Sadhana. On other days, I might cry as negative emotions come up. As we wash the windows of our minds, it's not uncommon to cry while releasing lots of negative emotions during any meditation or chanting. But today, as our hundreds of voices swell in devotional song, I start crying with gratitude to be in the company of so many saints, so much goodness. Whatever emotion I have turns into devotion.

After seven minutes of *Waa Yantee*, we begin chanting seven minutes of *Mool Mantra*, the opening lines of Japji Sahib. Just as

Japji Sahib is said to contain the total wisdom of the entire *Siri Guru Granth Sahib,* so Mool Mantra is said to contain the entire wisdom of Japji Sahib. As we sing it, we tap into the essence of condensed wisdom and we tap into our souls. As Snatam put it, chanting Mool Mantra "corrects you without your knowing it, because very simply you vibrate with its eternal truth, and it becomes your eternal truth."[7] It becomes very difficult to think wrong thoughts if you chant Mool Mantra. (See sidebar for how to chant Mool Mantra.)

Kundalini Yoga Aquarian Chants
Mool Mantra

Mool Mantra is the opening of *Guru Nanak's* Morning Bani, *Japji Sahib.* It contains the entire wisdom of Japji Sahib. Practicing it is good for the soul, literally.

Translation: *One Creator Creation. Truth Name. Being of Action. Without fear. Without vengeance. Undying. Unborn. Self-illumined. By Guru's Gift. RECITE! True in the beginning. True through all time. True even now. Nanak: Truth shall always be.* [8]

Pronunciation guide is in Appendix B. You can find a kriya using Mool Mantra in the Bani chapter.

How to Chant It

Chant *Ek Ong Kaar, Sat Naam, Kartaa Purakh, Nirbhao, Nirvair, Akaal Moorat, Ajoonee, Saibhang, Gurprasaad, Jap, Aad Sach, Jugaad Sach, Hai Bhee Sach, Naanak Hosee Bhee Sach* in any melody. But leave a slight pause (without taking a breath) between *Ajoonee* and *Saibhang,* and empower your chanting by emphasizing the "ch" sound at the end of *Sach.* No mudra or position was specified. Continue for 7

---

minutes as part of the Aquarian Sadhana. Mool Mantra may also be practiced for up to two and a half hours by itself.

After Mool Mantra, we begin seven minutes of chanting *Sat Siree, Siree Akaal.* Yogi Bhajan gave us this chant to carry us into the Aquarian Age. But it has another function. "Sat Siree Akaal is the Mantra that prepares us for death, for that moment when the *Prana* (life force energy) leaves the body, and the soul answers for all vibrations, all thoughts, and all actions. The penetration of this Mantra helps us to guide our lives so that we take the right course on a day to day basis, and are in the Infinite Flow at the time of death."[9] (See sidebar for how to chant Sat Siree, Siree Akaal.)

Kundalini Yoga Aquarian Chants
Sat Siree, Siree Akaal

This mantra is a combination of phrases from the *Siri Guru Granth Sahib.* Yogi Bhajan gave us this mantra to prepare ourselves for the Aquarian Age. We chant it to experience our deathlessness.

Translation: *Great Truth, Great Immortality, Great Immortality, Great Deathlessness, Great Deathlessness, Truth Name, Undying Image, Wow! Incomprehensibly Great is the Wisdom.*

Pronunciation guide is in Appendix B.

How to Chant It
Chant *Sat Siree, Siree Akaal, Siree Akaal, Mahaa Akaal, Mahaa Akaal, Sat Naam, Akaal Moorat, Waa Hay Guroo* in any

melody. No mudra or position was specified. Continue for 7 minutes as part of the Aquarian Sadhana. You may also sing it on its own for up to two and one half hours.

And now the musicians begin seven minutes of *Rakhay Rakhanahaar*, the exquisite *slok* (short verse) by Guru Arjan Dev that concludes *Rehiras Sahib*, the Sikh evening Bani. We chant it for success, and we chant it for protection for ourselves and for our communities. Often the most lilting tune of the morning Sadhana chants is the one that accompanies this mantra. "However, the effect is like a steel sword as used by the fiercest warrior you can imagine. This combination of sweet and fierce actually protects our innocence."[10] (See sidebar for how to chant Rakhay Rakhanahaar.)

Kundalini Yoga Aquarian Chants
Rakhay Rakhanahaar

This shabad by Guru Arjan Dev, the Fifth Guru, concludes the evening Bani, Rehiras Sahib. We chant it for complete protection and to allow the victory of God in our lives. It may also be practiced the way we practice Shabad Yoga. (See sidebar in the chapter on the Shabad Guru.)
Here's a translation:

O Savior God, save us all and take us across, uplifting and giving the excellence.
You have given us the touch of the Lotus Feet of the Guru, and our works are embellished with perfection.
You have become merciful, kind and compassionate, so our

mind does not forget You.

In the Company of the Holy, You carry us across from misfortune, calamities and disrepute.

The power-hungry, slanderous enemies You finish off in an instant.

That Master is my Anchor and Support; O Nanak, hold firm your mind.

Remembering God in meditation, happiness comes, and all sorrows and pain simply vanish. [11]

Pronunciation guide is in Appendix B.

How to Chant It

Chant the following in any melody. No mudra or position was specified.

Rakhay rakha_n_ahaar aap ubaari-an.
Gur kee pairee paa-i kaaj savaari-an.
Ho-aa aap da-i-aal manaho na visaari-an.
Saadh janaa kai sang bhavajal taari-an.
Saakat nindak dusht khin maa-eh bidaari-an.
Tis saahib kee tayk naanak manai maa-eh.
Jis simarat sukh ho-i sagalay dookh jaa-eh.

Continue for 7 minutes as part of the Aquarian Sadhana. You may also sing it on its own for up to two and one half hours.

The combination of sweet and fierce continues as we begin the 22 minutes of chanting *Waa Hay Guroo Jeeo,* an untranslatable song based on a Sikh Shabad that stirs the ecstasy of our souls. It's a sweet mantra, but people all around me are moving into *Vir*

Asana—literally "Warrior Pose," a posture used in the Sikh Amrit Ceremony that includes sitting on the left heel. (See sidebar for how to chant Waa Hay Guroo Jeeo.) Due to weak ankles, I don't join the multitudes in this *asana* (position), but curl up in my blanket and let the vibration of God's ecstasy seep into all my pores. This is a special time for me to acknowledge that God does all the work. Sometimes, I feel like I'm curled up in a little red wagon being pulled to my ultimate destiny by God and Guru.

Kundalini Yoga Aquarian Chants
Waa Hay Guroo Jeeo

This mantra from the *Siri Guru Granth Sahib* affectionately connects the Infinite ecstasy with the soul. *Vir Asana*, which is also part of the Sikh Amrit Ceremony, is a position of power. So this meditation creates victory of ecstatic consciousness.

Translation: *Wow! The Light! O my Soul.* (Technically, there is no translation of this one.)[12]

Pronunciation guide is in Appendix B.

How to Chant It

Sit in *Vir Asana* (Warrior Pose) by sitting on your left heel and bringing your right knee near your chest with your right foot flat on the ground. Place your palms together in Prayer Pose at the Heart Center. Focus your eyes on the tip of your nose without crossing your eyes. Chant *Waa Hay Guroo, Waa Hay Guroo, Waa Hay Guroo, Waa Hay Jeeo* in

---

any melody. Continue for 22 minutes as part of the Aquarian Sadhana. You may also practice it as a separate meditation for 11 minutes on up to two and one half hours.

By the time the *Waa Hay Guroo Jeeo* mantra ends, the sun is rising. We begin a final five minutes of chanting Guru Raam Daas Chant, a prayerful mantra of praise to *Guru Ram Das*, the Guru of miracles and the Fourth Sikh Guru. (The miraculous circumstances connected with this mantra appear in Chapter 2.) We chant it for humility, guidance, protection, and wise decision making. (See sidebar for how to chant Guru Raam Daas Chant.)

Kundalini Yoga Aquarian Chants
Guru Raam Daas Chant

This hymn of praise to *Guru Raam Daas*, the Fourth Sikh Guru, concludes the Aquarian Sadhana meditation cycle. Practicing it protects us, guides us and grants us humility.

Translation: *Great is the ecstasy of serving God.* Or: *The Servant of God brings us to the Light of ecstasy.* Or: *Wise, wise is the one who serves Infinity.*

Another meditation with this mantra appears in the sidebar in Chapter 2. Pronunciation guide is in Appendix B.

How to Chant It
Chant *Guroo, Guroo, Waa Hay Guroo, Guroo Raam Daas Guroo* in any melody. No special mudra or position is specified. Continue for 5 minutes as part of the Aquarian Sadhana. It may be practiced for up to two and a half hours on its own.

Slanting rays of light outline each of us as we listen for a minute or so in silence to the vibration of the mantra still resounding within us. Then the door to the Gurdwara opens, and we begin a short Gurdwara service. It's incredibly moving to see hundreds of people line up three-deep to bow at the Guru's Feet. What a gift it is to be in the Company of the Holy!

Although the pinnacle of Sadhana is reached at Summer Solstice (literally—we're some 7000 feet above sea level), this is the standard pattern for day-to-day Sadhana as Yogi Bhajan outlined it. We recite Japji Sahib. We practice Kundalini Yoga. And we chant this set of chants. We bow at the Guru's feet and listen to the Guru's word. (See sidebar for putting together the Aquarian Sadhana.)

Kundalini Yoga
Putting Together the Aquarian Sadhana

Here is the format for the Aquarian Sadhana:
Japji Sahib (if you have access to it)
Tune In!
Warm-up exercises (optional)
Any complete Kundalini Yoga Kriya
Short Deep Relaxation
Aquarian Sadhana Meditations
Long Ek Ongkars—7 minutes
Waa Yantee—7 minutes
Mool Mantra—7 minutes
Sat Siri, Siri Akaal—7 minutes
Rakhay Rakhanhaar—7 minutes
Waa Hay Guroo Jeeo—22 minutes
Guru Raam Daas Chant—5 minutes
Short Gurdwara or any Spiritual Reading from your
    faith tradition.

There are some variables. For people without direct access to a complete copy of the Guru, it's common to read at random from a Nit Nem or a book of Shabads instead of holding a short Gurdwara. At Solstice, the wake up call is generally earlier than it would be in our homes. And of course, there are usually fewer people elsewhere. But the program is much the same.

This isn't the only model for Sadhana however. (See sidebar for other Sadhana models.) Although more Sikhs of Punjabi descent than ever practice the Sadhana I've just described, the majority simply recite their Banis. Some also sing and listen to *Aasaa Di Vaar*, a lengthy hymn praising God. When I took *Amrit* (you'll get the whole story in the chapter on the Amrit Ceremony), the *Panj Pi-aaray* administering the Amrit told us to chant *Waa Hay Guroo* for our Sadhana, and gave us special instructions for how to do that. When my husband and I went to England to celebrate our 25th wedding anniversary some years ago, a Sikh official at Heathrow gave me an animated description of the best way to chant Mool Mantra while he was walking us to customs. Presumably this was his Sadhana, or a hefty part of it.

Kundalini Yoga
Other Sadhana Formats

Here is a sample of another Sadhana model:
Tune In!
Any Kundalini Yoga Kriya or Warm-Up Exercises
Short Deep Relaxation
One or two Kundalini Yoga Meditations

For a short evening Sadhana:
Tune In!
A Kundalini Yoga Meditation

Many of us practice special Sadhanas. I've currently got one going for 120 consecutive days. After Japji Sahib and a bit of Kundalini Yoga, I chant a particularly powerful mantra that is derived from the Bani *Jaap Sahib* by *Guru Gobind Singh,* the Tenth Guru. (See sidebar for how to practice this meditation.) This morning I woke up with a bad case of morning blahs and an infestation of worries. (I come from a line of Olympic-class worriers; so although meditating for years has decimated the ranks of the worry gremlins, it hasn't eliminated all of them...yet.) Well before I had completed the meditation, the blahs had vanished, the worries were fast dissolving, and I was feeling wonderfully energized and happy.

Kundalini Yoga
Gobinday Mukanday Meditation [13]

Practicing this mantra meditation balances the hemispheres of the brain, and releases fear, subconscious blocks and karmic debris. The mantra comes from *Jaap Sahib*, a Bani by *Guru Gobind Singh*, the Tenth Guru, and may be translated *Sustaining, Liberating, Enlightening, Infinite, Destroying, Creating, Nameless, Desireless.* [14]

How to Do It

Sitting with your spine straight, place your hands palms up on your knees keeping your elbows straight. Create *Gyan Mudra* by touching the tips of your index fingers to the tips of your thumbs, leaving your

---

other fingers straight. Focus at the *Brow Point*, the point between the eyes and a bit above them. Inhale deeply, and chant *Gobinday, Mukanday, Udaaray, Apaaray, Haree-ang, Karee-ang, Nirnaamay, Akaamay* on one breath, taking about 15 seconds per repetition of mantra. As you chant, pull in your navel and apply *Root Lock* (*Moolbandh*) by pulling up on your anal sphincter muscle and sex organ and pulling in on your navel. Make this Lock a little tighter with each repetition. Exhale. Continue for 31 minutes.

That, of course, is the whole point of practicing Sadhana, Kundalini Yoga, meditation and Naam Simran. We find our way through obstacles and release the ugly phantasms of our minds. One of the most amazing transformations I personally witnessed goes like this.

Many years ago, I met a lady whose life was a mess. She was divorced, having, in her words, "trashed a marriage" with a man who had cared for her and would have supported her. She was estranged from one of her two brothers and had had no contact with the other brother for a number of years. Not only had her son not contacted her for many months, but she was none too sure of his whereabouts. She was living in a place that was habitable, and that's the best you could say for it. She was suspicious of her neighbors. She was working for a temp agency at low wages and no benefits for people she didn't respect. Making ends meet was difficult.

As she was looking for a meditation practice that was "serious, but not grim," I invited her to join a friend and me for our marathon, once-a-week, two-and-a-half-hour meditation jamboree. She gratefully accepted. When she started the meditation, her only intention was to nourish her spirit. She had no intention of cleaning up her life. But that is exactly what happened. First, she landed a regular job with benefits working for people she respected greatly. The pay was only a little better, but the benefits made the money she had go further.

Then several things happened all at once. Her son began calling her nearly every week. Her cat got lost, and in the process of searching for it, she discovered that her neighbors were much nicer people than she had supposed. And one morning at work she felt an intuitive need to take an early break at a nearby restaurant. Whom should she see there but the brother from whom she had been estranged, who was eating a late breakfast. That chance meeting healed that relationship. Soon thereafter, she had the pleasure of visiting with the other brother. A month or so later, she moved in with the brother she had resolved her differences with, who lived in a nice home on a small farm.

What was the meditation we were practicing? Two and a half hours of Long Ek Ongkars—the mantra that begins our regular morning Sadhana chanting. Every year early on the morning of August 26, Yogi Bhajan's birthday, the entire 3HO community (Healthy, Happy, Holy Organization—begun by Yogi Bhajan in 1969 to share his teachings) chants this mantra for two and a half hours. That particular year, my friend and I had had such a sublime experience that we decided to get together to chant two and a half hours of Long Ek Ongkars each weekend. We did so for quite some time, including the period of time the lady's life healed.

Two and a half hours chanting Long Ek Ongkars is one of two special Sadhana meditations the entire 3HO community enjoy each year. The other occurs on Guru Ram Das' birthday, which 3HO Sikhs celebrate on October 9. (Most other Sikh holy days are on a lunar calendar, like Easter and Hanukah, which means the dates change from year to year.) Since 3HO Sikhs have a deep connection to Guru Ram Das, the orphan boy who rose to be the Fourth Sikh Guru, we celebrate his birthday by chanting and singing two and a half hours of Guru Ram Das Chant (the mantra that ends the regular Sadhana chanting) or two and a half hours of the Shabad *Dhan Dhan Ram Das Guru.* (See the sidebar for this Shabad in full.)

Shabad Yoga
Dhan Dhan Raam Daas Guru (Blessed, Blessed Is Guru Ram Das)

When you need a miracle, this is the Shabad to practice. Practicing 11 repetitions or more of this Shabad daily for 40 or more days makes the impossible possible and strengthens the ability to make the best decisions. This is the Shabad we sing for two and a half hours on Guru Ram Das' birthday. It's worth doing!

Remember to cover your head when practicing this or any Shabad. Pronunciation guide is in Appendix B. Further information on practicing Shabad Yoga is in the chapter on the Shabad Guru.

Several musical versions of this Shabad are available through the Resources listed in the back of the book.

Dhan dhan raam daas guru
Jini siri-aa tinai savaari-aa
Pooree ho-ee karaamaat
Aap sirajanahaarai dhaari-aa
Sikhee atai sangatee
Paarbrahm kar namasakaari-aa
Atal athaaho atol too
Tayraa ant na paaraavaari-aa
Jinee too(n) sayvi-aa bhaa-o kar
Say tudh paar utaari-aa
Lab lobh kaam krodh moho

Maar kadhay tudh saparvaari-aa
Dhan su tayraa thaan hai
Sach tayraa paisakaari-aa
Naanak too Lehnaa too hai
Guru Amar too veechaari-aa
Guru dithaa taa(n) man saadhaari-aa
Translation:
Blessed, Blessed is Guru Ram Das.
The One Who created you alone has embellished you.
Perfect is Your miracle.
The Creator has installed you on the throne.
Your Sikhs and the entire congregation bow and revere you
for manifesting the Supreme God.
You are unshakable, unfathomable and immeasurable.
Your extent is beyond limit.
Those who serve you with love
Are carried across the world-ocean.
Greed, attachment, lust, anger and ego
Have been beaten and driven out by you.
Honored is your place.
True are your bounties.
You are Nanak, you are Angad and you are Guru Amar Das.
So do I recognize you.
Seeing the Guru, my soul is sustained. [15]

In 2004, Guru Ram Das' birthday fell on a Saturday, three days after Yogi Bhajan passed away—which also happened to be the day his corpse was cremated. He had asked that we all celebrate his return to God. So we did. The atmosphere in the Eugene Oregon Gurdwara was more festive than at most weddings. Five musicians led the chanting for a half hour each, for a total of two and a half hours of chanting. I particularly remember Sat Pavan Kaur Khalsa chanting *Dhan Dhan Raam Daas Guru.* As I watched in amazement, Sat Pavan sang her heart out and played the harmonium while her arms encircled her bouncing, not-yet-two-year-old daughter.

Sat Pavan is no stranger to the miracle of chanting to Guru Ram Das. You've heard the story of how she was healed in the chapter titled "The Path of Paths." But the miracles started even before that. When she was eight, she spent hours in front of her altar with its pictures of the Golden Temple and Guru Ram Das. She wanted desperately to attend school in India, although her parents—especially her mother—felt Sat Pavan was much too young to go. So she chanted the Guru Ram Das Chant for hours and prayed that her parents would relent. At the very last minute, they did.

Miracles do happen as a result of Sadhana. Miracles do happen when we chant God's Name in any of its many forms. It may be something major, like an eight-year-old leaving home in a positive way. Or it may be the sweet inner singing in a heart that was once rock hard and miserable. However we practice it, Sadhana and Simran are blessings for those who practice them.

Chapter 9

Blessed by Sadhana

Viriam Kaur Khalsa's Story

The one called the Sikh of the True Guru
Should rise in the early morning to contemplate God's Name.
Guru Ram Das [1]

Many Sikhs who came to Sikhism through Kundalini Yoga were born Jewish. One such person is Viriam Kaur Khalsa, whose story exemplifies the blessings of *Sadhana* (spiritual practice, especially morning spiritual practice) and also why Sikhs consider it more blessed to live the life of a householder than to live as a hermit off in some cave.

Viriam Kaur lives with her family in Eugene, Oregon. She teaches *Kundalini Yoga* at the University of Oregon and at Yoga West, both in Eugene. She also works part-time as a bookkeeper and owns a billing service, Infinity Billing. But she says, "Aside from all that, I consider myself a stay-at-home mom. My true passion lies in raising my children and taking care of my family."

Her story is in her own words, except for some explanatory notes I have added in brackets. She has also provided some explanations of Jewish practices, which appear in the sidebars.

I was born to a Jewish family in Buffalo, New York. Both sets of grandparents came from Europe in the early 1900s. My maternal grandparents came from Rumania and settled in Toronto. My paternal grandparents came from southern Russia and settled first in Rochester, New York, and later moved to Buffalo.

My mother's family was fairly strict, more so than my father's.

There are 3 basic "levels" of Judaism in this country – Orthodox, Conservative and Reform. We were conservative and belonged to a conservative temple. My mother kept a kosher home [see sidebar], *and I attended Hebrew school for many years, had a Bat Mitzvah* [see sidebar], *went to temple almost every Saturday, and celebrated all the Jewish holidays. We changed the dishes at Passover time, and basically our family's social life was Jewish-oriented. Most of my parents' friends were Jewish and most of mine, as well.*

Viriam Kaur's Explanation of Keeping Kosher

Kosher refers to Jewish dietary law. Viriam Kaur explains two main components of it below. Other important items include not eating pork, shellfish or animals killed by hunting.

Keeping a kosher home means basically 2 things. The first is that meat and dairy products are never combined in one meal. (Fish is considered "pareve," which means it is neither meat nor dairy and so can be eaten with both.) It is ok to eat dairy before meat, but it is necessary to wait at least 1 hour (orthodox Jews wait 6 hours) before eating dairy after meat. This means you would never put milk in your coffee or tea after eating a meal with meat in it, or that you wouldn't eat mashed potatoes with butter at a meal with meat. The reason for this is it is believed meat and dairy do not mix well in the digestive system, and that is takes so long for meat to digest that Jews wait until it is digested before eating dairy.

The other main component is that in a kosher kitchen, there are 2 sets of dishes, pots, silverware, etc. for meat and dairy as they are not combined in any way in the preparation or eating process. Depending on how orthodox the home, different sides of

---

---

the sink may be used to wash meat and dairy, different sponges used, etc.

There are probably hundreds of laws about how food is to be prepared. An authorized person has the job of going around and inspecting kosher production facilities to make sure the food that is labeled kosher has indeed been prepared in a kosher way. Golden Temple cereal [manufactured in a plant established by Sikhs in Eugene] *has gone through the process and their cereal is labeled with the kosher label so people who keep kosher can eat it.*

Viriam Kaur's Explanation of Bar/Bat Mitzvah

A Bar (for boys) and Bat (for girls) Mitzvah is an initiation ceremony that takes place between the 12th and 13th birthday. The student prepares for months with the rabbi to read a portion of the Torah (Jewish holy book) at a Sabbath service. It is this ceremony that formally makes the student considered to be an adult in the Jewish community. In order for Jews to pray together, there must be a "minion" of 5 adults (the Jewish panj!). [Sikhs also do things in groups of 5 people; this is called a *panj.*] *After a child has his/her Bar/Bat Mitzvah, he or she is considered an adult in the community and can be counted as a member of the minion. Family and friends come to hear the child and there is a big celebration afterwards.*

Actually, I used to love being Jewish. I knew all the Hebrew prayers by heart, participated in the children's services at the temple, excelled in Hebrew school, etc. I used to get up early in the morning and recite the prayers before school. BUT...it was right around the time after my

Bat Mitzvah that things began to change for me. I think that's the time in a child's life when they become more aware of the world around them and begin to question how there could be so much evil in the world, how could God allow this to happen. I began asking questions in Hebrew school that my teachers could not satisfactorily answer. I began skipping class, and in one year I actually forgot almost all my Hebrew! I began to see that my parents' belief was in tradition and custom only, and it seemed to me that they had no real belief. I felt they had lied to me and misrepresented the religion to me. Basically I became an agnostic, and I remained one for many years.

I began practicing Hatha Yoga when I was 15 years old, when most of my friends were getting pretty heavily into drugs. It was a pretty confusing time. My brother gave me a book called Yoga, Youth and Reincarnation by Jesse Stearn. It was written by a journalist who went to a yoga camp and was very skeptical. As he wrote, he described in detail the exercises they were doing, and I would do them along with the book. The end of the book contained a glossary of all the exercises. I went to the library and took out every book I could find on yoga. There were maybe 10 of them. There were no classes at that time. I began doing yoga every day after school for about an hour. My diet also began changing; since I did yoga shortly before dinner, I found that I didn't want to eat heavily and started leaning away from meat. I began to eat lighter.

I continued practicing Hatha Yoga on and off for the next 8-9 years, right through high school and college. After college I was living in Pennsylvania, and a friend who did Kundalini Yoga took me to a class and invited me to Summer Solstice. [Viriam Kaur is referring to the celebration held on Sikh-owned land in New Mexico.] *I went to only one Kundalini Yoga class before going to solstice. I had never met any Sikhs and knew nothing about the lifestyle. I loved solstice and tantric* [White Tantric Yoga] *and the silence and the diet, but I did find the people and their dress rather strange!*

Anyway, the next year I started going to the Boulder ashram (I had moved to Boulder right before solstice) several times a week for yoga class. I felt like I began finding answers to questions I didn't even know

I had. I felt like I had finally arrived and I hadn't even known I was on a journey. I felt like I could stop now because I had found what I was looking for, and I hadn't even known I was looking for anything. I attended tantric when the Siri Singh Sahib [Yogi Bhajan] *came, and I got to know the people at the ashram. The following summer I again attended solstice and this time stayed for ladies camp* ["Ladies Camp" is the familiar term for Khalsa Women's Training Camp, a women's Kundalini Yoga camp held in New Mexico each summer]. *In those days ladies camp lasted for 8 weeks. There were 2 one-month sessions. I went for the first session and ended up staying for the 2nd session as well. By the end of the summer I had changed so much that I knew I wanted and needed to continue to grow and change in this direction, and the only way I could do that was to move into an ashram. I had met several of the women who lived in Eugene, and I decided to move there. It was really a fluke. I wrote the Siri Singh Sahib and asked him where I should go, and he said to let him know what I decided. I went back to Boulder, packed up my stuff and drove out to Eugene with the little dog I had somehow acquired at ladies camp that summer.*

Five weeks later the Siri Singh Sahib came for a tantric course. He engaged me to marry Viriam Singh, and we were married the next week. I was at that time basically a yoga student, and it was actually quite some time before I felt like I was a Sikh. I actually had a gigantic block against becoming a Sikh. I felt after my experience with Judaism that I couldn't trust a religion. I did believe in God again but could not trust organized religion, felt I had no relation with the Guru [Siri Guru Granth Sahib] *for many years. I talked with the Siri Singh Sahib about this many times, and he would always tell me "You are a Sikh. You are a very spiritual woman." But it took me a long time to "get over" the pain that the letdown of the Jewish religion had caused me. For me, it was Sadhana. I never missed Sadhana, and I still never miss Sadhana. The only time I miss is when I'm sick, and even then I put on the CD.* [She is referring to music for the Aquarian Sadhana chants.] *I am forever grateful to the Siri Singh Sahib for telling me to* get up in the morning and chant God's name. I know that I literally could not be alive without doing Sadhana; I can't imagine living without it. I honestly don't think I could get through my day. It's always been yoga and meditation for me, and my connection to the Guru has grown slowly over the years.

I want to add one thing. I was deeply wounded from my disillusionment with the Jewish religion, and as a result I was very resistant to accepting and giving myself to another religion. This problem didn't really resolve itself until my kids starting pre-school. They went to the pre-school at Temple Beth Israel here in Eugene. A friend's girls were going there, and I visited many schools and found that I liked that one best. I found that my association with the temple and the people I met there helped to heal me from my deep wounds, and I began to appreciate those things from the Jewish religion which were meaningful and beautiful to me and release myself from the hurt, which really didn't come from the religion at all but rather from my parents. I just lumped it all together at that age. Today many of my closest friends, and those of my kids, are from those pre-school days. Some of the kids have gone through school together and remain close friends. I have a warm and open relationship to the temple and my own Jewish history. I've gone to several Bar and Bat Mitzvahs and actually enjoy reading the Hebrew prayers and singing the songs I used to love so much.

There are many parallels between the 2 religions [belief in one God, no proselytizing, morning and evening prayers, covering the head at least during worship, etc.], but many differences as well and I am truly a Sikh, just as the Siri Singh Sahib said. To me the Jewish faith worships history, and in many ways hasn't brought that history into the daily life we live today. The Guru's words, however, remain as true today as when they were written. The depth of fulfillment I receive from yoga and meditation and the Siri Singh Sahib's teachings could not have ever been matched by the Jewish faith, for me.

Part III

Headless Saints

The Khalsa

If you desire to play at love with Me,
Place your head in the palm of your hand and come onto My Path.
On this road, place your feet,
Offer your head, and pay no attention to public opinion.
Guru Nanak [1]

Chapter 10

The Amrit Ceremony

Angelic beings and silent sages search for Amrit, the Undying Nectar;
This Amrit is obtained through the Guru.
Guru Amar Das [1]

That beautiful spring morning in 1699, the plain of *Anandpur* (literally "Town of Bliss") was carpeted with festive, excited people. For weeks, messengers on horseback had brought the word: *Guru Gobind Rai*, the Tenth Sikh Guru, was inviting all his Sikhs to come to Anandpur to celebrate *Baisakhi* (an Indian spring festival) with him on April 13. He requested particularly that they neither cut their hair nor shave beforehand. Many thousands— perhaps as many as 80,000—came.

In front of the assembled crowd was a mound of earth covered with a fine rug. Adjacent to this was a good-size tent. The assembled Sikhs sang *Japji Sahib* and other morning *Shabads* (Sikh hymns) with good cheer and delighted anticipation. They were going to see the Guru!

And then Guru Gobind Rai appeared. He was a short, sturdily built man, then 33 years old. That Baisakhi day his eyes were flaming and his face was fierce. He stood before the assembled throng with an upraised naked sword. And he asked for a head.

Silence. Disturbed, puzzled, whispering silence.

Guru Gobind Rai asked again if any of his Sikhs would give him a head.

A few people toward the back of the crowd began to slip away.

"Are none of you willing to offer your head to me?"

Thirty-year-old *Daya Ram* from Lahore stood up and said, "My head is yours." The Guru seized him and took him into the tent. People near the tent heard a thud. When the Guru emerged from the tent, there was blood on his sword.

"I need another head."

The consternation and whispering increased.

Guru Gobind Rai asked again.

More people in audience slipped away.

When the Guru asked a third time, *Dharam Das* of Delhi came up and offered his head. Again Guru Gobind Rai took the man into the tent, then emerged with blood dripping from his sword.

"My sword is thirsty. I need another head."

Despite the panic all around him, *Mohkam Chand* from the far off town of *Dwarka* immediately stood up and offered his head. Mokham Chand also entered the tent with Guru Gobind Rai, and the Guru emerged from the tent alone with yet more blood on his sword.

"I need another head."

The throng of Sikhs was rapidly disappearing, but *Sahib Chand* of *Bidar* stood up, placed his hands together, bowed his head, and said, "My head is at your disposal." He too entered the tent with Guru Gobind Rai. And again the Guru emerged from the tent solo with blood on his sword.

Before Guru Gobind Rai could even say the words to ask for another head, *Himmat Rai*, a lowly water carrier who had been sitting near the back of the crowd, flung himself at the Guru's feet and apologized for not responding sooner. He also entered the tent with the Guru, but this time, there was a lengthy wait before Guru Gobind Rai reappeared.

And this time, the five men emerged with the Guru. They were shining, smiling and radiant, beautifully dressed in fine new clothes and turbans. What was left of the crowd erupted with joy and relief, cheering the Guru's praises like fans of the winning team at a ballgame.

Guru Gobind Rai raised his hand, and the crowd fell silent. "In the time of *Guru Nanak*, only *Guru Angad* passed every test.

In my time, these five Sikhs have passed the test. There is no difference between them and me." He called these five, "the *Panj Pi-aaray*," the Five Beloveds. And the assembled again cheered like fans at a ballgame. Many wished they had given their heads to the Guru too! They were about to get their wish.

Since the time of Guru Nanak, when the Guru wished to initiate a disciple, he would put water in a vessel, stir it with his big toe, then have the disciple drink the water. (Feet represent our under-standing.) Guru Gobind Rai proposed to do something different.

First, he gave a stirring talk about the need to end all distinctions of caste and creed, to drink the same water and eat from the same pot, to treat each other with respect and reverence. Then he asked the five men to stand. Guru Gobind Rai filled a small iron cauldron or bowl (called a *bata*) with water and began reciting certain *Banis*—*Japji Sahib, Jaap Sahib, Tav Prasaad Swaiyay, Bayntee Chaupa-ee* and *Anand Sahib*—as he stirred the water with a double-edged steel sword.

As Guru Gobind Rai was stirring the *Shabad Guru's* vibration of courage and wisdom into the water, his third wife *Mata Sahib Devan* (also known as *Mata Sahib Kaur*) appeared at his side and placed *patashas* (sugar candy) in the water. Those who were to drink this water would become sweet and kind, as well as courageous and wise. Guru Gobind Rai commented that only women give birth, and today would be the birthday of the *Khalsa*—the Pure Ones who give their heads to God. Accordingly, *Mata Sahib Kaur* (who had no biological children of her own) is now known as the "Mother of the Khalsa."

When he had finished stirring this batch of sweetened Bani-drenched water, Guru Gobind Rai had each of the Panj Pi-aaray sit one by one in *Vir Asana* while the other four stood and chanted *Waheguru* continually. He poured water five times into the cupped hands of each man. Each time Guru Gobind Rai called out, *Waheguru ji ka Khalsa! Waheguru ji ki Fateh!* (The Khalsa belong to God! Victory belongs to God!) Each man responded with the same words. Guru Gobind Rai threw a small amount of water five times in each man's eyes, calling out the same words each time. And each time, each man responded, *Waheguru ji ka Khalsa! Waheguru ji ki Fateh!* Guru Gobind Rai sprinkled water five times on each man's head, again calling out *Waheguru ji ka Khalsa! Waheguru ji ki Fateh!* And each time, each man responded, *Waheguru ji ka Khalsa! Waheguru ji ki Fateh!* Guru Gobind Rai then placed his right hand on the head of each of man and chanted *Waheguru* five times, and each man chanted *Waheguru* after him.

When Guru Gobind Rai had completed this procedure with all five men, he had them all stand and drink the remaining water one by one from the same vessel. When the water was gone, he gave them each the surname of *Singh*, which means "Lion," an appellation given at that time only to princes. (The surname for women became *Kaur*, which means "Princess.") This was a radical departure for the times, as four of the Panj Pi-aaray came from low castes.

Guru Gobind Rai then gave them instruction. They were to love the One God, avoid all idolatrous actions, sing God's Praises, and read their Banis daily. They were to erase from their minds and actions all distinctions of caste. They were to feed and assist the poor, and come to the aid of anyone in need of protection. They were to make no alliances with practitioners of female infanticide. They were to wear turbans and maintain the five "k"s: wearing a steel bangle (*kara*) for identification, wearing *kacheras* (special underwear) as a reminder of chastity, never cutting their hair (*kesh*) out of respect for their Creator, using a wooden comb (*kangha*) to keep their kesh tidy, and carrying a *kirpan* (short steel sword or knife) to protect the weak. They were to be courageous and never to run from the field of battle. They were to greet each other by saying, *Waheguru ji ka Khalsa! Waheguru ji ki Fateh!*

Four things were forbidden. (These are called *kurehits*.) They were not to cut their hair. They were not to commit adultery or engage in sex outside a lawful marriage. They were not use tobacco. They were not to eat kosher meat (i.e. animals that had been bled to death). If they committed any of these actions, they would lose all benefits received from this initiation or baptism.

After these instructions, in the most unprecedented act on that day of unprecedented acts, Guru Gobind Rai placed his palms together in front of his chest, humbly bowed to the Panj Pi-aaray, and asked them to baptize him in the exact way he had baptized them. Never before had a Guru bowed to his own disciples and asked them to initiate him. What a great Teacher he was! What a profound way to inculcate humility and etch the Amrit procedure forever in their minds! So the Panj Pi-aaray repeated the entire process, including the instructions, and Guru Gobind Rai became *Guru Gobind Singh*.

Then Guru Gobind Singh invited everyone to give up their heads and their egos and partake of this *Amrit*—which literally means "Undying Nectar." In the days that immediately followed that first Amrit Ceremony, some 20,000 people were baptized as Khalsa Sikhs.

Countless people have taken Amrit since. One of them was me.

When I went to Los Angeles in April of 1988, I wasn't planning on taking Amrit. Oh, I had planned on taking Amrit someday—once I could recite all the Banis comfortably. But at the time, the only Banis I recited regularly were *Japji Sahib* in the morning and *Kirtan Sohila* at bedtime. Some Banis—Guru Gobind Singh's *Jaap Sahib*, for instance—I had never even attempted. Better to wait, I thought.

I actually went to Los Angles that year because I was pregnant and going through an emotional hurricane as a result of that pregnancy. Getting myself in top emotional shape to become a good mother was my priority. The best mental/emotional cleansing process I knew of was *White Tantric Yoga*, which I explained in How I Became a Sikh. But at the time, it looked as if the maze of my circumstances would block my attending White Tantric Yoga that whole year...unless I went to LA for Baisakhi.

I arrived in Los Angeles on Wednesday, April 6, in time to attend a special Gurdwara service at Guru Ram Das Ashram that evening. In the course of that Gurdwara, the *Siri Singh Sahib* gave a talk, which he concluded with details of upcoming Baisakhi events. He mentioned the Amrit Ceremony to take place on Sunday morning. Then he said, "Some few of us," and he turned and looked directly at me, "will march from the Amrit Ceremony to the Gurdwara." (The main Gurdwara on Sunday would be taking place at a much larger location than Guru Ram Das Ashram.) My decision to wait evaporated. I knew I would take Amrit that Sunday.

By Friday, I began bleeding. Nonetheless, I attended a meeting that evening for Amrit candidates. And when Sunday arrived, I did take Amrit even though I was pregnant and bleeding at the time.

I'm not sure I slept at all the night before the ceremony. Too excited! Too much to do! Around one in the morning, I got up, showered and washed my uncut hair (*kesh*). When I dressed, I put on *kacheras* (thigh-length underpants). I didn't own a *kurta* (tunic), but the people at a meeting I had attended for Amrit candidates said I could just wear a blouse belted with a cummerbund, tunic-style over pants, which is what I did. After my hair had dried a bit, I wrapped my turban as I had been instructed — leaving the top uncovered except for a *chuni* (a long, veil-like scarf). I put my *kangha* (wooden comb) in my hair and put my *kara* (steel bangle) on my left wrist. I had left my own *kirpan* (short sword) at home, so the people I was staying with very kindly loaned me one of theirs.

Around 2:45 am, I walked in the exhilarating night a few blocks to Guru Ram Das Ashram. A few people were already there. I was surprised to see a table outside the building laden with everything necessary for an Amrit candidate: karas, kanghas, kacheras, kirpans in abundance, plus some accessories. As I had no strap to hold my kirpan, I had tucked it into my cummerbund. So, after learning that I could take whatever I needed from this table, I selected a kirpan strap from the table, and transferred the kirpan to it.

More people arrived. We had quite a crowd on the sidewalk by 3:15 am when the van arrived with the Panj—as the Panj Pi-aaray is familiarly known. Actually, eight or nine men disembarked from that van—seven or eight sturdy-looking men who were wearing identical blue kurtas, and one tiny, elfin-faced, elderly man dressed in black. A couple of the men in blue toted suitcases. They all disappeared into the building.

Those of us outside the building had a long wait. Occasionally, we heard cries of *Waheguru ji ka Khalsa! Waheguru ji ki Fateh!* from within the building. I had figured that the suitcases contained all the paraphernalia necessary for the ceremony. But when one of the formerly blue-clad men emerged wearing a saffron-orange kurta, I realized that the suitcases contained more than just paraphernalia, and understood why the wait was so long.

But now I know that that the men had done much more than set up equipment and change clothes. Before the Panj Pi-aaray can examine the Amrit Ceremony candidates, they must first examine each other. Here's what happened behind those closed doors.

As part of set up for the ceremony, each of the Panj Pi-aaray washed a *Siri Sahib* (a four-foot long sword) and laid it in front of the Guru. After everything was ready and everyone had changed clothes, the *Granthi* (the person who would sit behind the *Siri Guru Granth Sahib* during the ceremony) stood with palms together before the Panj Pi-aaray, each of whom held a drawn Siri Sahib. During this time, someone else—perhaps it was the doorkeeper or the elderly man—took the Granthi's place behind the *Siri Guru Granth Sahib*. One of the Panj Pi-aaray (probably the

Head *Pi-aara*) asked the Granthi these questions:

"Do you keep your five *'k's*?"

"Do you read your Banis daily?"

"Have you ever committed any of the *kurehits*?"

"Have you ever betrayed the Khalsa, in thought, word or deed?"

After the Granthi said "Yes" to the first two questions, and "No" to the second two questions, the Head Pi-aara greeted the Granthi by exclaiming, *Waheguru ji ka Khalsa! Waheguru ji ki Fateh!* Then the Granthi bowed before the *Siri Guru Granth Sahib*, prayed to live to the purity of the Khalsa, and took his seat behind the Guru.

Then the Granthi called up each of the Panj Pi-aaray one by one and asked each of them the same questions. As each Pi-aara was found worthy to serve in the Amrit Ceremony, he bowed to the Guru and proclaimed, *Waheguru ji ka Khalsa! Waheguru ji ki Fateh!*

One of the Panj Pi-aaray — or perhaps it was the elderly man — then stood and offered an *Ardas* (standing prayer), requesting all blessings upon the ceremony about to begin. The Granthi then read a *Hukam* (literally "Command" — the random reading from the *Siri Guru Granth Sahib*).

After this Hukam, the doorkeeper appeared to those of us waiting outside. He stood in front of the closed door with a sword, which he wasn't holding it in a particularly menacing way. He invited those who were taking Amrit for a second time to present themselves, one by one, in front of the Guru.

Most of those who took Amrit when I did were taking it for the second time. (I've never heard of anyone taking Amrit for the *third* time, by the way, although I assume it would be possible.) There are only two reasons for taking Amrit a second time. Committing a kurehit intentionally (cutting one's hair or having a sexual fling outside a lawful marriage, for instance) breaks Amrit and flings its blessings out the door. To restore the blessings of Amrit after such an action, the person must undergo the Amrit Ceremony a second time. That's the first reason. The other reason to retake Amrit is to boost the blessings, to take the elevator up to the next level. That's what most of the people standing on the sidewalk were waiting to do: to take Amrit a second time to go to the next level up.

Once all of the people who were taking Amrit for the second time had been asked by the Panj Pi-aaray privately—but in front of the Guru—why they wished to retake Amrit, those of us who were taking it for the first time had our exam time. I was one of the first of these to go in.

The doorkeeper stopped me before I entered, asked if I was wearing all five "k"s, and asked me to remove my wedding ring. No one taking Amrit is allowed to wear any jewelry of any sort during the ceremony...other than their *kara* (steel bangle), of course. I divested my hand of the ring and put it in the pocket of my jacket, which I left outside the building near the doorkeeper.

I entered the building and bowed at the Guru's Feet, where I reverently laid an offering of $1.01. (The extra cent was to indicate my willingness to give myself 101% to the Guru.) Then I rose to face the identically saffron-clad Panj Pi-aaray who were standing so that I did not have to turn my back on the Guru to face them. They were probably holding drawn Siri Sahibs, but what I remember is five faces projecting great kindness and reverence...while doing their best to look stern. The Head Pi-aara, who stood in the center, asked me, "Why do you want to take Amrit?"

"Because my soul wants me to!" (That was the truest Truth. The way my spirit had been dancing since the decision to take Amrit told me clearly that this was indeed my soul's choice.)

The Head Pi-aara smiled in a cute, "Oh, that's nice!" kind of way. Then he asked if I was willing to read all the Banis. I smiled happily and nodded. After another question or two, he told me to return when everyone was invited back in.

The sidewalk wait was much shorter this time. After the Amrit candidates were all invited back in, we stood together on one side of the Gurdwara while the Head Pi-aara explained, among other things, that if any of us had second thoughts we could leave now, but once the ceremony started none of us could leave for any reason. He also humbly told us that he hoped we could understand his English. Then the Head Pi-aara (or it might have been the elderly man, who was still dressed in black) stood before the *Siri Guru Granth Sahib*, and gave an Ardas, asking blessings on the ceremony. After this, we all sat down. Then the Granthi read a Hukam in Gurmukhi, and the lady who had given instructions at the meeting for Amrit Ceremony candidates read the translation.

Those of us who were about to take Amrit then stood up to watch the preparation of the Amrit water. After one of the Panj Pi-aaray poured water into the *bata* (the iron cauldron), which was probably steadied with a rolled up towel or some other cloth, the lady who had given us instructions at the meeting for Amrit Ceremony candidates placed *patashas* (sugar candy) in the water. As it happened, the Panj, the Granthi and the doorkeeper for this Amrit Ceremony were all men, but they could just as well have been women or a mix of men and women. Any *Amritdari Sikh* (Sikh who has taken Amrit) in good standing and in good health may administer Amrit and assist in the Ceremony. But the person who places the sugar in the water for the Amrit Ceremony is representing Mata Sahib Kaur (the Mother of the *Khalsa*) and is therefore always a Khalsa woman in good standing. This is the only gender-specific duty anywhere in Sikhism. It is always a woman who insures that the new Khalsa will be sweet as well as spiritually strong.

While we stood and focused on the preparation of the Amrit water, the Panj Pi-aaray moved into position around the bata. Each man sat on the his left heel with his right knee up near his heart. (This is *Vir Asana*; for a photo of this pose, see the Sadhana chapter.) Holding this position, they placed their fingertips on the edge of the bata and focused like intense, kindly tigers on the sugar water. There was probably another man—perhaps the elderly man, perhaps someone else—standing guard with a Siri Sahib (four-foot long sword) over the proceedings. However, my eyes were on the Amrit-water-to-be most of the time so I have no clear recollection of this detail.

Truthfully, except for Japji Sahib, my knowledge of the *Banis* was little bigger than a tablespoon in those days, so my comprehension of the Banis being read was minimal at the time. I did notice as each Pi-aara recited a Bani that the Granthi followed along by reading silently in a *Nit Nem* (prayer book).

But now I understand that what happened went like this. The Head Pi-aara grasped the *Khanda*—a double-edged sword that's about a foot long—with his right hand, placing his right thumb on top. He moved the Khanda back and forth in the sugar water while reciting *Japji Sahib*, the Sikh morning Bani. When he completed it, he proclaimed *Waheguru ji ka Khalsa! Waheguru ji ki Fateh!* Then he passed the Khanda—without removing it from the sugar water—to the Pi-aara on his right, who did the same thing while reciting *Jaap Sahib* by Guru Gobind Singh. This same full procedure was followed by the remaining Pi-aaray, who recited *Tav Prasaad Swaiyay*, the complete *Bayntee Chaupee* with *Arill*, and all forty *pauris* (stanzas) of *Anand Sahib*. After reciting Anand Sahib and proclaiming *Waheguru ji ka Khalsa! Waheguru ji ki Fateh!*, the final Pi-aara passed the Khanda to the Head Pi-aara who continued stirring the Amrit water as all five men slowly rose, lifting the bata with the completed Amrit water—with the Khanda still in it—triumphantly into the air. I do remember the stretch in their arms and the boyish glee in their faces as they did this. Someone—maybe the lady who represented Mata Sahib Kaur—moved a small stool under the bata. The bata containing the Amrit water and Khanda was then reverently placed on the stool.

Sometimes the men and women about to partake of Amrit stand on opposite sides of the Gurdwara, and a candidate's name is called when it's that person's turn to come up, with men and women alternating as much as possible. But the way we did it was quite different. The Gurdwara we were in is L-shaped, with the Guru in the outside elbow of the L. All those who were waiting to be baptized—both men and women—stood together in the short arm of the L, and those who had just been baptized stood or sat in the long arm of the L. No one called our names. Instead, the Panj Pi-aaray requested that we come up to be baptized as the spirit moved us to do so. This allowed anyone with second thoughts to forgo the experience.

Of the thirty or so candidates present, I was about the fifth to go up to be initiated. Following the lead of those who preceded me, and with the help of one of the Pi-aaray, I sat in Vir Asana on my left heel with my right knee near my heart, and cupped my hands palms up with the right hand tightly over the left. I was facing the Guru. Starting with the Head Pi-aara, each member of the Panj scooped up a handful of Amrit water, proclaimed *Waheguru ji ka Khalsa! Waheguru ji ki Fateh!* and poured the Amrit into my hands. I drank each handful of Amrit quickly and responded *Waheguru ji ka Khalsa! Waheguru ji ki Fateh!* after each drink. There was a bowl resting on the floor beneath my hands to catch the inevitable drips.

After five handfuls of Amrit water, each member of the Panj Pi-aaray threw a small handful of Amrit in my eyes—each time calling out *Waheguru ji ka Khalsa! Waheguru ji ki Fateh!* and receiving my reply, *Waheguru ji ka Khalsa! Waheguru ji ki Fateh!* One Pi-aara was particularly fierce as he threw the Amrit. I thought it was funny. We're supposed to keep our eyes locked on the *Siri Guru Granth Sahib* without blinking or flinching during this. I didn't manage that perfection. I'm sure I blinked all five times. But I was also tickled by this part of the initiation and found myself grinning hugely during the process.

The Panj Pi-aaray next removed the chuni from the top of my head. I could feel them checking for the *kangha* (wooden comb) in my hair. Each member of the Panj Pi-aaray then scooped up a handful of Amrit water and proclaimed *Waheguru ji ka Khalsa! Waheguru ji ki Fateh!* as he poured the Amrit on my head. I responded in kind.

Then all five men laid their right hands on the top of my head. The standard protocol states that the Panj Pi-aaray recites *Waa Hay Guroo* five times with the candidate being initiated reciting *Waa Hay Guroo* after each repetition. But the way we were initiated was a little different. First, one member of the Panj Pi-aaray told me to chant *Waa Hay Guroo* by inhaling on *Waa Hay* and exhaling on *Guroo*. Then they chanted *Waa Hay Guroo* seventeen times (yes, I counted) while I chanted after them. One of them then placed the chuni back over my head.

I then bowed to the Guru, turned and faced the sangat with my hands together at my heart, and proclaimed *Waheguru ji ka Khalsa! Waheguru ji ki Fateh!* The sangat greeted me in the same way. As the next candidate came up to be initiated, I moved to the other arm of the Gurdwara—where I sat down cross-legged and began chanting *Waa Hay Guroo* as I had just been taught.

After chanting *Waa Hay Guroo* for what seemed like all eternity (and it probably *was* several hours), the Panj Pi-aaray looked around, and one of them asked if anyone else wished to be baptized. No response.

So they lined us all up standing in a semi-circle in the larger arm of the L facing the *Siri Guru Granth Sahib*. After removing the Khanda from the bata, one Pi-aara took the bata around this semi-circle and gave each of us a drink of the remaining Amrit water. We each drank directly from the bata. As I recall, there was still a bit of Amrit water left after all of us had had a good drink. So the Pi-aara took the bata to the elderly man and cheerfully tipped the rest of the Amrit water into the elderly man's mouth.

Instruction time! The Panj Pi-aaray may have been holding

Siri Sahibs during the instructions, but I remember the words better than I remember this detail. I do remember that the Head Pi-aara gave all the instructions, except for chanting *Mool Mantra*. This was the first thing we learned to do. Although most people who take Amrit can recite Mool Mantra in their sleep (and sometimes do!), the Panj Pi-aaray always carefully recite it line by line to the brand new Amritdari Sikhs, who repeat it back line by line.

We learned that we had gained new parents: Guru Gobind Singh became our spiritual father and Mata Sahib Kaur our spiritual mother. Our spiritual birthplace became *Anandpur Sahib*. We gained new names: *Singh* as the surname for men and *Kaur* as the surname for women. We learned that we had all gained the last name *Khalsa*, that we had joined the family of "Pure Ones." (See sidebar on Sikh Names.)

Sikh Names

Traditionally, Sikhs derive their names from the *Siri Guru Granth Sahib*, the Sikh Guru. When a child is born, the parents take a *Hukam* (the random reading from the Guru) and base the child's name on that Hukam's first letter. For instance, if the Hukam begins with the letter *a*, the parents might pick the name *Anand* (bliss) or *Amrit* (nectar) or *Ajeet* (victor). Often enough, the first name will have two, or sometimes even three, parts. My spiritual name *Siri Kirpal* is such a two-part first name.

With rare exceptions, Sikh first names are gender neutral. You really can't determine a person's gender by the first name alone. For instance, someone with the first name *Ajeet* might be either a man or a woman. *Singh*, which means "lion," is the gender designator for men.

Kaur, which means "princess," is the gender designator for women. So, *Ajeet Singh* would be a man, and *Ajeet Kaur* would be a woman.

The gender designator is often used as a last name, but not always. Western Sikhs as a rule take *Khalsa* (Pure One) as a last name. Complications arise in the USA due to the legal custom of children taking the father's last name. So you can easily find girls bearing the last name *Singh.* Some Indian Sikhs use family last names other than *Singh, Kaur* or *Khalsa,* and some Hindus also bear the last name *Singh.* In general, however, if any of these three words appear anywhere in a person's name, the person is a Sikh.

Receiving a Sikh name is not a requirement for becoming a Sikh. I know one lady who did not take a Sikh name when she stepped onto the Sikh path. But having one is helpful. Since Sikh names are taken from the *Shabad Guru,* the vibration of the name lifts the spirit and helps the individual become an embodiment of that Name. Also, a Sikh name points to the individual's farthest star, indicating the most difficult and most important thing a person must do to fulfill his or her destiny.

Originally, most Western Sikhs received their spiritual names by asking Yogi Bhajan for one. When he passed on, he bequeathed the job of naming people to one of his students. (See Resources for contact information.)

Then the Head Pi-aara told us what not to do—these are the *kurehits,* the actions that erase the blessings of Amrit. He told us never to cut our hair. He told us never to eat meat—and he made no distinction between kosher meat and any other sort of meat when he said this. He told us never to use tobacco, alcohol or recreational drugs—and there was no limiting this proscription just to tobacco. And then in his thick Punjabi accent, he said, "A Sikh, he must not commit adultery, except with his wife." No one laughed. Not even me. Okay, so I'll never have a *wife*, but I get the idea!

There were further instructions. We were enjoined to wear our turbans and five "k"s daily, to revere the *Siri Guru Granth Sahib* as our one and only Guru, to earn our livings righteously and share with those in need. The Head Pi-aara told us to recite *Waa Hay Guroo* with each breath and to chant it in the *Amrit Vela* (the hours before dawn). We were told to recite the following Banis daily: *Japji Sahib, Jaap Sahib, Tav Prasaad Swaiyay, Bayntee Chaupa-ee, Anand Sahib, Rehiras Sahib,* and *Kirtan Sohila.* If we had to miss a Bani, we could substitute Mool Mantra. I had thought that *Shabad Hazaaray* was a required Bani. I wasn't the only one. One lady piped up, "What about Shabad Hazaaray?" The Head Pi-aara responded that Shabad Hazaaray was fine to do, but strictly optional. Not everyone who administers Amrit agrees with that statement.

And finally we were told to always greet each other by proclaiming *Waheguru ji ka Khalsa! Waheguru ji ki Fateh!* This last point got reinforced throughout the day. Every time I turned to speak to anyone who had been part of the team that adminis-tered Amrit, he would instantly grin and say *Waheguru ji ka Khalsa! Waheguru ji ki Fateh!*

Each Pi-aara then one by one raised the Siri Sahib in his hand and called out *Bolay so nihaal!* (Speak and be joyful!) And we all sang out *Sat Siri Akaal!* (Truth is Great and Undying!)

Then we all sat down for a short Gurdwara service, the process of which is explained in detail in Chapter 6. We sang a Shabad, *Song of the Khalsa, Anand Sahib* plus the *Slok* of *Japji Sahib.* We stood for a brief Ardas, then sat for the Gurmukhi and English Hukam, which I believe was the following section from a *Vaar* (heroic poem in praise of God).

Slok Third Guru

One who knows Brahma is attuned to the Word; this is true Brahmin-hood.

They who enshrine God in heart and mind attract all psychic powers and all treasures of the earth.

Without the Guru, one receives not the Name: reflect and see.

Nanak, through perfect destiny, one attains the Guru and gathers peace through the four ages.

Third Guru

Whether old or young, the craving of egocentrics is not stilled.

But those who turn towards God are imbued with the word;

Losing ego, they are calm and cool.

They are inwardly content and hunger no more.

Whatever is done by those who are attuned to God's Name is approved by God.

Pauri

I am a sacrifice to the God-conscious devotees of God.

I seek the sight of those who contemplate God's Name.

Hearing God's Praise, I seek to recite it and inscribe it in my heart and mind.

I seek to praise God's Name with devotion and uproot all my sins.

Blessed, blessed and beauteous are all places and beings where my Guru plants his foot.[2]

Following this Hukam (or one remarkably like it), the Ceremony ended with *Gurprasaad*.

It was past 10 am when we finally left the Gurdwara. I was on high and not tired in the least, but I was also monumentally hungry and in dire need of a restroom as we had had no breaks whatsoever during the Ceremony. I was also in a quandary. There was no place I could go because the people I was staying with had already left for the main Gurdwara, which they had helped set up. The Siri Singh Sahib had said that some of us would march from the Amrit Ceremony to the big Gurdwara. But everyone was dispersing. And when the Siri Singh Sahib showed up, he simply disembarked from the chauffeured car, looked us over, then reentered the car and was whisked away. What was I to do?

As I was wondering how God was going to provide, a van drove up and a man on the sidewalk suggested with a gesture that I enter. I climbed into the van and was joined minutes later by the Panj Pi-aaray and the entire team of men who had administered Amrit, as well as a few other people. Instead of heading downtown for the Gurdwara, we headed into Beverly Hills where the van stopped in front of a (comparatively) modest house.

Standing on the entrance terrace that overlooked immaculately green grounds was Bibiji, the Siri Singh Sahib's wife, with her palms joined in a gesture of reverent greeting. She was clearly amused at my astonishment. At the time I thought I had arrived at the Siri Singh Sahib's own home, but was later to learn that that was not strictly true.

Once inside, we crossed a living room furnished only with sunlight and a cache of musical instruments in one corner. To the right was the dining room where we all selected a patch of carpeted floor to sit on. The Panj sat together across one wall, and I sat down in the farthest opposite corner. The Siri Singh Sahib came in and sat down on my immediate left, so that I was sitting at his right hand. It was a perfectly calculated social distance — just far enough, but too close for anyone other than a newborn babe to sit between us.

Langar (the communal meal) arrived quickly. As we ate, the Siri Singh Sahib discoursed at length in Punjabi with the Panj Pi-aaray. I noticed the Siri Singh Sahib fingering his *mala* (the Sikh version of a rosary) between bites of food and bytes of speech. Knowing that he was inwardly chanting *Waa Hay Guroo* each time he fingered a bead, I decided to chant *Waa Hay Guroo* with him.

Waa Hay Guroo! My mind filled with bliss. I saw the sound of that inward chanting reveal great Light, and heard Light-brilliant sound. *Waa Hay Guroo!* I gave my head and received Nectar in return. Not a bad deal! *Waa Hay Guroo!*

Some of you may be wondering what happened to the pregnancy. After I endured a couple of months of bleeding and inconclusive medical tests (and nearly daily frantic phone calls from my parents), the very dead fetal remnants were removed by D & C. During those months, I had to forgo all the vigorous Kundalini Yoga and strenuous meditations that had carried my spirit to this point. I was hit by the postpartum depression that attends the end of most pregnancies. But there was no baby, no apparent blessing, to heal that depression.

If I had had no other spiritual discipline to sustain me, I could have been like an orphaned bird that hasn't yet learned to fly. Had I not taken Amrit, the nagging sensation that I wasn't good enough to become a mother might have overcome me. But thanks to taking Amrit, thanks to reading Banis daily, my sorely-tested spirits did not plummet beyond recovery. Although I did indeed experience sorrow, my spirits soon began to rise. I have never been the same. It wasn't a child who was born. It was me.

Chapter 11

To Protect the Weak

Guru Gobind Singh gave us the sword,
To protect the weak from the merciless foe.
Gurudass Singh Khalsa [1]

One cold winter morning, Satya Kaur Khalsa drove to work over roads slick with ice. Understandably, she had no inclination to go anywhere else once she got to work. But after arriving on the job, she began receiving the inner message to drive to a certain store, using a particular back road shortcut. It was still early — too early for a break really, so she made a valiant attempt to ignore this message.

But the message kept broadcasting. So she obediently got in her car and drove off as the inner message directed her. As she came around the corner of a small country lane, she spied an elderly truck lying on its side, spinning its wheels. Satya had arrived just after the truck had hit a patch of black ice and overturned after skidding some 30 feet. A mother and her two children were trapped inside.

The truck had no regular window, but it did have a small plastic section that opened. Satya proceeded to pull the two children out through this small space. Then it was the mother's turn. Satya looked at the mother, and they both looked at the small opening. Satya is a small lady, and was recovering from severe spinal damage that had left her unable to lift anything heavier than 20 pounds for more than a year. The mother was substantially larger than Satya and substantially larger than the opening through which the children had been evacuated. As the mother looked at the space, she said, "I won't fit through that."

Satya mentally thought so too, but said out loud, "Yes, you will!" Then she reached down and began lifting the mother up and out. Another driver appeared and helped with the final lifting. Miraculously, the mother emerged through that small hole.

Also miraculously, neither the children nor their mother were injured by this misadventure. Shaken up, yes. Hurt, no. Someone came to transport the children to school. Satya stayed on the scene until the woman's fiancé arrived.

Afterwards, Satya expressed the deep satisfaction of following her intuition and serving in this tangible way. She recalled, "I did indeed feel the bliss of living as a Warrior-Saint at that moment."

Warrior-Saint? Yep. Sikhs are Warrior-Saints sworn to protect and champion the weak. Sometimes that means heavy lifting. And sometimes it means the Sword.

Just as you might get martial arts training for your child who was suffering from bullies at school, so too the Sikh Warrior-Saint stance began as a way of standing up to oppression. In 1606, *Guru Arjan Dev*, the Fifth Guru, was tortured and martyred on a trumped up charge. Before dying, Guru Arjan Dev commanded his son *Guru Hargobind* to sit fully armed on the throne of the Guruship and to maintain an army. So Guru Hargobind, the Sixth Guru, transformed his Sikhs—who had been a quiet, unassuming bunch of devotees—into a corps of Warrior-Saints, unbendable to the will of tyranny.

Some of those early Sikhs were confused. *Baba Buddha*, a now-elderly devotee of Guru Nanak, had invested *Guru Angad, Guru Amar Das, Guru Ram Das* and *Guru Arjan Dev* (the Second, Third, Fourth and Fifth Gurus respectively) with the symbols of their spiritual office. When Baba Buddha attempted to invest Guru Hargobind with the symbols of the Guruship, Guru Hargobind gently set aside the symbols worn by the first five Gurus and asked for a sword instead. So, Baba Buddha, who had no experience with swords whatsoever, brought a sword and placed it on the Guru's right side. (Right-handed people wear swords on their left side.) Then the Guru smiled and proclaimed that he would wear *two* swords—one on the right and one on the left—to indicate both spiritual and temporal power.

Guru Gobind Singh, the Tenth Guru, continued and codified this martial tradition, instilling courage and fearlessness into Sikhs by way of the Amrit Ceremony as we saw in the last chapter. As a result, Sikhs became "Headless Saints"—champions who would fight courageously against injustice and tyranny, and who would refuse to lie down and play dead or be suppressed themselves.

Please note that "courage" literally means "with heart." Violence for the sake of violence is repugnant to all true Sikhs. Equally repugnant is conversion by the sword. We're talking here about Warrior-Saints who have the heart to come through for others, no matter what the cost is to themselves. You've heard people say that they would be willing to "take a bullet" for someone else? Well, Amritdari Sikhs have the courage and the love to be willing to "take a bullet" for *anyone* in God's Creation.

And that explains numerous acts of courage. For instance, one evening in Eugene, Oregon, after the September 11 attacks, heads of news stations met with Sikh and Muslim leaders and the police in an attempt to educate the public and avert violence in the wake of the attacks in New York City and Washington, D.C. You could hear the intact of breath and gasps of surprise throughout the room when Snatam Kaur Khalsa—a tiny, sweet-faced lady—piped up and said, "I would be happy to be mistaken for a Muslim." Generally, although we strive to prevent misunderstandings, Sikhs tend to feel this way.

At an interfaith service I helped organize on September 11, 2004, a Mennonite pastor spoke of a man with pacifist principles who witnessed a half-witted man being beaten by some teenage boys on a train. That man had a moment of struggle with his pacifist principles, then said a prayer, got up and put his arms around the half-wit, greeting him as an old friend. The boys seemed puzzled and exited the train at the first opportunity.

At the time, I thought, "There's no difference between that and what a Sikh would do. The only difference is that a Sikh wouldn't struggle with inner principles before going to help. They'd just do it." My presentation followed the Mennonite pastor's. So I made the point that the interfaith services were the Sword of Truth I was raising to prevent the use of the sword of violence.

That's what a Sikh Warrior-Saint does. We raise the Sword of Truth. We negotiate, we teach, we try all possible means to resolve problems without violence. Many Sikhs, in fact, were (and are) in the Peace Movement. (You'll meet one in the next chapter.) But when the Sword of Truth no longer cuts, when we (or those around us) are facing actual physical attack (not a "maybe someday" attack), then and only then, we have not only the right, but the responsibility, to come to our own defense and the defense of others. No Sikh will knowingly allow tyranny to triumph. No Sikh will submit to bullying or accept the bullying of others.

Chapter 12

A Saint-Soldier in the Peace Movement

Guru Fatha Singh Khalsa's Story

Peace in this world, peace in the next,
Peace through meditation,
Dwell always on the Name of God.
Guru Arjan Dev [1]

Guru Fatha Singh Khalsa volunteers as a chaplain at the University of Toronto where he founded Peace Week in 2002. He teaches Kundalini Yoga and is the author of *Five Paragons of Peace: Magic and Magnificence in the Guru's Way* and other books. He is currently working on a biography of Yogi Bhajan. You can find his website and the Peace Week website in Resources.

He's an advocate of Truth, as you can see from the following very candid story. The words are Guru Fatha Singh's except for the glosses in brackets, which are mine.

I spent the first six years of my life in the northern Ontario city of Thunder Bay, and the next ten in Kingston, between Montréal and Toronto. My parents were wonderful. They did all the things parents ought to do: they paid for everything, they disciplined me, they taught me.

Because of their background, they took a bit of an extreme view of many things, though they tried to be as normal as possible. My father had served the Wehrmacht [German armed forces 1935-45] on the Eastern Front. You couldn't get him to say anything about it, though my mother said he had some medals he never showed and we knew he hated grated coconut because it reminded him of cat's teeth. They must have eaten a lot of cats during the retreat from Moscow.

My mother, for her part, convinced me that war was a bad thing by telling me pretty graphic stories of what it was like being bombed by the Americans and British and Canadians. She also described the food shortages. Most of the other boys in the neighbourhood were allowed bb guns to shoot up frogs and squirrels and groundhogs, as we lived near the country, but I was never allowed. If there was ever a sudden bang of any sort, my mother would jump. The war had shot her nerves pretty good.

So I took a pretty extreme view of things too. Truth and war and peace were for me a daily concern. Early on, I figured that everybody grows old, most of us not very well, and that became a concern. I saw most of these adults, so self-absorbed and serious...but put them in a party and give them some alcohol, and suddenly they are happy and gay! I never wanted to be like that.

I didn't like to be lied to just because of my age, just because the elders thought they had something over on me because of their God-damned age to tell us sweet stories of Santa Claus and the Easter Bunny. Why? I asked, did they go to all that trouble to lie, an entire generation lying to their young and their innocent. Isn't life fun enough, isn't it beautiful enough without lying and creating a phony culture of friendly ghosts?

Early on, I learned to distrust social consensus, the more so when I heard about the Jewish Holocaust and my mother denied it, and later tried to sugar coat it. My parents despised Jews. They said so. It certainly wouldn't have hurt their feelings if a few had been packed up and exterminated. But they knew you couldn't say that in the 1960s. In the 1930s maybe, but not in the 60s.

We went to church every second Sunday, to a beautiful gothic church downtown. The choir was nice, but the Sunday school was boring and I never fit in because I was always missing the previous Sunday's lesson. I preferred the alternate Sundays where I could lounge in my pyjamas. I never liked wearing the stuffy suits I had to wear to Sunday school, and besides, for all his good qualities, Jesus could seem *unreal at times. Maybe he was another Easter Bunny. Why did adults feel they had to keep the truth from children? I couldn't wait to grow up.*

At thirteen, I went to the World's Fair in Montréal. It was stunningly beautiful, and the motto was "To be a man is to feel that through one's life one has made a contribution to the world." I thought: Wow! To be able to do that! That would be wonderful!

Of course, the adults didn't teach us anything like that. Making a contribution to the world didn't even enter into the question. Everything was about making parents happy, getting good grades, staying out of trouble, telling the right lies, being quiet and submissive.

I started to read big books. I neglected my regular studies and read things like Socrates and Plotinus, Schopenhauer and Hegel, Orwell and Huxley, Sartre and Bertrand Russell, Freud and Jung, even Hitler and Marx, the Tibetan Book of the Dead and the Tibetan Book of the Great Liberation.

I really did not appreciate having my hair cut. I wanted to keep it uncut, but oh! the pressure to return and return to the barber. I knowingly ate meat for the last time when I was fourteen. I tried fasting too. I figured a better world was possible, it was just a matter of figuring out how to get there.

Finally, I turned sixteen and I knew that was the age you could legally live outside of your parents' care. [That was in the late 1960s and early 1970s in Canada; the legal age in Canada now, in the USA and at least some other countries is 18.] *I turned sixteen in February, then in May there was news that an anti-war demonstration in Ohio had gone very wrong. Four students had been shot and killed by the "national guard." What were they guarding, anyway? I decided if the peace movement needed volunteers to fill the streets and be shot by this mindless war machine, I would volunteer. That summer, I left home three times. Finally, the third time, I made it and hitchhiked to Vancouver* [in British Columbia]. *In Vancouver, I learned to meditate from a swami. I learned Hatha Yoga too. I had decided I would never submit myself to a short-haired guru, so I was fortunate to find these fine, longhaired teachers.*

A year and a half later, I hitchhiked back east to Toronto. I found a yoga class I could afford with the part-time janitor job I had. It cost twenty-five cents and turned out to be a Kundalini Yoga class. It was tough. The teacher was tough. But the relaxation was divine. After the third class, she asked whether I might like to live in their beautiful house and be a part of their community. They woke up at 3:30 each morning, she told me.

I spent the next six months thinking about it. Then I moved in. The rules were: 1) Rise early every morning and do your Sadhana [morning spiritual practice]. *(Three strikes and you move out.) 2) Teach one yoga class every week. 3) Write Yogi Bhajan every month. 4) Help with duties in the house. 5) Pay your rent.*

One thing led to the next. It was hard writing those letters at first, but eventually they became easier. Getting up was no problem. Teaching was fun. Helping was a joy. The rent always worked out.

We visited Yogi Bhajan at Cornell University that fall. My teacher suggested I wear a turban for our visit. It was this big and gawky thing on my head, but I afterwards discarded my toque and kept with the turban, and it got better, day by day.

The more I learned about the Sikh tradition, and that in fact my teachers were Sikhs, the more I liked it. I liked that it was open and nonjudgmental. I liked that it incorporated a physical and mental discipline of meditation and service. I liked the practical saint-soldier attitude. Frankly, in North America, wearing what looks like a skirt without a kirpan can look pretty effeminate – but with a proper kirpan, it rocks! [Guru Fatha Singh is referring to the kurta, a tunic worn in varying styles by both Sikh men and Sikh women, and to the kirpan, the short sword of the Sikh warrior-saint.] *And with a proper mala* [the Sikh rosary] *and turban, it is quite smart. I like Sikh Dharma. It is a simple, elegant, no-nonsense aptitude. Honest. Focused. And I wouldn't have it any other way. Thank God for Yogiji!*

Part IV

Living the Sound Way to God

Sikh Lifestyle & Life Transitions

God's devotees have this abundance as their capitol stock:
In conducting their affairs, they seek consultation with their Guru.
The support of God's Name is their capitol stock;
Ever and always, they praise God's Name.
Through the Perfect Guru, God's Name has been established within
them;
The treasury of God's devotees is inexhaustible.
Guru Amar Das [1]

Chapter 13

Get a Life: The Rehit

Virtue and vice do not come by mere words.
Actions repeated over and over are engraved on the soul.
Guru Nanak [1]

When Sat Pavan Kaur Khalsa was five or six years old, her father had a profound talk with her and her younger sister. He sat them down, and essentially explained that he and their mother might make mistakes, might go crazy, might divorce, might cut their hair, might leave the *Dharma* (in this context, "Dharma" means the Sikh path), and in any event, would someday die. That if these things happened, the two girls could always turn to the *Guru*. It would always be there for them and would always give them the right answers to their problems. As her father explained this, Sat Pavan began crying. Her father assured her that he and her mother weren't planning on actually doing any of those things. But she was not to see her parents as perfect beings. He didn't want the girls to be Sikhs through their parents only. He was asking them to be Sikhs in their own right. He was telling them to turn to the Guru, not secondhand, but on their own.

The lives of devout Sikhs do revolve around the Guru, and the Guru does provide outstanding answers to thorny questions. That doesn't sound so strange. But the funny thing is that the *Siri Guru Granth Sahib*, which has the sound current to change lives, is surprisingly silent on codes of conduct. Other than repeated injunctions to meditate on the Name of God and to sing God's Praises in the Company of the Holy, there are next to no commandments in the *Siri Guru Granth Sahib*. *Avoid actions that you will regret in the end* [2] is about it.

This lack of rules fortunately makes mincemeat of the human tendency towards rigidity and offensive fanaticism. Certain rules are critical for those of us who have taken *Amrit*, as we saw in the chapter on the Amrit Ceremony, but otherwise all actions in Sikhism are at the discretion of the devotee.

And yet *Sikh Dharma* is more a lifestyle than a belief system. Except for a belief in the One God Who Is Present In All and Who Is Totally Beyond All Comprehension, Sikhism is devoid of lengthy, elaborate beliefs. (You can check back to Chapter 1 for a brief summation of Sikh concepts.) You won't find us arguing about how many angels can dance on the head of a pin...except for fun. And you won't find us burning heretics. But there is a code of conduct—which we *never* attempt to foist onto non-Sikhs. This code of conduct is not embodied in the *Siri Guru Granth Sahib* however, but in the *Rehit Maryada* (Lifestyle for the Remembrance of Death), better known simply as the *Rehit*.

Unlike the *Siri Guru Granth Sahib*, the Rehit was not compiled by the saints who originally wrote the words. Although the Rehit started when Guru Gobind Singh established the Amrit Ceremony, it was only distilled in the late 1930s and early 1940s. It's based on the *Rehit Namas* (lifestyle writings) that have come down to us from *Guru Gobind Singh* (the Tenth Sikh Guru) and his followers, as well as admonitions that are imbedded in Sikh stories. Despite its late date, the Rehit contains much of what *Guru Nanak* (the father of Sikhism) taught.

Guru Nanak was an iconoclast and a rebel. He dispensed with the caste system, idolatry and superstitious foolishness. His very name, *Nanak*, means No Nonsense. For instance, there's the time he was in *Hardwar*, a place of Hindu pilgrimage on the Ganges, and spotted a group of devotees bathing in the river and throwing water eastward towards the sun. "Why are you doing that?" he inquired. "To propitiate our ancestors," came the answer. Hearing this, Guru Nanak proceeded to throw water to the west. "But the sun is in the other direction!" remonstrated the pilgrims. "Oh, I'm not offering water to the sun. I'm going to water my lands near Lahore," Guru Nanak replied. They were aghast. "But how can water here reach your distant crops?" "Well," said Guru Nanak cheerfully, "if your water can reach your ancestors and the sun, mine can surely reach my fields!" And to this day, although we do have ceremonies, devout Sikhs avoid superstitious acts and ancestor worship. That avoidance—as well as all avoidance of idolatry and caste—is part of the Rehit.

Notice that Guru Nanak wasn't a hermit living in a cave or a monk living in a celibate community. He was "watering" his fields. He actively participated in life, married and had children, as did all the Sikh Gurus, except for *Guru Harkrishan*, who died at age eight. Similarly, most Sikhs live householding lives as advocated by the Rehit. Sikhs believe that all creation is created by God, that God infuses all creation. We don't run from what God created. Doing so would just give power to the illusion of separateness. (That illusion is called *Maya.*) So we live in the world.

Much of the Rehit reflects this orientation towards the household. We view everyone as family. I remember the time my husband and I were in San Diego visiting my family. A lady picked us up in her van to take us to *Gurdwara*. We were parked outside another house waiting to pick up someone else, when a little Sikh girl (maybe five years old) got in the van, sat down right next to me, handed me a book and asked me to read her a story. I was touched by her trust. Because I was wearing *Bana* (the Sikh garb we'll be discussing in detail in the next chapter), she knew I was her "Aunt."

We display this same family attitude towards everyone. We'll be looking at the Sikh appetite for serving and feeding people in the chapter on Seva. We'll be looking at how Sikhs respect other faiths in the chapter titled "A Universal Path." And let me tell you, the Sikh capacity for hospitality can be mind boggling.

My husband and I were traveling through California on a

book tour in 2002 in connection with my first book. We had reserved the guest room at an ashram in LA, where several members of the Los Angeles *sangat* (congregation) live. But when we got there, we were told that the Siri Singh Sahib had asked them to host a couple of visiting dignitaries from India. (Presumably he had made this request without checking to see if the room had been reserved.) The men from India would have the guest room. Where were we going to stay? I knew God would provide, but what actually happened still astounds me.

One of the ladies in the ashram had looked a little puzzled when she saw Jim and me together. Although interfaith marriages between Sikhs and non-Sikhs aren't extremely rare, they aren't extremely common either. I explained that Jim was my husband. We also mentioned our predicament. After a brief consultation with her husband, she invited us to sleep in the same room she and her husband occupied. They put down an extra mattress for us in their bed-sitting room. And that's where we stayed. God bless them. There you have Sikh hospitality as advocated by the Rehit in living technicolor.

Because we live in the world, the Rehit tells us, "Earn your living righteously and share what you have with others." That means Sikhs work hard and strive to do their best at whatever they do. Usually "share what you have with others" manifests as charitable contributions, feeding the homeless, and such like. For example, a man (not a Sikh) in Vancouver, Canada, felt forced to put his injured dog to sleep because he had no money for the expensive surgery his dog needed to survive. A Sikh waiting in the veterinary clinic overheard the man's pain and paid for the dog's surgery.[3]

But sometimes, the injunction to "share what you have with others" manifests at a different level entirely. In 1975, Sat Jiwan Singh Khalsa, the first Sikh admitted to the Bar in New York state, was arguing his first case in court. Determined to do his best, Sat Jiwan Singh put heart, soul and meditation into it. Then mid-trial, the judge said in a deep authoritarian voice, "Let's take a recess. Mr. Khalsa, I want to see you in my chambers." As he accompanied the judge to his chambers, the new attorney expected at the very least a severe tongue lashing for committing some heinous breech of law or courtroom etiquette. Maybe he would be debarred! He couldn't think what he had done though. The judge sat down behind his gargantuan desk in a throne-like chair, looked intently at Sat Jiwan Singh, and said in his deep authoritarian voice, "Mr. Khalsa, can you help me relax?" Indeed, he could! (See the sidebar for what Sat Jiwan Singh taught the judge.)

Pranayam: Left Nostril Breathing

Pranayam refers yogic breathing practices. Left Nostril Breathing is a calming pranayam and helps us become receptive and relaxed, so this is what Sat Jiwan Singh taught the judge.

How to Do It

Block your right nostril with your right thumb. The fingers of your right hand point straight up. Breathe long and deep exclusively through your left nostril. To breathe long and deep allow your abdomen to expand as you inhale and contract as you exhale. Your shoulders move little or not at all. Deep abdominal breathing is the way a baby breathes. Continue for 3 minutes.

In the *Siri Guru Granth Sahib* is a Shabad by *Dhanna*, a Hindu saint and farmer, which expresses how strongly Sikhs believe that everything comes from God, and therefore the householding life is God's Will manifested. This Shabad is also in the *Aartee*, which was mentioned in the chapter titled "The Path of Paths." Here's the translation:

O God, this is Your Worship Service.
You arrange and resolve the affairs of those who perform Your devotional service.
Lentils, flour, and ghee, I beg of You.
These will gladden my mind.
I ask You for shoes and fine clothes and grains of seven kinds.
I ask You for a milking cow, a water buffalo, a fine mare, and a good wife.
Your servant Dhanna begs for this, O God. [4]

Don't get the idea, from this Shabad, that Sikhs view women as chattel. I wouldn't have become one, if that were true! The respect Sikhs extend to all God's creation includes respecting women, and equality between men and women is guaranteed by the Rehit. In fact, six of the ten human Sikh Gurus claimed their descent from a woman, *Bibi Bhani*.

Bibi Bhani was the daughter of *Guru Amar Das*, the Third Guru, and the wife of *Guru Ram Das*, the Fourth Guru. One day while Guru Amar Das was meditating, Bibi Bhani noticed that the chair Guru Amar Das was seated in was unbalanced and about to topple. She placed her hand under the wobbling leg and held the chair steady while her father and Guru meditated. When Guru Amar Das came out of his meditation, he was so touched by the sacrifice his daughter had made for him that he told her he would grant her any wish. Had she asked to become the next Guru, he would have been honor bound to give the Guruship to her. That may have been his intention. But this was

16th Century India, so the idea probably didn't occur to her. Instead, she asked that the Guruship remain forever in her line. Guru Amar Das granted this wish. He made Bibi Bhani's husband the Fourth Guru; all the remaining human Gurus were Bibi Bhani's descendants. You could say that all Sikhs today trace their spiritual lineage to this one woman.

Because Sikhs respect all life, motherhood is honored. 3HO Sikhs hold a party for the mother-to-be on the 120th day after conception, which is when we believe the soul enters the body of the fetus. No one belittles women who stay home with their children. No one belittles women who work outside the home either. And currently, since the *Siri Singh Sahib's* passing, the highest ranking ministers amongst 3HO Sikhs are women.

Of course, the Sikh respect for all of life does not mean that the Rehit encourages us to run wild. The operative word is "respect." Eating slices of watermelon is healthy; eating a whole truckload of watermelons all at once is not.

We are not required to fast—in fact, the newly bereaved are told to avoid fasting—but we are encouraged to "Eat less. Sleep less." Based on a rule set forth by Guru Gobind Singh, we completely avoid eating animals that are bled to death. Many Sikhs are vegetarians and eat no animals at all. Generally that includes no eggs, although most of us do eat milk products and honey.

The Rehit agrees with the Surgeon General and tells us to avoid the use of tobacco and recreational pharmaceuticals. Many Sikhs—including all 3HO Sikhs and most Amritdari Sikhs— avoid alcohol as well, considering it a recreational pharmaceutical. Some even avoid coffee.

We have no celibate priesthood (except, of course, for widowers and suchlike) and no monks and nuns, but sex outside a legal, monogamous marriage is not on the agenda of the Rehit. Premarital and extramarital sex are both rare among Sikhs. The result is comparatively stable marriages and few unwed pregnancies. Although the Rehit frowns on divorce, it does allow divorced and widowed persons to remarry.

We keep our bodies as God intended, which means no hair cutting, no shaving, no mutilating or mortifying our bodies, no tattoos, no body piercing and no circumcision. But, we're not stupid about it: surgery is allowed if necessary.

Sikhs dance and attend movies, plays, operas and sports events. Sikhs may wear fine clothes and jewelry...or blue jeans and boots. There's nothing in the Rehit against any of these. On the other hand, the Rehit—like a good mother—urges us to renounce greed, lust, anger, possessiveness, ego attachment, doubt and fear. If it's detrimental to our health and well-being, the Rehit tells us not to do it. But pretty much everything else is allowed in moderation.

The Four Pillars of this moderate, wholesome, serviceful lifestyle are *Bana, Banis, Seva* and *Simran. Bana* is Sikh garb, which we'll be looking at in the next chapter. We've already discussed *Banis*, the *Shabads* that Sikhs read on a daily basis. *Seva*, which we'll look at in more detail two chapters from now, is selfless service. But it also includes earning one's living right-eously, raising one's children consciously, all charitable giving and tithing, helping out a neighbor, and so on. *Simran*, which we covered in the *Sadhana* chapter, literally means "remembrance" and includes both remembering God's Name with every breath and singing the Guru's Word as a meditation.

And so we come full circle. The life of a devout Sikh revolves around the Guru. The Guru provides the foundation and two of the Four Pillars of the Rehit. The Rehit isn't IN the *Siri Guru Granth Sahib*, but it is OF the *Siri Guru Granth Sahib*. It's a wholesome, natural, kindly life. Thank God. Thank Guru.

Chapter 14

Bana: Dressed Up Royally

In the Guru's Court, I have been blessed with a robe of honor.
Guru Arjan Dev [1]

One dark Sunday evening in January, 2003, a friend and I entered the sanctuary of Salem Oregon's oldest church to attend an interfaith service honoring Martin Luther King, Jr. As I crossed the threshold, the Pauline Memorial A. M. E. Zion Church pastor—the chief organizer for the service—did a puzzled double take and inquired, "Are you one of the presenters?" I grinned and said, "Next year!" And next year, I *was* one of the presenters.

What was the lady pastor reacting to? *Bana*—the distinctive Sikh mode of attire.

If there's anything people react to about Sikhs, it's the way we dress. That's actually one of the reasons we wear our distinctive turbans and garb. It's extremely difficult to deny what you are three times before the cock crows if you're wearing a robe of honor proclaiming your identity.

Bana was the first gift *Guru Gobind Singh*, the Tenth Guru, gave the *Panj Pi-aaray* before he established the *Amrit Ceremony*, as we saw a few chapters ago. The distinctiveness of Bana establishes a Sikh's identity. Not only does it prevent a Sikh from running away, and insures that anyone who needs a Sikh can find one, it also endows the wearer with dignity. It's extremely difficult to act tawdry when you're dressed up royally.

In 1699, only princes of the blood and other high-ranking persons wore turbans. Stories tell of people fighting over the inheritance of special turbans. So Guru Gobind Singh insisted that all his Sikhs wear turbans as a statement of the nobility of those who are willing to give their lives for God. We've worn them ever since.

The nobility inherent in wearing a turban can have some interesting side effects. I have a friend who used to be a genuine starving artist, a modern-day Mimi—cold, hungry and sick. She had thought this was a noble and worthy way to be. Then she discovered Sikhism and started wearing a turban. She would look in the mirror, and see a beautiful princess looking back. Somehow, she felt the princess she had discovered herself to be deserved better than a life of abysmal poverty. So she is now revamping her life.

Wearing a turban has lots of benefits. It prevents sunburn to the scalp, keeps the cranial bones well-adjusted and hides gray hair and baldness. Many religious traditions ask their followers to cover their heads much the same way you would cover a pot to keep the heat in. Wearing a turban actually does prevent the Shabads that Sikhs sing from "going in one ear and out the other."

It also acts as insulation. I like to use an electrical analogy for this. When you're dealing with high-powered spiritual technologies, you're dealing with all the energy in the universe— much more energy than any atomic bomb. Just as you need insulation around an electrical wire in order to plug it in safely, so too you need insulation over the top of your head (the place where you connect with God's Infinite Energy) if you're going to use high-powered spiritual technologies without blowing a fuse.

Guru Singh Khalsa, who was the first of Yogi Bhajan's students to wear a turban, initially wrapped it in January of 1969 to protect his long 1960s rock star hair from the lacquer spray and sawdust while he was restoring antique chairs for the shop where Yogi Bhajan taught Kundalini Yoga. But when Yogi Bhajan questioned him about it, Guru Singh stated—to his own surprise—that he was wearing that turban to emulate his Teacher. Guru Singh soon discovered (as I did many years later) that wearing a turban focuses and calms the mind. The subtle pressure on the temples that a turban creates stimulates the pituitary, the seat of intuition.

With all these wonderful benefits, it's a pity so many Sikhs feel that turbans are primarily for men and strictly optional for women. Actually, the rules for *Amritdari Sikhs* (those who have taken Amrit) technically apply to men and women equally, which is why most Amritdari *3HO* Sikhs of either gender wear turbans.

However, just as there is a difference in male and female anatomy, so too there is a difference in male and female turbans. When I put on my turban, I start by coiling my uncut hair in a *Rishi knot* on top on my head. (A Rishi knot—named for the Rishis or yogis who wear them—is a tight hair bun placed on top of the head.) I position the Rishi knot toward the back center of my head to cover my *solar center*. (This is the spot that is open in a baby's head. Under it is the pineal gland, a light-sensitive organ.) Men position their Rishi knots near the front.

Why the difference? Very simple. As the yogis tell us, the position of the solar center is closer to the front for men and closer to the back for women.

Having secured my Rishi knot with a couple of bobby pins, I then cover the top of my head with a piece of white cotton. I use plain white cotton handkerchiefs. Many ladies cover the tops of their heads with cotton doilies.

Styles of turbans vary. To make mine, I cut five yards of white cotton gauze in half lengthwise and then fold them lengthwise a couple of times. (My husband helps with the folding process by holding one of the ends.) I wind a turban around my head, starting in front, working my way up, covering my ears and the ends of the handkerchief. Once it's coiled, I tuck the turban in at the top. The resulting turban resembles a short version of the one Nefertiti wears in the famous statuette. Many other Sikh ladies wrap their turbans like this, but styles do vary, and I haven't the foggiest notion how some turbans are wrapped. (Videos on turban tying for both men and women are offered on Sikhnet. See

Resources.)

Men stretch their six yards of more tightly woven cotton gauze on the diagonal. Men's turbans aren't folded the way women's turbans are. Because men's rishi knots are placed towards the front, their turbans look totally different once wrapped. Men also never wear a *chuni*.

A chuni is a gauzy, veil-like scarf that Sikh women wear. Many Punjabi women wear them exclusively, without the turban. I wear one over my turban when I'm out in public. It's prettier and more feminine than a plain turban. I've noticed that the general public respects me more when I wear a chuni. I even seem to drive better when I wear one. To prevent the chuni flying away in high winds, I pin it to my turban using a turban pin bearing a Sikh symbol.

After coiling the Rishi knot on top of my head, but before covering it, I stick a small wooden comb, called a *kangha*, in my hair. This is one of the 5 "k"s all Amritdari Sikhs keep about their persons. Each of these "k"s has at least one practical purpose and at least one symbolic purpose. Wooden combs are practical for combing long hair as they neutralize static better than do combs of other materials. The kangha symbolizes a Sikh's willingness to care for what God has given us.

Among other things, what God has given us is *kesh* (uncut hair), arguably the most important of the 5 "k"s. Like Christians and Jews, Sikhs believe that we are made in the image of God. By that we don't mean that we *look* like God, we mean that God *imaged* us. We're God's masterpieces—God's Mona Lisas. So we don't cut our hair—that includes no shaving of beards, no shaving underarms, and no shaving the legs—because that would mess with the image God made.

There's a lot of spiritual oomph in having uncut hair. It helps raise the *kundalini*—the energy of our latent potentials, and a derivative of *kundal*, which literally means a "lock of hair." You know how Samson was defeated when Delilah cut his hair? (The story's in the biblical Book of Judges.[2]) So we also don't cut any of our hair, because we don't want to destroy our strength. A lot of energy collects in the hair, as it's propensity for collecting electric static proclaims. Because hair (unlike fingernails and toenails) stops growing when it reaches its appointed length, the bodies of people with uncut hair don't waste nutrients attempting to grow it. And God knew what He/She/It was doing when He/She/It put beards on male faces. There's a center of energy there (called a *moon center*) that wearing a beard insulates and protects.

"Clean-shaven" is a complete misnomer. Shaving is actually a rather dirty custom, as anyone who has ever cleaned up the little hairs knows. Why a lady would want her man to shave is beyond me. It's no fun rubbing one's cheek against sandpaper...or 5 o'clock shadow. Unless you routinely wear gasmasks or are undergoing certain surgeries, shaving has no practical value...except for the people who make money on shaving gear.

Of the other 5 "k"s, it's no surprise that the thigh-length underwear called *kacheras* symbolize chastity. But it may be a big surprise that the practical value of thigh-length underwear is to insulate the thighbone, which yogic lore tells us helps to stabilize the body's calcium-magnesium balance. Kacheras from India generally have draw strings, which gives me some under-standing of the English word "drawers." I generally wear the sort of knee length underwear sold as "warm wear" here in the States. With either type of kacheras, we do our best to insure that kacheras are a bit loose in the crotch to allow air circulation to a part of the body that needs it.

Another of the 5 "k"s is the *kirpan*, the short sword or knife that Amritdari Sikhs carry about their persons. Like a number of Sikhs in the West, I usually fulfill this requirement with a Swiss Army knife in my pocket. I figure since the whole point of the kirpan is to save lives, a pocket knife with a can opener attached is likely to do the job best. The true kirpan has a curved tip and varies in size from children's models that are only a couple of inches long to two foot long swords. Sheaths vary from very plain to supremely elegant with fancy gold inlays.

It's unfortunate that the mere possession of a kirpan so often gets law-abiding Sikhs in trouble. School children especially run into problems if they carry a kirpan, and I know of several cases where Sikhs were hauled into court on concealed weapons charges. The word "kirpan" stems from the root word *kirpaa*, which means kindness, compassion, mercy, grace, etc. So the kirpan is an instrument of mercy. It is only used for protection and to save lives...and to cut *Gurprashaad*, as we saw in Chapter 6. It's a symbol of our willingness as Warrior-Saints to give our lives for others if God so wills. And because it's a deeply sacred symbol to us, Sikhs rarely ever misuse a kirpan.

Every Sikh also wears a *kara*, a steel bangle bracelet. Men wear them on the right wrist; some women, including me, wear them on their left. This member of the 5 "k"s family puts steel in our auras (the *aura* is the body's electro-magnetic field) and reminds us that we belong to God. You can see it as a wedding band reminding us that we are ultimately wedded to God. You can see it as a manacle: I'm handcuffed to God and God is handcuffed to me. You can see it as an identification badge. In any case, it's a reminder of Who a Sikh belongs to.

When Guru Gobind Singh gave us Bana, he included a few other items: *kurta* (tunic), cummerbund and *churridars* (leggings). Styles vary. The cummerbund stimulates the navel area and aids digestion. The kurta and churridars serve our physical modesty. These items, however, are more optional than the turban and 5 "k"s. Many Sikh men wear suits and ties to work. Indeed, many Punjabi Sikh men wear Western clothes exclusively, except for the turban and the 5 "k"s. I generally wear white cotton pants and top—with a skirt over the pants if it's a more formal occasion. I've seen lots of Sikhs of all descriptions wearing blue jeans and T-shirts. As long as it's modest and graceful, Sikhs may wear it.

You may have noticed that I mention the color white a lot. White is the color of light. It reflects the full spectrum of the visible and invisible rainbow. Yogis know that wearing white expands the aura by three feet total (a foot and a half on each side). Since a person with a strong aura remains inspiring and radiant in the face of negativity, hostility, or challenging circumstances, most 3HO Sikhs wear white more often than not. But it isn't a requirement. For Punjabi people, white is the color of mourning, and is generally reserved for widows and funerals. Even 3HO Sikhs do wear other colors. I interviewed Sat Pavan Kaur Khalsa for this book right after a Gurdwara service to which she wore an elegant deep-rose kurta/churridars set with a pattern of stylized leaves and flowers embroidered in pastel colors.

So, let us understand: Bana is the costume Sikhs wear for the part we play in God's drama. If an actor shows up wearing the wrong costume, it confuses the audience and lowers the actor's credibility. That's why we wear Bana. But the costume is never more important than the actor's actions (i.e. *Rehit* and *Seva*), nor more important that the script (i.e. the *Shabad Guru* as embodied in the *Siri Guru Granth Sahib*, the daily *Banis* and *Naam Simran*), nor more important than the Playwright (i.e. God).

Long before I became a Sikh or had even seen one, a Hindu lady once explained to me what Sikhism is about, and all she talked about were the 5 "k"s. At the time, I thought it was the dumbest thing I had ever heard. I still do. A religion based on special underwear?! Ridiculous! There's a passage in the *Siri Guru Granth Sahib* that says, *Through robes, one meets not with God.*[3] Yes, my hair is uncut and I'm wearing a steel bangle, the other 5 "k"s and a turban as I write this. And I wear these things proudly as a badge of honor. Bana lets our inner light shine out, and that serves to inspire and uplift people. But please understand, Sikhs wear Bana to enhance our spirits; we don't enhance our spirits in order to wear Bana.

Chapter 15

Seva: An Appetite for Service

Those who remember God help others generously.
Guru Arjan Dev [1]

Today is Saturday. About 10:45 am, Krishna Singh Khalsa and I pull into the parking lot of the "Service Station." It's in a modest modern structure—a former bank that now houses a community police station and a social services office—located in a less than scenic part of town. It also houses a facility run by St. Vincent de Paul in Eugene that provides a day room with food and clothing, plus shower, laundry, telephone and mailing facilities for homeless and low-income adults. Every other Saturday, Sikhs in Eugene contribute hot organic nutritious vegetarian meals here as part of The Lotus Project—a large healing vision and Krishna Singh's brainchild.

Krishna Singh takes a small table out of the trunk, while I remove a box with utensils, paper bowls and paper cups. We unload an urn, a pot of *Yogi Tea* (a hot spice drink) and two pots of *kitcharee* (an Indian dish of mung beans and rice). (See sidebar for kitcharee recipe.) Ordinarily it would be just one pot of kitcharee, but today a family in the Eugene *sangat* is contributing extra food.

Recipe for Kitcharee

Kitcharee (also known as mung beans and rice) is a wholesome and nourishing one pot meal. There are almost

---

as many recipes of it as there are people who make it. All measurements, especially for the spices and vegetables, are variable. There are a lot of ingredients, but it's easy to make if you use a slow cooker.

1 cup mung beans
7-8 cups water or vegetable stock
1 cup Basmati rice
2 stalks celery, chopped
1-2 carrots, chopped & peeled
1 large stalk broccoli, chopped, or other vegetables (green beans, red cabbage, kale, zucchini, etc.)
1 heaping tablespoon turmeric
1/4 teaspoon kelp powder
1 heaping teaspoon paprika
1/4 teaspoon *garam masala* (an Indian spice mix), optional
1 heaping tablespoon dried parsley
1 teaspoon ground cumin
1 teaspoon ground coriander
Dash of black pepper
Olive oil (or other oil or *ghee*) for sautéing ginger and onion
1 inch ginger root, peeled & minced
1 large onion, chopped
Several cloves garlic, minced

Soak the mung beans overnight in water to cover. Be sure to remove any little stones that may be lurking in the mung beans. The next morning drain the mung beans, and throw out the water they have soaked in.

Place the mung beans in a slow cooker with 6 cups fresh

water or vegetable stock. Let the mung beans cook, preferably for several hours. Then stir in the Basmati rice and another 1-2 cups water or vegetable stock. Add the herbs and spices, then the vegetables.

Place enough olive oil (or other oil or ghee) in a skillet to cover the bottom. Sauté the ginger root and onion in the oil until the onion is lightly caramelized. (If desired, you can cook the turmeric and cumin with the onion before adding them to the pot.) Add the onion/ginger mix to the cooking mung bean mixture. (I pour some water into the emptied skillet, scrap up any onion that has stuck to the pan, and pour the water and onion scraps into the slow cooker with the mung bean mixture.) Then mince up some garlic and add it to the pot. Once the mixture comes to a boil, turn the slow cooker heat to low. Cook for several hours. Stir occasionally and add more water or stock if necessary.

Serves 6 as a one pot meal. Serves more if there are other dishes.

As we walk by, a lady sitting to the side of the walkway looks up and smiles. We walk past two desks into the medium-sized room where a group of 20-30 people are watching what looks like a Spiderman movie. Krishna Singh sets up the table and pours the Yogi Tea into the urn while I take the plates and cups out of the box.

By 11 am we're ready to serve. After Krishna Singh makes his announcement, a few of the men amble up. He chats with the men while I pour cups of Yogi Tea and he dishes up the kitcharee. There are no lines forming and no jostling—the men and a couple of women amble up one by one or in very small groups. A few are skeptical of the tea, so I offer them half cups to try out. Invariably, they come back for a full cup.

After twenty minutes we're out of the Yogi Tea. So Krishna Singh washes up the urn and two of the pots, while I dish up the remaining kitcharee. By 11:30 am, we're out of food, and everyone who wanted food is fed. As we lug the empty pots back to the car, one of the men calls out, "Thank you!"

I answer, "Our pleasure!" And it is.

It has been the pleasure of Sikhs to feed people from the very beginning. *Guru Nanak*, the founding father of Sikhism, was the despair of his own father, who saw his meditating son as a ne'er-do-well. The father urged Nanak to do something profitable, such as become a merchant, making the best investments possible. To this end, the father gave Nanak (who was not yet enlightened or married or a Guru) some money to make purchases, and off Nanak went to the nearest large town. On his way back from town, Nanak spotted some holy men, who were naked and hungry. Nanak went back to town, took all his earnings, and used it to feed and clothe these holy men. By Nanak's standards, this was the best investment possible.

It's the best investment by Sikh standards also. Feeding people is a favorite Sikh service (*Seva*). At the Golden Temple (*Hari Mander Sahib*) in *Amritsar*, volunteers feed some forty to seventy thousand people on an average day with the number increasing exponentially to well over a million people on special occasions. When you sit down to *langar* (the communal meal) at the Golden Temple, you may be sitting next to a beggar or a business tycoon, a devout Sikh or a tourist. Total strangers have come up to me and told me that Sikhs fed them when they were stranded in a foreign country. At the Council for the Parliament of the World's Religions held in Barcelona in July of 2004, Sikhs provided free meals for all the participants, serving an estimated 20,000 meals. A friend who is a Religious Science minister emailed me that all the delegates from her denomination spoke glowingly of the food, "the wonderful atmosphere in the tent, and the kindness of those providing the experience and the food." Providing free meals to everyone is common in Gurdwaras with a large enough sangat. It's been said, "In Amritsar nobody goes to sleep hungry."[2] I look forward to the day when enough Gurdwaras in enough places are providing food for everyone so that no one goes to sleep hungry anywhere.

There is much more to Seva than feeding people. *Seva* (selfless service) is one of the pillars of *Sikh Dharma* (Sikhism as a spiritual path) and an indelible part of the Sikh psyche . We've already seen examples of Seva in other chapters, and in the chapter titled "A Universal Path," we'll see Sikhs initiating interfaith services and hear the historical story of the Sikh man who founded a group that served (and still serves) the wounded on both sides of battlefields, more than 150 years before the Red Cross was founded.

In common with members of most faiths, Sikhs are involved in relief work to this day. For instance, in the wake of the December 26, 2004, tsunamis, several young Sikh men and women from the USA helped with clean-up and reconstruction in the tsunami-struck areas. The ones I heard of traveled under the auspices of UNITED SIKHS, a U.N. affiliated, multi-national, non-profit organization originally organized in New York in 1999, that acts for the good of all without regard to race, religion, creed, gender or age.

UNITED SIKHS' relief work embraces the United States as well as foreign countries. For instance, after Hurricane Katrina hit New Orleans, they assisted their fellow Sikhs by rescuing the Guru (i.e. the New Orleans Gurdwara copy of the *Siri Guru Granth Sahib*). Of course, it might be more accurate to say that the Guru rescued itself, because, after hiring a boat and two rescue experts and slogging through waist-deep muddy water and fearing that the retrieved copy of the Guru would need to be cremated, the UNITED SIKHS team discovered to their aston-ishment and joy that the *Siri Guru Granth Sahib* was floating peacefully on a wooden *palki* (in this case, a table used as the Guru's palanquin), untouched by the mud and the turbulence and the water. But in the wake of that same disaster, UNITED SIKHS also fed at least 1300 evacuees and provided bedding, clothing and medical assistance.[3]

It isn't just Sikh groups that aid the unfortunate. Sikh individuals do too. One stellar example is Bhupinder Singh Kohli, who has discovered numerous ways to aid those in distress in his own area of India. After witnessing an accident that proved fatal because there was no ambulance to move the injured to a hospital quickly, Bhupinder Singh turned his own car into a free hospital transport vehicle. Three months later, grateful sangat members of his local Gurdwara provided Bhupinder Singh with a genuine ambulance to provide even more effective service—which is still free.

Bhupinder Singh then noticed rich patients dumping their medicines after they got well. So he began collecting unused and unexpired medicines from doctors and patients. These medicines go to charitable dispensaries for distribution to the poor and sick. The amazing thing is that Bhupinder Singh does all these things while working at a bank and caring for his own bed-ridden father.[4]

Sikhs also consider working in the world with excellence and compassion in an income-producing job to be a form of Seva. It isn't just Sikhs in the healing professions who feel this way. I've heard Sikhs speak of their jobs making nutritious granola as a service to humanity.

Uplifting and freeing people's spirits can be another form of Seva. This is something of a 3HO specialty. 3HO Sikhs have initiated programs to bring Kundalini Yoga and meditation to chronically and terminally ill patients, to incarcerated and at-risk youth, to drug addicts and to adult prisoners.

One such program is the Guru Ram Das Center for Medicine and Humanology, which helps chronically or terminally ill patients using the techniques of Kundalini Yoga. The Center's director wrote of a late-stage colon cancer patient in this program, who lived four years beyond his prognosis and who died at peace after saying, *I have discovered a world beyond my intellect, and this has been an extraordinary experience. Now, to me, every place is an altar, every experience is a blessing. Life has become magical, even though I am doing the same routine.*[5] Other men and women in the program have also been blessed with a peaceful transition, and many have been blessed with longer lives.[6]

Then there's Y.O.G.A. (Your Own Greatness Affirmed) for Youth, which helps uplift incarcerated and at-risk youth through yogic techniques. After four to eight sessions, eighty percent of them become noticeably less prone to physical and verbal violence, and many show other lifestyle improvements as well. One young man in the program said, "Yoga helps you deal with rage—it calms the heart. I like it."[7]

Many Sikhs, including me, have gone into prisons to teach Kundalini Yoga to adult felons. In April 1986, just as I was beginning to think of myself as a Sikh, I was asked to take over the Kundalini Yoga class established by Sikhs in Salem at the Oregon State Penitentiary (a men's maximum security facility). The transformations I witnessed in that prison were profound and moving. I was privileged to watch several men quit smoking, which was still allowed—and very common—in prisons at the time. But the most moving experience occurred after I'd been teaching there about three years, when one man came up to me after class. He told me he was in on his second murder charge. (That's rare, by the way, despite what you read in murder mysteries. Usually murders are a one-shot deal.) Through wet eyes, he told me that he had planned on breaking out of prison by "taking" one of the guards, but discovered he couldn't do it. He pleaded to know what had I done to him. I explained that the only freedom anyone ever has is inward. Later, when another convict badmouthed the guards, our repentant murderer said, "The guards are our brothers."

And that's the underlying rationale behind Seva. Sikhs see God in all. We know the whole human race to be one family under God indivisible. We serve everyone with devotion as a way of serving God with devotion. We're all One.

Chapter 16

Dancing to God

Meherbani Kaur Khalsa's Story

I dance, and so my mind dances.
Guru Amar Das [1]

Meherbani Kaur was born in a small farming and oil industry community in the high desert region of Utah. She says, *My family has its roots deeply planted in the Mormon religion with my ancestors coming across the plains as pioneers following Brigham Young. My religion of origin gets a lot of negative press and comment, but I have to say that my attitude about being raised in this culture is positive. My maternal grandparents were musicians, and grandmother was the church chorister. My first exposure to vibration came gathered around the piano singing as a family, rehearsing hymns and also singing in children's choirs.*

But even at a young age, she questioned the Mormon concept of serving only other members of the Mormon church. And so, she wondered if Mormonism was right for her spirit and began an intense study of other paths.

At age 18, she had her first in-depth experience with other paths when Transcendental Meditation came into her life. This included a friend on that path teaching her how to do *Puja* (Hindu prayers) offerings to the Hindu deities. Meherbani Kaur says, "I had my personal mantra before I knew what was happening."

Her next discoveries came in massage school, when, at the age of 21, her world exploded open—learning *Chi Gong* and waking in the *Amrit Vela* to practice *Tai Chi*. (Both Chi Gong and

Tai Chi are stylized Chinese martial arts forms usually practiced for their health benefits. The Amrit Vela is the time before dawn when the spirit is most active; this is the time *Kundalini Yoga* practitioners—and members of many other spiritual traditions— do spiritual practice.)

She says, *Spirit loudly spoke to me after school was complete that Portland, Oregon, was the place to move. About a year after arriving here, I attended a Classical Indian dance performance, and with tears streaming down my face was beckoned by the gods to learn this divine art form.* For 12 years, she has studied and performed Classical Indian dancing. Currently, she creates moving *Celestial Communications* (meditative dance in the Kundalini Yoga tradition) using Kundalini Yoga technology with Indian dance postures.

And then, at the age of 24, all her previous explorations coalesced, and she was introduced to and began to study Kundalini Yoga. She says, "I have been blessed with teachers who have never separated Sikhism from Yoga teaching." She has always experienced the Presence of the Guru during *Sadhana* (spiritual practice), especially since an *Ardas* (standing prayer) and *Hukam* (literally "Command," the random reading from the *Siri Guru Granth Sahib*) always end the morning program. She experienced that *Guru Ram Das* (the Fourth Sikh Guru) "delivered the message that this path is where my soul's growth lies." And then she adds, "The awareness developed by practicing Kundalini Yoga is what made hearing the call possible."

She says, "Being a Sikh means everything to me. It is my soul's destiny." She feels very blessed to have the teachings of the *Siri Guru Granth Sahib* (the Sikh Guru), which, along with *Dharma* (the path of righteous spiritual action), *Bana* (Sikh garb) and *Banis* (Sikh poem/prayers) possess a truth that resonates deeply for her.

She says, *It hasn't always been easy to bow. It took many years to fully understand and give myself to this lifestyle. In the beginning I kept being drawn again and again to the Gurdwara* [Sikh Temple or service]. *Sitting amongst the women, I was always wondering what force brought me there. One day as ten men rapidly chanted Waa Hay Guroo* [the most ecstatic of Sikh mantras] *all levels integrated inside. I realized the Guru was bringing me to the Gurdwara; Sikhism is my path. Instead of the sensation of searching, I was filled with gratitude.*

She currently serves the Sikh community as the director for community Gurdwara services. She says, *It is important to me that all who come feel welcome and involved. It is this attitude and openness the former director held, and it allowed me to form my relationship with the Shabad Guru* [Guru of divine song and sound] *and develop my commitment.*

Meherbani Kaur lives in Portland, Oregon, where she works as a licensed massage therapist. She is also taking undergraduate classes with an eye towards attaining a degree in Oriental Medicine.

Chapter 17

Marriage: Two Bodies/One Soul

They are not married who are together in body, but separated in spirit.
They are married who have two bodies and one soul.
Guru Amar Das [1]

At last the big day arrives! My husband and I are going to go through the *Anand Karaj*, the Sikh Wedding Ceremony.

In seventeen days, we will celebrate the 31st anniversary of our civil wedding ceremony. None of our non-Sikh friends and relations think it strange that a Sikh would want to have a Sikh wedding ceremony, even after more than three decades of wedded bliss. But a few Sikhs are puzzled. "But I thought you were already married!" they say questioningly. When I tell them, "It's my heart's desire to go through the Anand Karaj. Who else am I going to go through it with?!" they laugh as if to say, "The joke's on me!" No one goes through an Anand Karaj by proxy.

We're not going to have as big a production as is usual with Punjabi wedding festivities, which can last several days. Jim isn't riding in on a horse, although some Western grooms do. We've dispensed with the not-so-small fortune in fancy clothes and 24-carat gold jewelry, usually studded with gemstones, that are de rigueur for Indian weddings. And heaven forbid! I'm not going to henna my hands the way a Punjabi bride would do. But it's taken a major effort nonetheless.

As June 7, 2003, dawns, we drive to Eugene from Salem with my mother and brother Charles, who will help us prepare the auditorium we've rented for the occasion. Today will be blazing hot, but as the auditorium roof is more than two stories up, we will be spared the worst of the heat.

The caretaker of the building arrives and lets us in. We have just enough time to move the chairs and clean up the space a bit before the men with the rented carpets arrive. Like nearly every major Sikh ceremony, the Anand Karaj is performed in the Guru's Court—it's embedded in a *Gurdwara* service. The carpeting will provide padding for everyone who will be sitting on the floor.

We cover the carpeting with clean white sheets, starting with the carpet on stage. Jim and Charles set up the stand Jim created for the canopy. A bunch of people arrive: the courier delivering the cake, a friend looking over the sound system he will tend during the ceremony, other friends bringing the Guru's paraphernalia, and the courier delivering flowers—large beribboned vases of red and white carnations, yellow rosebuds, fresh Baby's Breath, and greenery. As my husband and brother hoist up the canopy, I fill the basins with water for hand washing and foot washing. My mother ties red and yellow balloons on trees around the building. A lady friend and I set out the flower vases and place burgundy red velvet *ramalas* with gold trim and decorations on the *palki sahib* (the altar/throne/bed on which the Guru sits). Today there are more flowers, but set up for a wedding and many details of the service are basically the same as for any Gurdwara service.

Where has the time gone? The musicians are arriving, and so are the guests. Everyone in the *sangat* (congregation) gets invited to a Sikh wedding. To honor this custom, we've invited all the members of Jason Lee United Methodist Church, which my husband attends in Salem. The pastor and her daughter are here. So are our family members, plus friends from at least five different faith traditions. Some of the guests arriving are sangat members whose names I don't know. That's part of the fun of a Sikh wedding.

Jim and I quickly change into our wedding clothes. Jim is wearing the green tunic with yellow sash I made him for our original civil ceremony. Although a Punjabi bride would wear a red or passionate pink outfit, that didn't suit my Western sensibilities, so I am wearing a full-length, white-on-white, embroidered cotton dress and carrying a small bouquet of red carnations rimmed with ferns and adorned with dried Baby's Breath. My husband is tickled that the bride and groom are changing into their wedding finery in the same room. Not the usual scenario!

Although I don my best gold-embroidered *chuni* (long veil-like scarf), I do not cover my face. *Guru Amar Das*, the Third Guru, once severely reprimanded a lady who veiled her face in his presence. She wasn't a bride, but the rules for a woman's (or a man's) conduct in the presence of the Guru apply as much to a wedding as to any other situation. As the *Siri Guru Granth Sahib* is equal to the original human Gurus, it deserves the same respect. So, no face veiling.

As we return to the entrance hall, where our guests are congregating, the minister arrives carrying the *Siri Guru Granth Sahib* on his head. I boom out, "Cover your heads, and remove your shoes. The Guru's coming through." It's around 10:30am: time for the service to begin!

Traditionally, Sikhs prefer morning hours for their weddings. (Afternoons and evening are reserved for funerals and other sad occasions.) Fresher hours just seem more appropriate for fresh commitments.

A Sikh wedding has no formal procession for either the bride or the groom. Since I am the on-time-or-early sort (very rare among Sikhs!), I'm one of the first people to arrive at the Guru's Feet. My youngest niece is with me, so I show her how to bow. The minister and the young man who will be our *Granthi* have already done *Prakash* (opening the Guru) by the time we arrive, but we are able to listen to the opening *Hukam*, the Guru's opening word for this service. I'm pleased that this Hukam comments on the blessings received by turning to God and Guru, because that's what I hope this service will be.

Gradually, as we listen to *kirtan* (Shabads set to music and sung), the rest of our guests arrive. Sikh wedding always start with at least one Shabad. Many Shabads in the *Siri Guru Granth Sahib* use the imagery of the happy marriage as a metaphor for the merger of the soul with God. Naturally, these Shabads are preferred as the prelude to wedding ceremonies. Today we are starting with *Vas Mayray Pi-aari-aa Vas Mayray Govindaa*, a lovely Shabad whose translation follows.

Dwell, O My Beloved, Dwell, O My Lord of the Universe.
O God, be kind to me and dwell within my mind.
I have obtained the fruits of my heart's desire, O My Lord of All.
Beholding the Perfect Guru, I am transported with wonder.
God's Name is received by the happy soul-brides, O My Lord of All.
Night and day, their minds are in bliss.
God comes to us by greatest good fortune, O My Lord of All.
Ever earning spiritual profit, we laugh with joy.[2]

After another Shabad, the lead singer takes over and plays a short rendition of the *Saa Taa Naa Maa* mantra, the *Panj Shabad* or Shabad of five notes. (The words literally mean *Infinity, the world of form, negation, rebirth*.) This is quite unusual at weddings, but our minister has asked for it specially. Thinking it over, I'm not surprised. There's a line in the Guru that says, *The marriage is performed with glory, and the Panj Shabad resounds within the bride's mind.*[3] (Yogi Bhajan taught many meditations with the Panj Shabad; see the sidebar for one of them.)

Kundalini Yoga
Meditation to Arouse Mercy and Compassion [4]
Originally Taught on January 31, 1977

Saa Taa Naa Maa—also known as the Panj Shabad—is the *mantra* of regeneration. It is the mantra *Sat Naam* broken into its component parts. Practicing it balances the hemispheres of the brain and improves intuition. Yogi Bhajan taught many meditations containing the Panj Shabad. Practicing this one grants us the compassion we need for a happy marriage. It also enhances our life force energy.

Remember to tune in before practicing this meditation, if you have not already done so. See the sidebar in Chapter 2.

How to Do It

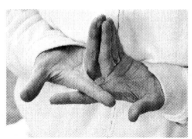

Sitting with your spine straight in any comfortable meditative position, place your hands at the level of your heart. The backs of your little fingers, ring fingers and middle fingers press against each other; your index fingers cross over one another, and your thumbs are stretched out to the sides. The palms face up. Close your eyes. Inhale completely in 4 or 8 or 12 or 16 equal parts while mentally chanting *Saa Taa Naa Maa*, one syllable per part. Hold the breath for the same length of time as the inhale was while mentally chanting *Saa Taa Naa Maa* as many times as you chanted it on the inhale. Exhale in as many parts as the inhale, being sure to expel all the air, and again mentally chant *Saa Taa Naa Maa*, one syllable per part. Hold the breath out the same length of time while mentally chanting *Saa Taa Naa Maa* as many times as you chanted it on the inhale. (Word to the wise: if you are a beginner, start with an inhale of 4 parts—one full *Saa Taa Naa Maa*. Work up to 16 parts—4 full *Saa Taa Naa Maa* mantras.) Focus on the breath and mantra. Time is open.

The minister stands and welcomes everyone. Because half of the people in the sangat today are non-Sikhs, he explains how Sikhs always welcome people of all faiths. Then he calls us up front. Jim and I sit together directly in front of the Guru, with Jim on my right. Our families sit immediately behind us.

And now the musicians strike up with *Keetaa Loree-ai Kamm*, the Shabad that opens the Anand Karaj, which translates as follows.

Whatever works you long to accomplish, speak of them to God,
Who shall bring all projects to completion as the True Guru
*   testifies.*
In the Company of Saints, you shall taste the Ambrosial Treasure.
The Destroyer of Dread is the Merciful Savior of His servants.
O Nanak, sing God's Praises, and you shall see the Invisible God. [5]

Our friend Heminder Singh comes up as we stand with our family for the *Ardas*, the standing prayer. Traditionally, only the couple, their families and the person reciting the Ardas stand at this time. (But looking back at the photos, I think at our Anand Karaj a high percentage of the congregation stood. That's okay. We're all family!) There will be another Ardas later for the whole congregation. This Ardas is shorter and sums up the blessings each family wishes to shower on the couple getting married.

After Heminder gives this Ardas for us, we all sit down to listen to the Hukam for the couple. The Granthi lifts the ramalas and takes a random reading—first in Gurmukhi, then in English. I feel so blessed! Our wedding Hukam is long, but blissful. This is the first part of it in translation:

> *Make an effort, O fortunate one, and dwell on God, the King,*
> *Contemplating Whom one experiences peace, and all one's miseries*
>   *and doubts depart.*
> *Be not lazy in reciting God's Name.*
> *Meeting with the Saints, one goes not to Death's abode.*
> *One is neither afflicted by fear nor sorrow, and is forever blissful.*
> *Recite God's Name with the tongue on every breath.*
> *The Beneficent, Bountiful, Bliss-giving God is merciful and yokes*
>   *you to the service of the Treasure of Virtue.*
> *Nanak says, "Recite God's Name and be not lazy in contemplating*
>   *God."* [6]

Our minister then gives a talk about the Anand Karaj—how it is like walking a maze to arrive at four successively higher levels of experience. Using the Panj Shabad he had asked the lead singer to play, he explains that we start with the mundane, duty-bound, workaday world, and as the ceremony progresses, we ultimately arrive at the ecstasy and bliss of union with God. This is why I have so deeply desired to go through this ceremony. *Anand Karaj* literally means "Creating Bliss." It is the process of taking two people with two separate souls and turning them into One Soul with two bodies—a consummation greatly to be desired.

My mother then comes up to connect us with the *palaa* (the

wedding shawl). In the ordinary way it would be my father, but as my father is deceased, my mother has accepted this job. She places one end over Jim's right shoulder. Draping the palaa across Jim's back, she hands the other end to me.

Punjabi brides often carry fruits and nuts in their end of the palaa to symbolize a fruitful and prosperous union. It's a neat custom, but one we are following today in spirit only. Our palaa is unusual: it's made from two and a half yards of lace curtain valance material—not suitable for carrying fruits and nuts.

As my mother places the palaa, the musicians sing a *slok* (short verse) translated as follows.

Praise and slander, O Nanak, I have utterly banished.
I have totally abandoned all worldly affairs.
I have seen all relations to be false,
Now that I am attached to Your Robe, O God.[7]

The minister now invites my family to go up on stage and sit behind the Guru. As a show of support, they will stand when we make our rounds. Traditionally in Punjabi families, only the bride's brothers stand behind the Guru during a wedding. Western Sikhs have extended that custom to include all family and friends who are willing and able to stand. During the ceremony, I am deeply touched to see that one or two of my Sikh friends are standing for us. As both our mothers are unable to sit on the floor, neither is behind the Guru. Both are in chairs, but will stand for us during the ceremony.

We are nearly ready for the *Lavaan*, the Sikh wedding song. *Guru Ram Das*, the Fourth Guru, wrote the Lavaan for his own 16th Century wedding to *Bibi Bhani*, whose story is in the *Rehit* chapter. Sikhs have used the Lavaan for weddings ever since.

The minister explains that we start the first round at the level of duty and mundane but righteous living. Then he asks if we're ready. We nod. The Granthi lifts the top ramala and reads the first *pauri* of the Lavaan in Gurmukhi. My brother Paul then reads the translation in English.

> *Proceeding forth into the first nuptial round*
> *God grants you instruction for the daily duties of married life, O Beloved.*
> *Rather than reciting the Vedas by rote, be constant in the performance of your righteous duty, and errors of the past will be washed away, O Beloved.*
> *Be confirmed in righteousness and repeat God's Name, as Semitic Scriptures urge as well.*
> *Reflect upon the Perfect True Guru and all your sins and errors will depart.*
> *By greatest good fortune, ecstasy effortlessly arises as thoughts of God, of God, fill the mind.*
> *Slave Nanak proclaims that in the first round, the marriage ceremony has begun.* [8]

As the musicians start playing this first section of the Lavaan, Jim and I bow in unison with our foreheads to the floor. Then we rise to our feet. Jim walks in front of me as we climb the stairs and walk around the Guru in one clockwise circle.

Now I understand why we walk *four* times instead of one. Part of my mind is still chattering about what needs to be done, and it doesn't quit until the first round ends. As we bow at the Guru's Feet in unison at the end of the first round, I'm grateful we have three more rounds to go. If it were only one round, I would have missed it.

Some of you may be wondering why Jim is walking in front. Why not walk side by side? Sikhs circle the Guru during the Anand Karaj to indicate that our lives center around the Guru, and that the Guru is the chief witness to the ceremony. We are performing this ceremony to receive the shower of the Guru's blessing on our union. If we were to walk side by side, one of us

Marriage: Two Bodies/One Soul

would be shielding the other from the Guru's blessing, which is hardly what we're doing this for. To receive the full measure of the Guru's blessing on both halves of a marital union, we must walk single file.

So, if someone has to go first, why isn't the Sikh leading the non-Sikh in a Sikh ceremony? Very simple. The Sikh gender-designator for a man (*Singh*) literally means "lion." The Sikh gender-designator for a woman (*Kaur*) literally means "princess." Now, I ask you, if you're going to hold a procession with a princess and a lion, wouldn't you rather put the lion in front of the princess, instead of the princess in front of the lion?

We repeat the process for the second round, but the experience is very different. The minister explains that the second round is about releasing old patterns so that new and better patterns can form. The Granthi reads the second pauri of the Lavaan in Gurmukhi. Then Paul's eight-year-old daughter Jaime, my youngest niece, reads the translation.

In the second nuptial round, God leads you to the True Guru, O Beloved.

With a heart filled with awe of the Fearless God, all prideful ego dissolves, O Beloved.

In awe of the Immaculate God, sing God's Praises and see God everywhere.

God is the Soul of creation, the Master of the Universe, Who pervades all places, everywhere.

Deep within you, and outside you too, there is only One God.

Meeting together, God's Servants sing and rejoice.

Servant Nanak proclaims that in this second round, the divine music resounds. [9]

As the musicians begin playing this second pauri, as we bow in unison and begin our second perambulation, I *do* feel deep awe and gratitude that God is granting us this blessing. And in that inner space of gratitude and awe, a miracle happens. Before this day, a friend wrote me from Toronto saying, "God and the angels will be with you on your wedding day. God willing, I'll join you in spirit, too." I had taken that as merely a kind thought. But then it happens. I'm nearly in tears as I experience hundreds of souls thronging the room—God's saints and angels, our missing friends and relations. I can identify some of them—two ladies whose husbands are here, and two of my spiritual brothers. Jim later tells me with wet eyes that he experiences this too, these hundreds of souls thronging in spirit to bless us. He identifies the same two ladies, plus his father, who passed away a week and a half before this wedding. All the spirits blessing us are still there as we bow in unison at the end of the second round.

The third round is much like the second for us. But the words are different. The minister comments on the rejuvenation inherent in the third round. The Granthi reads the third pauri in Gurmukhi, and Paul reads the translation.

In the third round, the heart fills with Divine Love, O Beloved.

By good fortune, I have met God in the Company of the Saints, O Beloved.

I have found the Immaculate God, singing God's Praises and reciting God's Word.

By good fortune, the humble Saints attain God and tell the unspoken story.

Within the heart resounds the Name of God, God, God.

Meditating on God, the great destiny inscribed on the forehead manifests.

Servant Nanak proclaims that in the third round, the Love of God awakens in the heart. [10]

The musicians play the third pauri as we go through the same motions—bowing in unison before and after our clockwise single file walk—and again experience hundreds of souls blessing us.

It's time for the fourth round. The air becomes electric. This is what we're all waiting for. The minister talks about merging into Infinity in the fourth round. The Granthi reads the fourth and final pauri of the Lavaan. Jaime reads the translation.

> *In the fourth round, I have effortlessly found God in my heart, O Beloved.*
> *Turning to the Guru, I have met God effortlessly,*
> *And my body and mind are filled with sweet delight, O Beloved.*
> *God is sweet to me. I am pleasing to God day and night.*
> *I overflow with God's love.*
> *I have obtained my Lord Master, the fruit of my heart's desire.*
> *God's Name resounds within and around me.*
> *God merges with His holy bride, whose heart blossoms with the Holy Name.*
> *Servant Nanak proclaims that in this fourth round, we have obtained the Immortal Lord.* [11]

As the musicians start the music for the fourth round, as we bow, there is an electric surge of energy. The overwhelming awe of the last two rounds falls away. I can feel joy dancing like a band of festive angels. We rise and take our walk. We rise to be showered with flowers.

As we were making the third round, I could see some of the women and girls in the sangat passing out handfuls of flower petals to everyone, except the Granthi, the musicians, and of course, me and Jim. These petals come from a kind neighbor who let me pick a bucketful of roses and peonies the day before the wedding. We're about to get showered with those petals. As we pass Paul and Jaime, who are sitting next to the musicians, I can see Paul ask if it's okay to throw the flowers now. Yes! He does. So do other on-stage family members. As we begin the home stretch of our final walk in front of the Guru, the entire sangat is on their feet, pelting us with petals. What a joyous gift! What a blooming blessing!

As the Lavaan ends, while the petals are still flying, the musicians sing *Vee-aaho Hoaa Mayray Baabulaa*, the Shabad that concludes the Anand Karaj. Here's the translation:

My marriage is performed, O my father!
Through the Guru's Teachings, I have obtained God.
The darkness of ignorance is banished,
For the Guru has blazed the light of divine knowledge.
The knowledge bestowed by the Guru radiates light and dispels darkness.
I have found God's priceless jewel.
The disease of ego has left me, and my pain is gone.
By the Guru's Teachings, my Self has eaten up myself.
I receive my spouse, the Lord of Immortal Form
Who never dies and never goes away.
My marriage is performed, O my father!
By the Guru's Teachings, I have obtained God. [12]

By Sikh standards, we are now married in spirit whether a minister is officiating or not. With our Sikh wedding, our union is now cemented in our one soul. But even so, after the sangat settles back down, the minister makes the usual pronouncement.

It's fortunate that grapes are in season, because they are the only fruit we both like. We've got a whole bowl of them. We each pick up one grape and simultaneously feed each other. This is the first act of every Western Sikh marriage—feeding each other a piece of fruit simultaneously in acknowledgement that each person will put the other first.

Since Jim and I were already legally married, we do not exchange rings. If we were going to exchange rings, this would be the place in the service to do so—after sharing fruit. Punjabi couples, however, exchange rings the day before the actual wedding as part of their much lengthier festivities.

228

The service ends like any Sikh Gurdwara service with the Song of the Khalsa, *Anand Sahib*, Ardas and Hukam.

While *Gurprashaad* is distributed during *Sukhasan* (the ceremony of closing the *Siri Guru Granth Sahib*), Jim and I distribute the rest of the grapes to everyone present. Usually, there is only enough fruit to distribute to family and a few friends. So the caterer's assistant looks overcome with emotion when I hand him two grapes. But this is what it's all about: we gave to each other so we can give to everyone. We joined our souls so that we can know the One Soul we all share. We're all family. Let us sit and eat together. Let us eat cake!

Jim and I originally had a "love match," which means we picked each other, the way most people in Europe and the Americas do. Sikhs certainly allow such matches. One Punjabi lady told me that her parents told her they would make the arrangements if there was someone she fancied.

But notice that the parents would make the arrangements. A high percentage of all Sikh marriages are arranged, usually by parents or other relatives. One mother explained that this practice should really be called an "assisted marriage," rather than an arranged marriage, because nowadays the prospective couple generally get together once or twice to determine if they like each other.

In any event, whether it's a love match or an arranged one, the couple will only marry after receiving the blessing of their parents or guardians. (Before his passing, the Siri Singh Sahib acted as a surrogate parent for nearly all his students—arranging and blessing marriages and engagements.)

This is not as backward a practice as Western sensibility makes it out to be. Arranged marriages are often preferable to the Western variety. Here are some reasons:

"Love is blind," which means a lovesick couple may not see the faults in each other. Parents can generally do a better job of weeding out the insane, the violent, and the addicted than their children can. One Punjabi lady friend told me how her father kept his eyes on the man he planned for her to marry—visiting the prospective son-in-law occasionally to be sure he had no bad habits. Her marriage was very happy. So while arranged marriages may not be perfect, they often provide fewer nasty surprises.

People in arranged marriages rarely deal with in-laws from hell. The in-laws picked them, after all. One lady was rhapsodizing so enthusiastically over the beautiful, sweet and devout bride she and her husband had found for their (very willing!) son that I told her, "You're more in love than your son is!"

Marriages based on sexual attraction alone do wither in time as hormones head south in the winter of our lives. But marriages based on the mutual respect, companionship, family, and shared values that arranged marriages often provide tend to endure. Such marriages often bear the sweetest fruit as time goes by. Love matches can certainly provide this...but only if the love is real.

People who are raised knowing their marriages will be arranged exude a confidence that people panicking to find a spouse never attain. I remember one unengaged young man who told me with perfect confidence that he would marry a Punjabi girl when his job settled down. Such people rarely develop the habit of flirting, because there's simply no need to.

There's one other reason arranged marriages may work where Western-style marriages may fail. Most of us know people who seem constitutionally unable to find a good mate for themselves. If you put such a person in a room with twenty possible suitors, all but one of whom would be an excellent spouse, such a person would invariably pick the one person in the whole room who wouldn't be good for them. But such people can be happily married...if the marriage is carefully arranged.

My friends Ravi Singh and Dya Kaur Khalsa are a case in

point. Today they are one of the happiest, most united couples it is my personal privilege to know. But they started out with an extravagant dislike for each other.

They have a great deal in common. They were born approximately six months apart—Ravi Singh in September of 1946 and Dya Kaur in April of 1947. Both became Sikhs in 1974. Both endured seven years of misery in marriages that ended in divorce before they became Sikhs. Both lived in *3HO ashrams* and worked for Sikh-run businesses for more than a decade before they married each other. Both were (and are) regular attendees of both group *Sadhana* and Gurdwara. And both have *Kuja Dosha Mars*.

Kuja Dosha Mars is an afflicted position of Mars in *Vedic astrology* that disrupts smooth and happy relationships. (Vedic astrology isn't strictly speaking a Sikh thing, but it's often used by Sikhs, especially for determining marital compatibility.) Left to their own devices, people with this position will always pair up with a shark—-someone who will abuse them. But if matched correctly, two people with equally balanced Kuja Dosha Mars afflictions make excellent spouses for each other. The afflictions in this case cancel each other out. Unfortunately, people with this affliction will not pick each other, tending instead to ignore the one person divinely intended for their happiness.

Dya Kaur and Ravi Singh both have this configuration. And sure enough, they didn't like each other when they met in Tucson in the mid-1970s. Dya Kaur had just arrived in Tucson to work for the 3HO Alcohol and Drug Rehab Program. Ravi Singh was just leaving Tucson to head for El Paso, where he would drive the first Golden Temple Health Foods truck. From time to time, he'd drive the truck on business into Tucson, where he and Dya Kaur would "dramatically ignore each other."

By 1982, Dya Kaur was living in Los Angeles and had attended Khalsa Women's Training Camp (KWTC) for many years. There, Yogi Bhajan had shared with the women how to communicate, how to raise their children, how to deal with men, and how to be strong and happy as women in strong and happy households. So in 1982, Dya Kaur wrote to the Siri Singh Sahib and told him she had learned enough from him at KWTC that she might be capable of a good marriage now, and asked him to find a husband for her. His reply simply said, "Guru Ram Das has heard your prayer, and will take care of it." She heard no more on the subject for two years.

In the interim, Yogi Bhajan started teaching Kundalini Yoga classes at a lovely park in Los Angeles, which Dya Kaur would attend before work. Ravi Singh would be there too, having returned to Los Angeles (where he had worked before) after Dya Kaur wrote her letter. They would both sit up front at the feet of the Master and studiously ignore each other.

And then health problems drove Dya Kaur to seek medical advice. A medical doctor gave her medication for low thyroid and suggested she also see a counselor. The counselor Dya Kaur went to see was Dr. Bibiji Inderjit Kaur, the Siri Singh Sahib's wife, a licensed therapist, who said, "You need to be married." Dya Kaur told her about the letters. Bibiji replied that she would talk to the Siri Singh Sahib about it.

Soon thereafter, Dya Kaur was at a business luncheon with the Siri Singh Sahib. The man sitting next to the Siri Singh Sahib got up and said he had a dentist appointment. So Dya Kaur quietly moved into the vacated chair in order to hear the Siri Singh Sahib better. As the meeting ended, the Siri Singh Sahib turned to Dya Kaur and said "O, by the way, I have a husband for you." Without saying who the man was, the Siri Singh Sahib got up and left.

This cliffhanger left Dya Kaur wildly unhappy. Deciding she needed to talk to someone, she suggested to a lady friend that they have lunch together. So four days after the Siri Singh Sahib had mentioned this prospective husband, the two ladies went to lunch at a hole-in-the-wall restaurant with good vegetarian food. And that's where they were when the pay phone began to ring and ring and ring. Someone picked it up and said, "Is Dya Kaur here? The Siri Singh Sahib is calling her from New Mexico!"

He told her, "My dear Daughter, I'd like you to go over and talk to Ravi Singh." She knew what he was really saying.

"But sir! he doesn't like me!"

In a light, funny voice, he said, "Don't worry, he's my good Son, just go talk to him."

So after work, she went. She arrived on the doorstep of the ashram Ravi Singh was living in around 6pm. And she waited about four hours.

Ravi Singh had a tough landscaping job in those days and got home tired and dirty around 10pm to discover Dya Kaur waiting for him. He knew why she was there. No one had told him, but he knew. He also knew that matchmakers in India research numerous aspects of the histories of the prospective couple (their family histories, financial histories, educational histories, and so on). So faced with this lady on his doorstep, Ravi Singh decided they would do things by the book. They would sit down and discuss these aspects of their histories with each other—a process that was to take them about a month.

He also told Dya Kaur to call him when she was ready to leave for group Sadhana so he could walk with her. She was impressed by this considerateness as walking several blocks alone—as she had been doing—in Los Angeles around 4am takes some courage.

For about a month they would walk together to group Sadhana. They would also sit on the front steps of Guru Harkrishan Ashram, where Dya Kaur was living, and work on their histories. Dya Kaur wasn't thrilled by the impersonal nature of this process. She didn't like Ravi Singh's ugly old chartreuse Ford Pinto either. Her antagonism and her unhappiness were both firmly in place.

But Ravi Singh was at peace with the situation. At one point, the Siri Singh Sahib asked them if they were engaged yet, and

Ravi Singh said, "I am, but she's not!"

Then a 3HO healer from Mexico arrived to give some workshops in Los Angeles. Dya Kaur went to him for a treatment. As the healer was balancing her, she looked at her *Third Eye* (the point centered between the eyes and a bit above them) and saw a beautiful, radiant male face. Ravi Singh! She exclaimed, "O my God, the Siri Singh Sahib's right! He's in my Third Eye!" (The "He" in Dya Kaur's Third Eye was Ravi Singh...not the Siri Singh Sahib! The presence of a man in a woman's Third Eye indicates a deep, intimate soul connection. The Third Eye is also known as the *Brow Point*.) Her antagonism vanished.

Ravi Singh was shocked when Dya Kaur invited him in for tea that October evening. She had never done any such thing before. But the moment she realized he really was the man for her everything changed. They got along just fine and decided that evening to get married at Summer Solstice in New Mexico the following June.

But the Siri Singh Sahib had other ideas. As a thank you for bringing them together, Ravi Singh and Dya Kaur gave the Siri Singh Sahib eleven gold and silver coins. After opening the package, the Siri Singh Sahib told Dya Kaur to open her hands. Then he poured the coins into her palms and counted them. "On the eleventh day from now you get married," he proclaimed.

Typically, Sikh engagements are short, although not usually *this* short. While eleven days is certainly shorter than average, I've talked to two Sikh men who married the day after their engagements. I had the privilege of attending a wedding held less than a week after the Siri Singh Sahib told the couple they couldn't get engaged, but they could get married. But some engagements periods last much longer. Yogi Bhajan himself was engaged for two years before getting married. Two months, however, is about standard.

Eleven days later was a Friday, sometimes known as Love

Day—perfect for what was unfolding. Ravi Singh and Dya Kaur married on November 9, 1984, in the morning immediately after Sadhana, early enough for everyone in the sangat to attend and still have time to get to work. They had no time before the big day to get new clothes, so they made do. Ravi Singh wore his best go-to-Gurdwara *kurta*. Dya Kaur's "something borrowed" was the wedding dress loaned by the friend who was present for the historic phone call. On the other hand, at Dya Kaur's request, Ravi Singh did get new glasses to replace the heavy, dark, broken pair he had.

The Siri Singh Sahib made it plain that the only honeymoon they could have would be sitting outdoors and eating honey by the light of the moon. Ravi Singh planned to move into Guru Harkrishan Ashram with Dya Kaur after the wedding. So, they paid for everyone in that ashram to "go on the honeymoon" for them—leaving them alone in the ashram for a weekend.

Now they say they've been "honeymooners for years." With marriage, Dya Kaur's medical problems and unhappiness evaporated like ice in July. Both of them also dropped the worst of their personality quirks. Dya Kaur's domineering stance transformed into wifely solicitousness. Ravi Singh's pickiness transformed into kind attention to detail. As the Siri Singh Sahib later commented, "It's a miracle that two such perfect idiots could make one such perfect couple!"

Chapter 18

Death: Going Home to God

Death, which the world dreads, gives joy to my mind.
By death alone, one is blessed with perfect supreme bliss.
Kabir [1]

Har Darshan Kaur Khalsa received the call in the late afternoon of Wednesday, January 22, 1997. Her friend, Amrit Kaur Khalsa, was dying of lymphoma, and the doctors were discontinuing treatment. If Har Darshan wished to see her friend one last time, she would have to make the trip from Chapel Hill, North Carolina, to Knoxville, Tennessee, quickly.

About three weeks previous, Har Darshan had visited the hospitalized Amrit Kaur. Creating a sacred space in Amrit Kaur's hospital room were a photo of the Golden Temple and Singh Kaur's *Mool Mantra* tape playing non-stop. Someone from the *sangat* (congregation) was always present. Due to Amrit Kaur's lymphoma, Har Darshan and all other visitors had to wear masks before entering the room. And getting food for a vegetarian who could only eat cooked food was difficult at best. Nonetheless, although Amrit Kaur was putting her affairs in order as best she could from a hospital bed, there was still hope.

Har Darshan meditated after the phone call and knew she had to make this trip. So, the next day, January 23, Har Darshan drove six hours, wending her way through the winter Appalachians. She arrived in Knoxville around 2:30 pm and had about half an hour in the hospital room with Amrit Kaur before Amrit Kaur's sister arrived around 3 pm from Oklahoma. Har Darshan and the other Sikhs stepped out into the hallway to allow the sisters some private time with each other.

So, Har Darshan was out in the hallway with members of the Knoxville sangat when she suddenly knew intuitively that Amrit Kaur had passed on. A few minutes later they received the official word that Amrit Kaur had crossed the finish line at 3:18 pm. True to character, Amrit Kaur had waited for both her sister and her friend to arrive before passing away. Also true to character, Amrit Kaur had died a *keshdari* Sikh (a Sikh with all hair intact). Ten days before dying, she had begun a course of chemotherapy that her doctor had predicted would cause all her hair to fall out in ten days. She died on the tenth day with all hair intact instead.

Sikhs believe our lives are measured in breaths—not in minutes or days. When Amrit Kaur breathed her last required breath, she watched the complete story of her life unfold for three seconds and passed judgment on it. Our lives really do flash before our eyes at the moment of death. Since we have reason to believe that Amrit Kaur lived from her soul, she probably was able to view even the worst life episodes without flinching.

According to Yogi Bhajan's account of his own near-death experience, Amrit Kaur would then have been offered the choice between a warm, dark, secure place and a cold, bright, challenging path.[2] Choosing the warm, dark, secure place is choosing to return to the womb and to reincarnate for yet another lifetime. Choosing the cold, bright, challenging path is choosing to return Home to God.

Some Sikhs may feel comforted by the idea that they will have further lifetimes with loved ones. But that's not what the *Siri Guru Granth Sahib* advocates. It speaks often of "the fire of the womb" and of "the pain of births and deaths." Here's a sample of what it says about reincarnation from the *Bani* (Sikh prayer) *Sukhmani Sahib*:

Sometimes, one attains the Company of the Holy...

> *One's light blends with the Light.*
> *Then the coming and going of reincarnation end,*
> *And one obtains eternal peace.* ³

Perhaps a God-conscious Sikh might reincarnate for some God-given purpose. But while Sikhs don't believe in Heaven and Hell as real afterlife places, a Sikh who focuses on the Guru's words will generally consider choosing another incarnation as tantamount to choosing hell and choosing to return to God as tantamount to choosing heaven.

Upon receiving the official word of death, all the Sikhs in the corridor, plus a few of Amrit Kaur's non-Sikh friends, trooped back into Amrit Kaur's room. There, they followed Sikh custom and recited *Japji Sahib* (the morning Bani) and *Kirtan Sohila* (the bedtime Bani). Then they chanted *Akaal* (literally "timeless" or "deathless") five times.

Sikhs focus on the Name of God throughout life in order to have a conscious death. Especially, we like to be chanting *Waheguru* or reciting Japji Sahib when we die. A moribund human can be in a coma and still be chanting *Waheguru* inwardly at the moment of death, because the soul isn't bound by the limitations of mind and body. But if a person has not chanted *Waheguru* or any of the other of God's Names while crossing the finish line, the survivors can chant for them. This is why we chant *Akaal*—to aid the soul on its way home to a safe reunion with God.

Chanting *Akaal* reminds the soul that it is eternal and immortal, liberates it from the earth's gravitational pull, and frees it to return to God. There's a story told here in the Pacific Northwest of a man with some vicious habits who was related to a lady in the Sikh community in Eugene, Oregon. He died, and the lady and her husband chanted *Akaal* for him. Later, she mentioned his death to Yogi Bhajan and asked, "I wonder what so-and-so is going to come back as?" Yogi Bhajan replied, "What do you mean, 'What is he coming back as?' You chanted *Akaal* for him, didn't you?" The lady responded, "Well, you know, he did such-and-such and such-and-such. So I was wondering what kind of life form he would come back as." Then Yogi Bhajan explained, "He's not coming back. He may have done everything wrong. But he did one thing right: he had friends who chant the *Naam* for him." (You can find information on this technique in the sidebar.)

How to Chant *Akaal* for the Dead[5]

Chant *Akaal* (it's pronounced "uh CALL") out loud extending the second syllable. Chant it at least 5 times. Eleven to thirty-one minutes are recommended. There is no special mudra and no special posture. It is best to start chanting within 72 hours of clinical death. The optimum situation is for 5 or more people to chant Akaal for 31 minutes for 17 days in a row starting with the day of death. But even one person chanting only one time will have an impact.

Chanting *Akaal* can be rescue work, as it was in the case of the Sikh lady's relative. In Amrit Kaur's case, it was more the kindness of friends—a bon voyage from the pier of life as the soul's ship sails off into the sunset.

Sikhs don't believe in a vindictive and punitive God. We don't believe in Heaven and Hell either, except as states of mind. In the *Siri Guru Granth Sahib*, the Hindu/Sufi saint *Kabir* says, *What is Hell and what is Heaven? The Saints reject both of them.*[4] We do believe in *reincarnation*—a soul moving through many lifetimes before it returns Home to God. Indeed, the *Siri Guru Granth Sahib* tells us that most souls go through 8.4 million lifetimes (i.e. as insects, little sea creatures with ridiculously long scientific names, birds, mammals and other creatures) before achieving the blessing of a human birth. We also believe that the cycle of reincarnation ends in God's most loving embrace...if the soul is released by a conscious death.

If the *Hukam* (literally "Command"—the message from the Guru) that the Knoxville sangat received the morning following Amrit Kaur's death is any indication, Amrit Kaur was indeed reuniting with God. Here's the translation:

The Creator of all is One.
The One Whose Name is Truth
Is realized by True Guru's Grace.
Friends have come into my home.
The True One has brought about this union.
When it pleased God's Mind, I spontaneously met them.
By meeting the chosen ones of God, I found peace.
I have obtained the very thing my mind desired.
By meeting the Holy in devotion, my mind remains pleased day and
*   night.*
Beauteous are my home and mansion.
The unstruck melody of five sounds resounds as loved friends come
*   into my home.*
Come, my dear friends. Sing songs of joy, O sister friends.
Sing the true songs of joy.
So shall you win God's favor
And your paeans of praise shall be sung through the four ages.
My Spouse has come into my home.
The place is adorned, and by the blessing of the holy word, my affairs
*   are adjusted.*
By applying the salve of the great elixir of enlightenment to my eyes,
I have seen God's form in the three worlds.
Meet me, my sister friends, and sing with zest the songs of rejoicing
For my Beloved Spouse has come into my home.

My mind and body are dewy with Nectar,
And within me is the jewel of God's Love.
In my mind is the invaluable gem.
I contemplate the Supreme Essence.
All beings are beggars.
You are the Bestower of boons.
You give to all people.
You are the All Knowing, Enlightened Controller of the inner Self.
You Yourself have created the world.
Listen, my sister friend, the Charmer has charmed my heart.
My body and mind are drenched in Nectar.
O God, the All-Pervading Self of the world,
This world is Your true play.
True is Your play, O Inaccessible and Infinite God.
Who except You can make me understand this?
There are many adepts, strivers and wise ones.
But without Your Grace, who can call himself anything?
By Guru's Grace, one steps out of the wild dance of birth and death.
By Guru's Grace, the mind gains ease.
Nanak says, "Our demerits are burnt by the Holy Word.
Becoming virtuous, we attain to God. [6]

This Hukam sustained Har Darshan and her friends throughout the day, especially as they prepared Amrit Kaur's corpse for cremation. Even with lifeless corpses, Sikhs maintain the privacy of the deceased. Where possible, five people who are the same gender as the deceased prepare a Sikh corpse for cremation. So five Sikh ladies, including Har Darshan, performed this final act of love for Amrit Kaur.

Har Darshan described the process of preparing Amrit Kaur's corpse as "very meditative and very beautiful." First, with the help of buckets provided by the funeral home, the ladies bathed the corpse with water. They used natural sponges and water from the Golden Temple (*Hari Mander Sahib*) in *Amritsar*—both of which were a nice touch, but optional. Maintaining Amrit Kaur's modesty, the five ladies uncovered only one part of Amrit Kaur's dead body at a time. Then, the five ladies bathed Amrit Kaur's corpse with homemade yogurt made by a sangat member the night before. This yogurt the ladies enhanced with sandalwood oil—another optional, but nice touch. Here again, they maintained the privacy of Amrit Kaur's dead body by uncovering only one part at a time. They did not wipe off the yogurt. Leaving yogurt on a dead body helps slow the process of decay somewhat. This is helpful as Sikhs don't embalm or pretty up their dead. Har Darshan commented that it was comforting feeling the coldness of Amrit Kaur's stiff body. It assured the five ladies that the body they were preparing for cremation was indeed an unoccupied shell.

Then the five ladies dressed Amrit Kaur's dead body for her reunion with the Beloved. Sikhs prefer, if possible, to use brand new *Bana* (Sikh garb) to dress a corpse for its return Home. Fortunately, one of the Sikh sisters preparing Amrit Kaur's body had just been to India and was able to provide beautiful new Bana for the occasion. According to Har Darshan, dressing a stiff corpse is very difficult. It took all five women to do it. (Har Darshan personally recommends making death Bana ahead of time with extra-wide Velcro closures.) As with all devout deceased Sikhs, Amrit Kaur's death Bana included all five "k"s— *kesh, kacheras, kangha, kara, kirpan.* One of the five women combed out Amrit Kaur's hair, put it in a *Rishi knot* and wrapped a new turban around Amrit Kaur's lifeless head.

Once a dead Sikh is bathed in yogurt, dressed in new Bana and all five "k"s, the corpse is usually wrapped in a rose-water-scented white sheet. But instead of a sheet, the five spiritual sisters of Amrit Kaur who prepared her body for cremation used five white rose-water-scented *dupatas* (long, wide, fringeless and usually opaque shawls). The ladies liked the grace of this extra refinement.

Har Darshan was in such an altered state during this process that she has no idea how much time elapsed. Throughout the entire procedure, the five Sikh ladies chanted *Mool Mantra* (the opening lines of Japji Sahib). Sometimes one or more of them would need to stop and cry for a bit, but the whole process was ultimately very elevating and sustaining.

The next day they held the memorial service. Sikh memorial services vary widely. Some are formal, and some are informal. Some are held in funeral homes. Some are held in a Gurdwara, or in a large hall turned into a Gurdwara for the occasion. Some are held just before cremation with the mortal remains present in an open or closed casket. Some are held seventeen days or even more after a death, in which case the corpse will not be present at all...except, perhaps, as ashes. The contents of the service will vary as well. I attended a memorial service for a drowned ten-year-old girl consisting primarily of a talk in Punjabi and the recitation of Japji Sahib and *Sukhmani Sahib*.

Amrit Kaur's memorial service was quite different. That lovingly prepared corpse was in a closed wood cremation casket in the funeral home. A framed photo of a happy and beautiful Amrit Kaur smiled on the assembled. As few Sikhs lived in Knoxville in those days (the sangat has grown exponentially since then), most of the people present were non-Sikhs. So the sangat sang lots of contemporary Sikh songs in English.

Ordinarily, a sangat will serve *Gurprashaad* containing an added mix of poppy, cardamom, sesame, sunflower and pumpkin seeds after a memorial service. (See sidebar for the recipe.) Besides the regenerative symbolism of seeds, this combination also sustains the bodies of mourners who partake of them. It wasn't practical to make Gurprashaad, however, so the Knoxville sangat improvised. Amrit Kaur had been well loved, and a bakery she patronized provided free cookies, which the sangat distributed to everyone as a sort of "cookie prashaad."

Recipe for Five Seed Gurprashaad

To a completed batch of Gurprashaad (see recipe in Chapter 6), add a mixture of poppy, cardamom, sesame, sunflower and pumpkin seeds—no less than 1/4 part seeds and no more than 1 part seeds to any completed batch of Gurprashaad.

At the end of the service, everyone threw flower petals on Amrit Kaur's casket as they would have thrown them on her living form if she were getting married—which in a sense, she was. After the service, many people commented on how moving the whole experience was. Amrit Kaur's cattle-ranching sister stated that she had never really understood what Amrit Kaur had seen in Sikhism before, but now she (the sister) understood.

Right after the memorial service was the cremation. Although organ donation is allowed, Sikhs are always, always, always cremated after death. Not only does this hygienic custom save precious land for the living, but it also is good for the soul. It's important for the soul's evolution that it not attach to the flesh and blood vehicle that carries it around during any given life. Those unfortunate souls that attach to the earthly vessel often become ghosts and do not pass beyond the Earth's electromagnetic field after death. Cremating dead bodies and scattering the ashes help prevent such a tragedy.

After Amrit Kaur's memorial service, all the Sikhs—plus Amrit Kaur's biological sister and a few of her non-Sikh friends—stayed for the cremation ceremony, which, in line with Sikh practice, began and ended with an *Ardas*. In between, they chanted over the howling of the flames, alternately reciting Japji Sahib and Kirtan Sohila, first in *Gurmukhi* and then in English, for the entire two hours or so it took for the flames to do their job. All that was left afterwards were some ashes, a few bones that were later ground up, and Amrit Kaur's *kara*—her steel bangle. As Har Darshan said, "It sinks in how transitory this life is!"

This wasn't the complete end, however. They also held an especially moving Gurdwara worship service the next day, which was a Sunday. Also, usually after a death, a sangat or Sikh family will hold an *Akhand Path* or *Sahaj Path* for the dead. (See the *Path* chapter for more information.) Listening to the Guru's word can be extraordinarily healing and comforting for the survivors. Like Har Darshan, many of the Sikhs attending Amrit Kaur's rite of passage lived out of area and had to return home right away, so there weren't enough people to complete an Akhand Path in a timely fashion. So, the Knoxville sangat asked the sangat in Espanola (which was, and still is, the largest *3HO* sangat in the USA) to hold their next Akhand Path in Amrit Kaur's honor.

Following a death, Sikhs often read Sukhmani Sahib and chant *Akaal* for 17 days because that's how long it generally takes for the soul to cross the Earth's electro-magnetic field. Some families continue reading Sukhmani Sahib for months or even years as this Bani is particularly helpful for comforting the bereaved. Because Sukhmani Sahib is such a very long Bani, Har Darshan and her friends divvied it up and each recited a section of Sukhmani Sahib at a synchronized time of the day for 18 days. They also chanted *Akaal* for Amrit Kaur for 17 days.

Today Har Darshan speaks with upwelling gratitude of the sacredness of the Sikh approach to death. "I am just so grateful for the technology we have," she says. Many of us feel the same way.

Ultimately, all the technology of the Sikh path is designed for the day of death. In fact, the *Rehit Maryada* (the Sikh code of conduct) literally means "lifestyle for the remembrance of death." We live rich and full lives in the world, so there is little chance that in the final hour we will regret an unlived life. And we give service (*Seva*) to all, so there's little chance of regrets for deeds undone.

But there's more to it than that. You many recall back in the Bani chapter the elderly man who was reciting his *Banis* in preparation for his death. Reading Banis—especially Japji Sahib, Kirtan Sohila and Sukhmani Sahib—is one of the ways a Sikh prepares throughout life for the inevitable end.

Then there's *Sadhana* (spiritual practice). For Sikh and non-Sikh Kundalini Yoga practitioners, Sadhana includes *Sat Siree, Siree Akaal*, a *mantra* specifically designed to help us prepare for the day of death. (See the Sadhana Chapter for more information on this mantra.) But individuals may practice other—or extra—Sadhanas. One lady found that the mantra *Ang Sang Waa Hay Guroo* helped her face her approaching early death. (A meditation with this mantra is in the sidebar.)

Kundalini Yoga
Ang Sang Waa Hay Guroo Meditation [7]

Practicing this meditation is good for preventing and releasing anxiety and the hysteria that anxiety can produce. It also is good for clarity of mind and strengthens the *Pranic Body*, which means that it enhances our life force energy.

Ang Sang Waa Hay Guroo (which rhymes with "Young Sung") means "the ecstasy of God is in all my limbs." This mantra reminds us that the power of God is within us, that it's not an outside thing.

How To Do It
Tune in if you have not already done so. (See sidebar in the chapter on Yogi Bhajan.) Pronunciation guide is in

---

Appendix B.

Focus at the brow point. Inhale slowly as you mentally chant *Ang Sang Waa Hay Guroo* once. Hold the breath and mentally chant *Ang Sang Waa Hay Guroo* 4 times. Exhale thoroughly as you mentally chant *Ang Sang Waa Hay Guroo* once. No hand position and no sitting position were specified, but keep your back straight and  your chin tucked in enough that your neck is in line with your spine. (I am demonstrating this meditation in a chair, but you may also sit in any comfortable cross-legged position.) Continue for 11-31 minutes.

Most importantly, devout Sikhs focus on God's Name with every breath as much as possible. Doing so tunes us in to God's every word. So when God calls us Home from the playground of life, it's easy enough to come running joyously Home.

Many years before he died, Yogi Bhajan commissioned and had erected a tombstone for himself, which reads:

Born: Zero
Died At One.

And that's what Sikh spiritual practice does: it takes those who are nothing and transforms them so that death may reunite them with the One. [8]

Chapter 19

A Universal Path

See brotherhood with all as the highest order of yoga,
And conquest of the mind as conquest of the world.
Guru Nanak [1]

In October of 1675 as the rainy season ended, *Guru Teg Bahadur* and a few of his followers camped in a garden outside *Agra*. Calling to the shepherd boy who was tending sheep and goats nearby, Guru Teg Bahadur drew a diamond-studded gold ring from his finger and gave it to the boy, requesting him to go to town, purchase a few sweets and bring them back. He also gave the boy an exquisite and costly shawl to carry the sweets in. Guru Teg Bahadur was on his conscious way to the most unusual martyrdom the world has ever witnessed.

Earlier that year, a group of devout and learned Hindus from Kashmir had approached Guru Teg Bahadur with a terrible problem. Due to persecution from *Aurangzeb*, the bloodthirsty and bigoted *Mughal* Emperor, Hindus in Kashmir were facing wholesale conversion to Islam or wholesale slaughter. They wanted neither. The Emperor's Viceroy in Kashmir had given them six months to make up their minds. As this grace period came to an end, divine guidance sent them to Guru Teg Bahadur with a plea to save them.

As Guru Teg Bahadur sadly pondered the best course to take in this grave situation, his son *Gobind Rai*, who was then 9 years old, entered the room and inquired, "Father dear, you are so sad and silent today. What can be the matter?"

Guru Teg Bahadur explained the situation to Gobind Rai and said, "Some great and brave soul is needed to offer his life."

Gobind Rai pointed out, "Who is greater and braver than you?" This cheered Guru Teg Bahadur greatly, for he now knew that his son was ready to receive the mantle of the Guruship, young though he was. With the issue of the Guruship settled, Guru Teg Bahadur could offer himself as a sacrifice for the Kashmir Hindus.

So, Guru Teg Bahadur told the Kashmir delegation to go en mass to Delhi and tell the Emperor, "Guru Teg Bahadur, the Ninth Sikh Guru, sits on the throne of the great *Guru Nanak*, the protector of faith and religion. First make him a Muslim. Then all people, including ourselves, will adopt Islam of our own accord."

When the delegation gave its message, the Emperor was delighted with the news. All he had to do was convert one man to convert a whole nation. What a bonanza! So, he sent two officers to summon Guru Teg Bahadur. When the officers arrived at the Guru's domicile in *Anandpur*, Guru Teg Bahadur received them graciously. He replied to the summons with a written promise that he would come to Delhi after the rainy season ended.

Before the rainy season ended, Guru Teg Bahadur ordained his son Gobind Rai as the Tenth Sikh Guru. (Guru Gobind Rai was later to become *Guru Gobind Singh*, as we saw in the chapter on the Amrit Ceremony.) Then, taking a few trusted Sikhs with him, Guru Teg Bahadur began his slow journey to Delhi, stopping at various towns and blessing his Sikhs along the way. When Aurangzeb sent officers to Anandpur to seize the Guru, they found him gone.

So, Guru Teg Bahadur knew what was coming to him when he handed the shepherd boy that costly ring and shawl. The shepherd boy honestly took the ring and shawl to a confectioner's shop, where the confectioner was astonished to see a lowly urchin with such valuable items. He assumed the worst and hauled the lad off to the nearest police. Under examination, the shepherd boy protested his innocence and told the full story of the noble man and his companions in the garden just outside Agra. Strange as the story was, the police went to investigate. Sure enough, there the men were. Guru Teg Bahadur answered all questions candidly. Then he and his companions were arrested and taken to Delhi.

When they arrived in the Emperor's presence, Aurangzeb fulminated against Hinduism and anyone who would tolerate such "superstitious" faiths. Then he offered Guru Teg Bahadur and his Sikh companions numerous enticing material rewards if they would accept Islam. As you can guess, someone who could give up an extremely valuable diamond ring wasn't going to be tempted by anything so minor as a high ranking job. Guru Teg Bahadur further stated, "O Emperor, you and I and all people must walk in God's Will. If it were the Will of God that there should be only one religion, God would never have allowed Islam and Hinduism to exist at the same time."

Guru Teg Bahadur and his companions were then imprisoned and tortured. But no torture broke their spirits. Their tormentors tied one of Guru Teg Bahadur's companions—*Bhai Mati Das*-- between two logs, then sawed him in half lengthwise from head to crotch while Guru Teg Bahadur watched. What happened to the other companions varies from story to story, but whatever happened, Guru Teg Bahadur never flinched.

Eventually, Guru Teg Bahadur was given a choice: he could perform a miracle and save himself, or he could accept Islam, or he could die. At this, Guru Teg Bahadur wrote some words on a piece of paper. He requested that this paper be tied around his neck and explained that it was a charm to protect him from beheading. The executioner obliged. Shock! There was a mighty gasp from the assembled crowd when the executioner's sword severed Guru Teg Bahadur's neck. Then they examined the paper, which said, "I gave my head, but not my faith." This, then, was the miracle—that in an age of severe religious intolerance, one man would give his life and keep his own faith to save members of a faith not his own.

Not only can Sikhs claim the first saint to give his life for members of another religion, but also the first holy scripture in the world formally designed as an interfaith document. As we saw in the chapter on the Shabad Guru, *Guru Arjan Dev* chose to include Shabads by Muslim and Hindu saints in the *Siri Guru Granth Sahib* as well as Shabads by Sikh Gurus and their followers. He did this purposefully. At that time and place, Muslims were burning Hindu books, and Hindus deemed Muslim writings untouchable. It was a major departure from the prevailing prejudice to include writings of saints of both religions in a single document.

Furthermore, Sikh willingness to serve everyone of all faiths is legendary. *Seva Panthis*—those on the path of selfless service— are deeply respected in India. They are the descendants and followers of *Bhai Kanaiya,* one of Guru Gobind Singh's disciples. In 1705 while *Guru Gobind Singh* was reinforcing the defense of Anandpur Sahib, his followers brought word that Bhai Kanaiya had been seen giving water to the enemy wounded as well as to Sikh soldiers. So Guru Gobind Singh sent for Bhai Kanaiya and asked him about it. Bhai Kanaiya folded his hands and said, "Master, since I have come into your presence, I see God every-where. Amongst the wounded, I fail to distinguish between Sikhs and Hindus and Muslims." Guru Gobind Singh smiled, commended Bhai Kanaiya for his holiness, bade him continue to serve everyone irrespective of caste or creed, and even gave him medicinal ointments to enhance his work with the wounded. To this day, Sikhs serve people in this same spirit.

Sikh tolerance and appreciation of other faiths is not restricted to a few great saints. Respect for all faiths runs deep and strong in the psyches of all Sikhs I've met.

As an example, I remember the time I was helping set up for a *Gurdwara* service at the Portland State University campus ministries building. A couple of young Punjabi family men and I had completed our task and were waiting for the *kirtan* players to arrive when we heard the Chinese Christian group in the upstairs room strike up a hymn. I cheerfully suggested that we could just chant *Waheguru* to the tune of the hymn while we waited. One of the men looked up, his face filled with surprising light, and said, "They're doing the same thing we are, aren't they?" It wasn't a question.

Given the directives from Sikh history and given the depth of respect Sikhs feel for everything God made, including all religions, it's not surprising that Sikhs are in the forefront of today's interfaith worship movement. If anyone in Oregon can be called the matriarch of this movement, it's my dear friend and spiritual sister, Siri Kaur Khalsa Harris. Here's her story:

When Siri Kaur was a toddler in a playpen, she could hear babies crying, even when no other babies were present. Siri Kaur, who was born in October of 1941 in Eugene, Oregon, to a Yanktonia Dakota Sioux father and a Comanche mother, attributes this auditory experience in part to her sensitivity to the pain of children traumatized by World War II, even though she carried that experience with her long after the war ended. Her sensitivity to the pain of others was to become a gift to us all.

Buoyed by inward experiences of God's ever-present love, Siri Kaur managed to survive both polio and unspeakable horrors that would have killed or embittered most people. Then, on December 22, 1984—after violent and abusive men were out of her life and she was finally happily married—her youngest son was killed in a tragic accident at the age of 14. She was devastated. The inner voice that had sustained her through untold trauma began telling her, "Your son was a great yogi. Contact the Yogi." Repeatedly, insistently, she heard this message urging her to "Contact the Yogi." So her husband Bill Harris, a big, burly, black, Baha'i police sergeant with a heart as tender as spring foliage, began hunting immediately for "the Yogi" who could help his wife, and spoke with someone connected with Yoga West in Eugene on December 23. Since Yoga West and the Eugene Sikh *sangat* are like Siamese twins, Siri Kaur met Eugene's Sikh community as a result of this contact, read in an *Akhand Path* the following January, fell in love with the Shabad Guru, and has been on the Sikh path ever since.

A few months later she met "the Yogi" in person. To her surprise, Yogi Bhajan proved to be someone she had met in a vivid out-of-body experience some dozen years earlier. In that visionary experience, she and Yogi Bhajan had been walking together as associates in a magnificent garden with beautiful trees that were fruiting and flowering at the same time. All the people in this garden wore delightful smiles, as they worked with grace and cheerfully appreciated both their own jobs and the work of everyone else. This was the way things should be, she and Yogi Bhajan agreed. This was the design in the etheric realms for a glorious future on earth.

In the Summer of 1996, God granted her the blueprint for manifesting this vision. The *Siri Singh Sahib* had appointed Siri Kaur as a senator to the Eugene Sikh Community Administrative Council. As she pondered how to best serve the community in this capacity, she began to meditate. She experienced a Great Silence (the capital letters are hers), signaling the approach of a Great Presence. That loving Presence strongly requested that she "initiate a regular coming together of devotion of all faiths," especially for those in pain or in painful times to come. Siri Kaur, who is a soft-spoken, modest, somewhat shy lady with a speech impediment, was floored. Surely there were other people better suited to this task! Gentle laughter showered upon her. The gentle, laughing Presence told her to get some paper and write down the principles it was giving her. The Great and Loving Presence providing this inspiration told her, "This will be vital to the community and, with enough heart, the world."

After a lengthy and extended vision, during which Siri Kaur

wrote down the Divine Guidance, she attempted to implement it. On a lazy, warm August evening in 1996, she suggested to the Eugene Sikh Community Administrative Council a plan for implementing regular interfaith services, without telling anyone of the divine inspiration behind it. The Council was under-whelmed. No one was interested. That confused her. Why had she gotten such a clear vision if it was going to be rejected? And it also relieved her. She was off the hook.

And then came the 9-11 attacks. The days of complacency had ended. Again, Siri Kaur presented this idea to the Council, again without mentioning its Divine Source. By this time, Sikh Dharma International had sent a directive to all ministers urging them to begin this very thing—a series of regular interfaith services devoted to peace. Snatam Kaur Khalsa, a young minister, informed the Council of this directive, and the whole community mobilized behind it.

Siri Kaur and Snatam Kaur formally presented the proposal for a series of interfaith worship services at an interfaith meeting held at Eugene's First Christian Church right after the attacks. Though the steering community turned the proposal down, two members of the committee—a Baha'i and the pastor of First Christian Church—took it on as their personal project. The pastor offered First Christian Church as the location for these gatherings, thinking that they would last only a few months.

October 11, 2001, witnessed the first service, with 75 or more people in attendance. Today, some 250 to 300 people attend these services, which have been held on the eleventh of every month at the First Christian Church ever since, with new people flocking to the services all the time. Their September 11 services invariably draw a standing-room-only crowd of six to seven hundred. One of the local newspapers now hosts a regular column written by members of the Eugene interfaith community, and several communities in Oregon and elsewhere have been inspired to emulate the example set by the interfaith community in this moderately sized city.

Siri Kaur did eventually share the Divine Vision underlying her interfaith proposal. Today, the stated purpose of the Interfaith Prayer Services is "...to bring together people from different faith communities in the spirit of harmony and growing appreciation, and to nurture confidence on the universal power of love and unity for all." It's an interfaith vision. It's a Sikh vision.

Sikhs can claim the first saint to give his life for members of *another* religion. Sikhs can claim the first consciously designed interfaith scriptures in the world. Sikhs can claim a group of people serving the wounded on both sides of fields of battle more than a century and a half before the International Red Cross was founded. And Sikhs can claim visionaries who are building a more tolerant world in the face of our current world turmoil. Deep in the marrow of our faith we see God in All. As *Guru Nanak*, the First Sikh Guru, said when he was camping outside Mecca and was berated for falling asleep with the soles of his feet pointing in the direction the *Kaaba*, "Please point my feet where God is not."

Epilogue

Shall We Dance?

You should see us dancing at Summer Solstice in the Jemez Mountains of New Mexico! As the festivities and the days of meditation draw to a close, Sikhs and non-Sikhs join together in a big dance. One year as the dance began, I reached out my hands to the people on either side of me to begin a line dance. I'd done that before and always had, oh, a dozen or so people join the line. But this year was different. Within minutes the whole group was dancing in a huge, joyful circle. Within minutes we were all united.

This is the message I hope to leave you with. We can get along despite our differences. We can reach out our hands to each other. All of us can dance together in the circle of life. Sikhs have proclaimed this from the beginning. We will feed you, we will serve you, and we will give our lives for you regardless of our differences. In God we all dwell. Shall we enjoy the mansion of God's Love together? Shall we dance?

Appendix A

A Chronology of the Sikh Gurus

1469	*Nanak* is born in mid-April at *Talwandi* (now *Nankana Sahib*) 35 miles southwest of Lahore in what is now Pakistan. (But his birthday is now celebrated in November.)
1479	Amar Das is born in a village near what will become Amritsar.
1496	Nanak dives into the *Bein River* and emerges 3 days later enlightened. Becoming *Guru Nanak*, the First Sikh Guru, he undertakes a series of journeys.
1504	*Bhai Lehna* (later Guru Angad) is born on March 31.
1534	*Jetha* (later Ram Das) is born in October near Lahore.
1539	Guru Nanak's light merges in the Light (i.e. he passes away) after passing the Guruship to Bhai Lehna, who becomes *Guru Angad*, the Second Guru.
1552	Guru Angad passes the Guruship to Amar Das, who becomes Guru Amar Das, the Third Guru, on March 29. Guru Angad's light then merges in the Light.
1563	Arjan, the son of Ram Das and *Bibi Bhani* (the daughter of Guru Amar Das), is born in *Goindwal* in mid-April.
1574	Guru Amar Das turns the Guruship over to Ram Das, who becomes *Guru Ram Das*, the Fourth Guru. The light of Guru Amar Das then merges in the Light.
1577	Around this time, Guru Ram Das begins building the city of *Amritsar*.
1581	Guru Ram Das passes the Guruship to his son Arjan, who becomes *Guru Arjan Dev*, the Fifth Guru. The light of Guru Ram Das merges in the Light.
1588	Guru Arjan Dev begins construction on the *Hari Mandir Sahib* (now known as the Golden Temple).

1595	Hargobind, son of Guru Arjan Dev and his wife *Ganga*, is born in *Wadali*, a village outside Amritsar.
1601	Guru Arjan Dev completes construction of the Hari Mandir Sahib.
1604	Guru Arjan Dev completes the compilation of the *Adi Granth* on August 15. It is installed in a gala ceremony at the Hari Mandir Sahib on August 30.
1606	Guru Arjan Dev is martyred in June in Lahore. Hargobind is ordained as *Guru Hargobind*, the Sixth Guru, and begins the Sikh Warrior-Saint practice.
1621	Teg Bahadur, son of Guru Hargobind and his wife *Nanaki*, is born on April 1 in Amritsar.
1630	Har Rai, son of Guru Hargobind's son *Baba Gurditta*, is born on February 26 at *Kiratpur*.
1645	Guru Hargobind ordains his grandson Har Rai as *Guru Har Rai*, the Seventh Guru. Guru Hargobind's light merges in the Light.
1656	Harkrishan is born on July 7 to Guru Har Rai and his wife *Krishan Kaur*.
1661	Guru Har Rai ordains his 5-year-old son Harkrishan as *Guru Harkrishan*, the Eighth Guru. Guru Har Rai's light merges in the Light.
1664	Guru Harkrishan dies at age eight of smallpox. On the basis of the Guru's dying words, his uncle Teg Bahadur is ordained as *Guru Teg Bahadur*, the Ninth Guru.
1666	Gobind Rai is born in *Patna* on December 26 to Guru Teg Bahadur and his wife *Mata Gujri*.
1675	Guru Teg Bahadur is martyred in Delhi. His son Gobind Rai becomes *Guru Gobind Rai*.
1699	On April 14, Guru Gobind Rai institutes the *Amrit Ceremony*. This is the birthdate of the *Khalsa*. Guru Gobind Rai becomes *Guru Gobind Singh*.
1705	Guru Gobind Singh dictates the current version of the *Siri Guru Granth Sahib*.

1708   In October, Guru Gobind Singh ordains the Siri Guru Granth Sahib as his successor and the Guru of all living Sikhs. Guru Gobind Singh's light merges in the Light as he dies of the wounds inflicted by an assassin.

Appendix B

Pronunciation Guide

The more accurately we pronounce the shabads and mantras, the greater the effect is on consciousness. Here is a system for pronouncing the Gurmukhi transliterations in the sidebars and in Appendix C.

Note: Throughout the text of this book, I have used common spellings of Sikh words. Some conform to this pronunciation system, and some don't. Where the spelling does *not* conform to this system of pronunciation, I have given the pronunciation in parentheses after the word in the glossary.

Vowels: Long vowels are held slightly longer than they are in English.

Long Vowels include:

aa as in *father*
ay as in *say*
ai as in *mess*
ee as in *seen*
oo as in *soon*
o as in *so*
au as in *cow*
Short Vowels include:
a as in *but*
i as in *win*
u as in *put*
Consonants:
Most consonants are pronounced the way they are in English.
g as in *guy*
j as in *jaws*
The notation *(n)* after a vowel means that the previous vowels

are nasal sounds.

The sound *ng* is a nasal sound. In mantras, this nasal sound is accented.

The *r* in Gurmukhi is made by touching the tongue to the upper palate just above the teeth. It will sound almost like a *d*.

The letters *v* and *w* are interchangeable in Gurmukhi. The actual sound is somewhere between the two.

Aspirated Consonants: Where an *h* immediately follows a consonant, we expel extra breath to create the sound. Note that *th* is pronounced as it is in *Thailand*.

Retroflexed Consonants: *Retroflexed* sounds are made by flipping the tongue to the upper palate where the hard palate meets the soft palate, allowing the tongue to flip forward to complete the sound. Retroflexed consonants are indicated by an underline.

Notes:

Eh is pronounced like it is in English.

Ek rhymes with *neck*.

Accent: The accented syllable in a word is the first syllable with a long vowel. Where a word has only short vowels, the accent is on the first syllable.

Appendix C

The Complete Bayntee Chaupa-ee (God, Please Give Me Your Hand)

Bayntee Chaupa-ee was Guru Gobind Singh's prayer and Shabad for protection. It's one of the Banis used in the Amrit Ceremony. Keep in mind as you read this that *Guru Gobind Singh* was embattled from the age of nine, but lived to be 42 years old. He never harmed the wounded, never harmed prisoners, never took territory for himself, and never refused an offer of friendship from a former enemy.

Because *Bayntee Chaupa-ee* is difficult to find in its entirety, I include the whole thing here. It is sometimes sung as a Shabad in Gurdwara. We may chant Bayntee Chaupa-ee during *Sukhasan* (the process of closing the *Siri Guru Granth Sahib* for the day) if the Gurdwara is held early in the day.

The pronunciation guide is in Appendix B.

Paatishaahee Dasvee Kabyobaach Bayntee Chaupa-ee.
Hamaree karo haath dai rachhaa.
Pooran ho-i chit kee ichhaa.
Tav charanan man rehai hamaaraa.
Apanaa jaan karo pratipaaraa.
Hamaray dusht sabhai tum ghaavaho.
Aap haath dai mo-eh bachaavaho.
Sukhee basai moro parivaaraa.
Sayvak Sikh sabhai kartaaraa.
Mo rachhaa nij kar dai kariyai.
Sabh bairan kau aaj sanghariyai.
Pooran ho-i hamaaree aasaa.
Tor bhajan kee rehai pi-aasaa.

Tumeh chhaad ko-ee avar na dhiyaa-o.
Jo bar chaho so tum tay paa-o.
Sayvak Sikh hamaaray taaree-a-eh.
Chun chun satr hamaaray maaree-a-eh.
Aap haath dai mujhai ubariyai.
Maran kaal kaa traas nivariyai.
Hoojo sadaa hamaaray pachhaa.
Sree asidhuj joo kariyaho rachhaa.
Raakh layho mu-eh raakhanhaaray.
Saahib sant sahaa-i piyaaray.
Deen bandh dustan kay hantaa.
Tumaho puree chatur das kantaa.
Kaal paa-i brahmaa bap dharaa.
Kaal paa-i sivajoo avataraa.
Kaal paa-i kar bishan parkaasaa.
Sakal kaal kaa kee-aa tamaasaa.
Javan kaal jogee shiv kee-o.
Bayd raaj brahmaa joo thee-o.
Javan kaal sabh lok savaaraa.
Namaskaar hai taa-eh hamaaraa.
Javan kaal sabh jagat banaayo.
Dayv dait jachhan upajaayo.
Aad ant aykai avataaraa.
So-ee guroo samajhiyaho hamaaraa.
Namaskaar tis hee ko hamaaree.
Sakal prajaa jin aap savaareee.
Sivkan ko sivgun sukh dee-o.
Satrun ko pal mo badh kee-o.
Ghat ghat kay antar kee jaanat.
Bhalay buray kee peer pachhaanat.
Cheetee tay kunchar asthoolaa.
Sabh par kirpaa drisht kar foolaa.
Santan dukh paa-ay tay dukhee.
Sukh paa-ay saadhan kay sukhee.

Ayk ayk kee peer pachhaanai.
Ghat ghat kay pat pat kee jaanai.
Jab udakarakh karaa kartaaraa.
Prajaa dharat tab dayh apaaraa.
Jab aakarakh karat ho kabahoo.
Tum mai milat dayh dhar sabhahoo.
Jaytay badan srisht sabh dhaarai.
Aap aapanee boojh uchaarai.
Tum sabhahee tay rehat niraalam.
Jaanat bayd bhayd ar aalam.
Nirankaar nirbikaar nirlambh.
Aad aneel anaad asambh.
Taa kaa moorh uchaarat bhaydaa.
Jaa kau bhayv na paavat baydaa.
Taa kau kar paahan anumaanat.
Mahaa moorh kachh bhayd na jaanat.
Mahaa dayv kau kehat sadaa shiv.
Nirankaar kaa cheenat neh bhiv.
Aap aapanee budh hai jaytee.
Barnat bhinn bhinn tu-eh taytee.
Tumaraa lakhaa na jaa-i pasaaraa
Kih bidh sajaa pratham sansaaraa.
Aykai roop anoop saroopaa.
Rank bhayo raav kehee bhoopaa.
Andaj jayraj saytaj keenee.
Utabhuj khaan bahur rach deenee.
Kahoo fool raajaa hvai baithaa.
Kahoo simat bhiyo sankar ikaithaa.
Sagaree srisht dikaa-i achambhav.
Aad jugaad saroop suyambhav.
Ab rachhaa mayree tum karo.
Sikh ubaar asikh sangharo.
Dusht jitay uthavat utapaataa.
Sakal malaychh karo ran ghaataa.

Jay asidhuj tav sarnee paray.
Tin kay dusht dukhit hvai maray.
Purakh javan pag paray tihaaray.
Tin kay tum sankat sabh taaray.
Jo kal ko ik baar dhi-ai hai.
Taa kay kaal nikat neh aihai.
Rachhaa ho-i taa-eh sabh kaalaa.
Dusht arisht taray tatkaalaa.
Kirpaa drisht tan jaa-eh nihariho.
Taa kay taap tanak mo hariho.
Ridh sidh ghar mo sabh ho-ee.
Dusht chhaah chhvai sakai na ko-ee.
Ayk baar jin tumai sambhaaraa.
Kaal faas tay taa-eh ubaaraa.
Jin nar naam tihaaro kahaa.
Daarid dusht dokh tay rahaa.
Kharag kayt mai saran tihaaree.
Aap haath dai layho ubaaree.
Sarab thaur mo ho-o sahaa-ee.
Dusht dokh tay layho bachaa-ee.
Kirpaa karee ham par jag maataa.
Granth karaa pooran subh raataa.
Kilabikh sakal dayh ko hartaa.
Dusht dokhiyan ko chhai kartaa.
Sree asidhuj jab bha-ay da-i-aalaa.
Pooran karaa granth tatkaalaa.
Man baanchhat fal paavai so-ee.
Dookh na tisai bi-aapat ko-ee.
Arill:
Sunai gung jo yaa-i so rasanaa paava-ee.
Sunai moor chit laa-i chaturtaa aava-ee.
Dookh darat bhau nikat na tin nar kay rehai.
Ho jo yaakee ayk baar chaupa-ee ko kehai.
Swaiyaa:

Paa-i gehay jab tay tumaray tab tay ko-oo aankh taray nehee aanyo.

Raam raheem puraan kuraan anayk kehai mat ayk na maanyo.

Simrit shaastra bayd sabhai baho bhayd kehai ham ayk no jaanyo.

Sree asipaan kripaa tumaree kar mai na kehyo sabh to-eh bakhaanyo.

Doharaa:

Sagal du-aar kau chhaad kai gehi-o tuhaaro du-aar.

Baa-eh gehay kee laaj as gobind daas tuhaar.

Translation:

God, please give me Your Hand and protect me.

Please fulfill my mind's desires.

May my mind remain attached to Your Lotus Feet.

Please make me Your Own and cherish me.

Please destroy all my enemies.

Give me Your Hand and save me.

May my family live in peace.

May all serviceful Sikhs dwell in peace, O Creator.

Protect me with Your Omnipotent Arm.

May all my enemies be destroyed today.

May my hopes be fulfilled.

May my thirst for chanting Your Name continue unabated.

May I never forsake You. May I meditate only on You.

May I receive from You those gifts I long for.

Help my serviceful Sikhs cross over.

Single out my enemies and kill them.

Please give me Your Hand and save me.

Destroy the fear of death from within.

Please be on my side forever.

O Wielder of the Great Sword of Justice, please protect me.

Protect me, O Protector.

O Beloved Master, Helper and Support of the Saints,

O Friend of the poor, Destroyer of tyrants,

You are the Lord of all fourteen worlds.

As ordained by God, Brahma obtained a body.

As ordained by God, Shiva was incarnated.

As ordained by God, Vishnu appeared.
All this is the Play of God.
God created the Yogi Shiva,
And created Brahma, the king of the Vedas.
The One Who fashioned the whole world:
I bow in humble adoration to That One.
God created the whole world,
And the demigods, demons and spirits.
From beginning to end, the One is incarnate.
Let everyone know: That One is my Guru.
I humbly bow to That One
Who has created all beings,
Who bestows happiness on all virtuous servants,
Who destroys the evil and wicked in an instant,
Who knows what is within each and every heart,
Who knows the sufferings of the good and the bad.
From the tiny ant to the enormous elephant,
God casts an Eye of Grace on all.
When the Saints suffer, God suffers.
When the Holy are happy, God is happy.
The One knows the cares of everyone.
The One knows the secrets of every heart.
When Creator projects Creative Power,
Creation appears in countless forms.
When the One draws Creation back into Oneness again,
All living beings are reabsorbed.
All beings who have come into this world
Describe God according to their own understanding.
O God, You remain detached from everything.
Only the learned and wise understand this.
O Formless One, Unstained, Unmarked.
O Primal Being, Pure One, without beginning, Self-Created.
Only fools claim to know God's secrets.
These secrets are not known to the Vedas.

The one who sets up a stone idol as god
Is a complete fool, and knows no different.
One who keeps calling Shiva "the Great God,"
Knows not the secrets of the Formless God.
According to their understanding,
People describe God in their own ways.
Your extent and limit cannot be known.
How the universe was first created cannot be known.
One Form of Unparalleled Beauty
Appears as a beggar or a king at different places.
The One Who created all forms of life
Created nature's abundant vegetation.
Sometimes sitting joyfully as an Emperor,
Sometimes sitting as a Yogi, Detached from all,
The entire creation unfolds as a wondrous miracle.
From the beginning, through the ages, there is One Unchanging,
    Self-Created One.
Now, O God, please give me Your Protection.
Save my Sikhs and destroy all those against them.
Destroy our enemies who engage in evil and wickedness.
Destroy all scummy evil-doers on the field of battle.
O Wielder of the Sword, those who seek Your Sanctuary,
May their enemies meet a terrible death.
Those who fall at Your Feet, O God,
Please release them from all suffering.
Those who meditate on the Almighty One, even once,
Death cannot approach them.
God will totally protect them forever.
Their troubles and enemies will vanish in an instant.
When God casts an Eye of Grace,
They are instantly freed of all suffering.
All worldly and spiritual powers come to them in their own homes.
Their enemies shall not touch even their shadows.
Whoever remembers You, O God, even once,

Shall be saved from the noose of Death.

That person who chants Your Name

Shall be freed from poverty and the attacks of enemies.

O Wielder of the Sword, I seek Your Sanctuary.

Please give me Your Hand and save me.

Please be my Helper and Support in all places.

Please protect me from the evil plots of my enemies.

The World Mother blessed us with her grace.

The Granth was completed at the perfect time.

All residual sin and evil deeds are erased and destroyed.

The wicked and cruel are reduced to ashes.

When the Supremely Great, All-Powerful Sword became Merciful,

The Granth Sahib was completed perfectly.

Reading it, the mind's desires are fulfilled.

You shall not be afflicted again with pain.

Arill:

Listening to this is like the mute who tastes sweetness, smiles, but cannot speak.

Listening to this, even a fool becomes clever and wise.

Sorrow, pain and fear cannot come near that person

Who chants this Chaupa-ee even one time.

Swaiyaa:

Since I have grasped Your Feet, I have beheld nothing else.

Many speak of Ram and Raheem, of the Puraanas and the Koran, but I do not follow the teachings of any one of them.

The Smritis, the Shaastras, and the Vedas all talk of God's many mysteries, but I know none of them.

O Supreme Sword, bless me with Your Mercy; I cannot speak unless You speak through me.

Doharaa:

Having left all other doors, I have come to Your Door.

Please preserve the honor of Gobind, Your slave. [1]

Notes

Part I
1. Bhai Gurdaas. "Namo, Namo, Namo, Namo." From *Shabad Kirtan.*

Chapter 1: Introduction: What's a Sikh?
1. Guru Nanak, Raag Dhanaasree, *Siri Guru Granth Sahib,* p.685.
2. Guru Nanak, Japji Sahib, *Siri Guru Granth Sahib,* p.4.

Chapter 2: The Sun Shall Rise in the West:
1. A Sikh saying.
2. Bhai Gurdaas. Vaar 29, Pauri 15.
3. Yogi Bhajan. *Aquarian Times,* Winter 2005, "Wisdom from Yogi Bhajan," p.81.
4. Yogi Bhajan. *Aquarian Times,* Summer 2001, "Dear Yogiji," p.55.
5. Guru Nanak. Raag Soohee. *Siri Guru Granth Sahib,* p.730.
6. Guru Arjan Dev. Sukhmani Sahib. Raag Gauree. *Siri Guru Granth Sahib,* p.262.
7. The quotation is in *The History of Sikh Dharma in the Western Hemisphere,* p.14. The rest of the story is from "There's More to Mantra Than Meets the Ear," *The Science of Keeping Up,* Fall/Winter 2000, p.12-3.
8. Yogi Bhajan taught this meditation on April 23, 1979. Previously unpublished. Transcript calls it the Meditation to Give Your Children Values.

Chapter 3: How I Became a Sikh: Siri Kirpal Kaur's Story
1. Guru Arjan Dev. Sukhmani Sahib, Slok before Asṭapadi #20. Raag Gauree. *Siri Guru Granth Sahib,* p.289.
2. S.S. Shanti Kaur Khalsa. *The History of Sikh Dharma of the Western Hemisphere,* p.11-2.

3. Excerpted from *Victory & Virtue*, p.9-10.

Chapter 4: Shabad Guru: The Sound Way to God
1. Bhai Gurdaas. Vaar 13, Pauri 2.
2. Guru Arjan Dev. Raag Maajh. *Siri Guru Granth Sahib*, p.96.
3. Ibid.
4. Guru Arjan Dev. Raag Maajh. *Siri Guru Granth Sahib*, p.96-7.
5. Guru Arjan Dev. Raag Maajh. *Siri Guru Granth Sahib*, p.97. These four poem/letters form the opening of Shabad Hazaaray, one of the Banis.
6. Mohan means "enchanter," one of the Names of God. Guru Arjan Dev. Raag Gauree Chhant. *Siri Guru Granth Sahib*, p.248.
7. Ibid.
8. Guru Arjan Dev. Raag Soohee Chhant. *Siri Guru Granth Sahib*, p.783.
9. This information comes from *The History of Sikhism (Guru Nanak Dev to Guru Gobind Singh)*, p.251.
10. The Slok in question is number 54 on p.1429 of the *Siri Guru Granth Sahib*. Bhai Mani Singh compiled Guru Gobind Singh's writings in a separate volume some years after the Tenth Guru died.
11. Guru Arjan Dev. Raag Bilaawal. *Siri Guru Granth Sahib*, p. 827. Benefits referenced from *The Psyche of the Golden Shield*.
12. Guru Arjan Dev. Raag Bilaawal. *Siri Guru Granth Sahib*, p. 827.

Part II
1. Guru Gobind Singh. Raag Raamkalee.

Chapter 5: Banis: The Daily Word
1. Guru Arjan Dev. Raag Maajh. *Siri Guru Granth Sahib*, p.103.
2. Yogi Bhajan taught this kriya on July 23, 1977. Reference is *Slim & Trim*, where it is called Glandular Balance and Gain

in Energy.

3. Guru Nanak Dev. Japji Sahib, *Siri Guru Granth Sahib*, p.1. (The complete Japji Sahib appears on p.1-8.)

4. Guru Nanak Dev. Japji Sahib, *Siri Guru Granth Sahib*, p.8.

5. Guru Nanak Dev. Japji Sahib, *Siri Guru Granth Sahib*, p.5.

6. Crowder, Dena. "The Eighty Fourth Step," *Aquarian Times*, Spring 2002, p. 45.

7. Guru Nanak Dev. Raag Bilaawal. *Siri Guru Granth Sahib*, p.795.

8. Guru Gobind Singh. Jaap Sahib, Pauris #189-196. (The entire Jaap Sahib appears in the *Dasam Granth*, p.1-10.)

9. Yogi Bhajan taught this meditation on August 1, 2001. Reference is *Meditations for the New Millennium*, where it is called Naam Nidh Kriya.

10. Guru Gobind Singh. Tav Prasaad Swaiyay. (These appear in the *Dasam Granth*, p.13-15.)

11. Guru Amar Das. Anand Sahib, Pauris #1-5. Raag Raamkalee. *Siri Guru Granth Sahib*, p.917. (The entire Anand Sahib starts on p.917 and ends on p.922.)

12. Guru Arjan Dev. Raag Goojaree. *Siri Guru Granth Sahib*, p.495.

13. Benefits for this Shabad appear in *The Psyche of the Golden Shield*.

14. Guru Nanak. Raag Gauree Deepakee. *Siri Guru Granth Sahib*, p.12 and p.157.

15. Guru Arjan Dev. Sukhmani Sahib, Astapadi 14, Pauri 4. Raag Gauree. *Siri Guru Granth Sahib*, p.281. (The entire Sukhmani Sahib appears on p.262-296.)

Chapter 6: Inside the Guru's Court: How Sikhs Worship

1. Guru Ram Das. Raag Goojaree. *Siri Guru Granth Sahib*, p.492.

2. Kabir. Raag Gauree. *Siri Guru Granth Sahib*, p.325.

3. Guru Arjan Dev. Raag Siree. *Siri Guru Granth Sahib*, p.44.

4. Hymns in Praise of Guru Ram Das. *Siri Guru Granth Sahib*,

p.1402.

5. Anonymous.

6. Livtar Singh Khalsa. Song of the Khalsa. Used by permission.

9. Guru Arjan Dev. Sukhmani Sahib, Astapadi 4, Last Pauri. Raag Gauree. *Siri Guru Granth Sahib*, p.268.

10. Guru Gobind Singh. Chandi ki Vaar. However, the byline, the lines that begin "Great is Guru Gobind Singh...," and all the lines that follow are by an unknown author or group of authors, probably in the late 19th Century or early, early 20th Century.

11. The first four lines are two couplets from *Panth Prakaash* (published in 1880) by Giani Gian Singh. However, in Gurdwaras today, we misquote the fourth line. The remaining two lines are by Guru Gobind Singh's disciple, Bhai Nand Laal.

12. Guru Arjan Dev. Raag Bihaagara Chhant. *Siri Guru Granth Sahib*, p.547-8.

13. Guru Nanak. Japji Sahib, Mool Mantra. *Siri Guru Granth Sahib*, p.1.

Chapter 7: The Path of *Paths*

1. Guru Gobind Singh. From Bayntee Chaupa-ee.

2. Guru Teg Bahadur. Slok #1. *Siri Guru Granth Sahib*, p.1426.

3. Guru Nanak. Raag Dhanaasree. *Siri Guru Granth Sahib*, p.13 & p.663.

4. Guru Gobind Singh. Jaap Sahib, Last Four Lines.

5. Yogi Bhajan taught this set on February 27, 1985. Reference is *Self Experience*, where it is called To Release Stored Pain and Refresh Yourself.

6. Taken from "A Miracle During World War II" by Bhai Ranjit Singh, Jalandhar, India.

7. Guru Arjan Dev. *Siri Guru Granth Sahib*, p.1362.

Chapter 8: Sadhana: Early in the Morning Our Song Shall Rise to Thee

1. Guru Ram Das. Raag Soohee. *Siri Guru Granth Sahib*, p.733-4.
2. Guru Singh Khalsa. Rise Up, copyright 1971. Used by permission.
3. Words by Reginald Heber, 1783-1826.
4. Yogi Bhajan taught this set in the summer of 1983. *Kundalini Yoga for Youth & Joy*, p.44-45.
5. Snatam Kaur Khalsa. March 31, 2003. "Community Sadhana for the Aquarian Age."
6. Ibid.
7. Ibid.
8. Guru Nanak. Japji Sahib, Mool Mantra. *Siri Guru Granth Sahib*, p.1.
9. Snatam Kaur Khalsa. March 31, 2003. "Community Sadhana for the Aquarian Age."
10. Ibid.
11. Guru Arjan Dev. Slok from Vaar of Raag Goojaree. *Siri Guru Granth Sahib*, p. 517-8.
12. *Siri Guru Granth Sahib*, p.1402.
13. Yogi Bhajan. *The Mind: Its Projections and Multiple Facets*, p.156.
14. Guru Gobind Singh. Jaap Sahib, Pauris #94-5. (The entire Jaap Sahib appears in the *Dasam Granth*, p.1-10.)
15. Satta and Balwand. Raag Raamkalee. *Siri Guru Granth Sahib*, p.968.

Chapter 9: Blessed by Sadhana: Viriam Kaur Khalsa's Story

1. Guru Ram Das. Slok from Vaar of Raag Gauree. *Siri Guru Granth Sahib*, p.305.

Part III

1. Guru Nanak. Slok. *Siri Guru Granth Sahib*, p.1412, #20.

Chapter 10: The Amrit Ceremony

1. Guru Amar Das. Raag Raamkalee, Anand Sahib. *Siri Guru Granth Sahib*, p.918.
2. From Vaar of Sorath by Guru Ram Das with Sloks by Guru Amar Das. *Siri Guru Granth Sahib*, p.649-50.

Chapter 11: To Protect the Weak

1. Gurudass Singh Khalsa. Sikh National Anthem, copyright 1974. Used by permission.

Chapter 12: A Saint-Soldier in the Peace Movement: Guru Fatha Singh Khalsa's Story

1. Guru Arjan Dev. Raag Dhanaasree. *Siri Guru Granth Sahib*, p.683.

Part IV

1. Guru Amar Das. Siree Raag. *Siri Guru Granth Sahib*, p.28-9.

Chapter 13: Get a Life: The Rehit

1. Guru Nanak. Japji Sahib. *Siri Guru Granth Sahib*, p.4.
2. Guru Amar Das. Anand Sahib. Raag Raamkalee. *Siri Guru Granth Sahib*, p.918.
3. Reported in *The Vancouver Province*, January 8, 1999.
4. Dhanna. Dhanaasree. *Siri Guru Granth Sahib*, p.695.

Chapter 14: Bana: Dressed Up Royally

1. Guru Arjan Dev. Siree Raag. *Siri Guru Granth Sahib*, p.73.
2. *Holy Bible*. Book of Judges, chapters 13-16.
3. Guru Amar Das. Slok. *Siri Guru Granth Sahib*, p.785.

Chapter 15: Seva: An Appetite for Service

1. Guru Arjan Dev. Sukhmani Sahib, Astapadi #1. *Siri Guru Granth Sahib*, p.263.
2. Farzana Contractor. "At the Golden Temple, There's Always

a Meal for the Hungry," Upper Crust, October-December 2001.

3. From the UNITED SIKHS website, www.unitedsikhs.org.

4. "Karsewa," *The Times of India*, August 5, 2004.

5. Shanti Shanti Kaur Khalsa, Ph.D. "What Happens When We Die Consciously?" *Aquarian Times*, Fall 2003, p.35-6.

6. Ibid.

7. From a Y.O.G.A. for Youth flyer. See also www.sikhnet.com archives and www.yogaforyouth.org.

Chapter 16: Dancing to God: Meherbani Kaur Khalsa's Story

1. Guru Amar Das. Raag Goojaree. *Siri Guru Granth Sahib*, p.506.

Chapter 17: Marriage: Two Bodies/One Soul

1. Guru Amar Das. Slok. *Siri Guru Granth Sahib*, p.788.

2. Guru Ram Das. Raag Gauree Maajh. *Siri Guru Granth Sahib*, p.173.

3. Guru Nanak. Raag Soohee Chhant. *Siri Guru Granth Sahib*, p.765.

4. Yogi Bhajan taught this meditation on January 31, 1977. Reference is *Kundalini Winter Lectures 1977*, p.138-9.

5. Guru Ram Das. Pauri. Vaar of Siree Raag. *Siri Guru Granth Sahib*, p.91.

6. Guru Arjan Dev. Slok and Chhant. Raag Aasaa. *Siri Guru Granth Sahib*, p.456. The full Hukam actually continues onto p.457.

7. Guru Arjan Dev. Slok. *Siri Guru Granth Sahib*, p.963.

8. Guru Ram Das. The Lavaan, Raag Soohee Chhant. *Siri Guru Granth Sahib*, p.773.

9. Guru Ram Das. The Lavaan, Raag Soohee Chhant. *Siri Guru Granth Sahib*, p.773-4.

10. Guru Ram Das. The Lavaan, Raag Soohee Chhant. *Siri Guru Granth Sahib*, p.774.

11. Ibid.
12. Guru Ram Das. Chhant. Siree Raag. *Siri Guru Granth Sahib*, p.78-9.

Chapter 18: Death: Going Home to God
1. Kabir. Slok. *Siri Guru Granth Sahib*, p.1365, #22.
2. Based on Yogi Bhajan quote in Guru Terath Kaur Khalsa, Ph.D. *Dying Into Life*, p.148.
3. Guru Arjan Dev. Sukhmani Sahib. Raag Gauree. *Siri Guru Granth Sahib*, p.278.
4. Kabir. Raag Raamkalee. *Siri Guru Granth Sahib*, p.969.
5. Taken from *The Aquarian Teacher*, p.239.
6. Guru Nanak. Raag Soohee, Chhant. *Siri Guru Granth Sahib*, p.764.
7. Taken from the Brief on Grief on the IKYTA website.
8. Photo of this tombstone appears on p.8 of *Aquarian Times*, Winter 2005.

Chapter 19: A Universal Path
1. Guru Nanak. Japji Sahib. *Siri Guru Granth Sahib*, p.6.

Appendix C
1. Guru Gobind Singh. The Complete Bayntee Chaupa-ee.

Glossary

Non-English words are spelled phonetically according to the pronunciation guide in Appendix B. Those not spelled phonetically are followed by the phonetic pronunciation in parentheses.

3HO: Healthy, Happy, Holy Organization; a non-profit organization begun in 1969 to promote Kundalini Yoga and the teachings of Yogi Bhajan Aad Guray Nameh, Jugaad Guray Nameh, Sat Guray Nameh, Siree Guru Dayvay Nameh: *I call upon the primal Guru, I call upon the Guru of the Ages, I call upon the True Guru, I call upon the Infinitely Great Divine Guru*; mantra for protection and knowledge; the opening lines of Sukhmani Sahib, a Bani by Guru Arjan Dev

Aagi-aa Bha-ee Akaal Kee: Literally, *The Order Has Come from the Undying One*; Shabad sung/recited right after the Ardas in a Gurdwara service; written by Giani Gian Singh and Bhai Nand Laal

Aartee: Literally "Worship Service"; in Sikh practice, a special collection of Shabads played traditionally after an Akhand Path

Aasaa: One of the Indian Raags; the word literally means "hope" or "longing"

Aasaa Di Vaar (Aasaa Dee Vaar): Lengthy hymn praising God in Raag Aasaa

Adi Granth (Aadee Granth): Literally "Primal Knot"; version of the *Siri Guru Granth Sahib* compiled by Guru Arjan Dev

Adi Shakti (Aadee Shaaktee): Literally "Primal Power"; the name of a Sikh symbol that features a double-edged sword in the middle of a circle flanked by a pair of long swords; also the name of a popular Sikh mantra

Adi Shakti Mantra (Aadee Shaaktee Mantra): *Ek Ong Kaar Sat Naam Siri Waa Hay Guroo*; also known as Long Ek Ongkars,

Morning Call and Long Chant; mantra found on doorways at historical Sikh holy sites in Goindwal and Amritsar; one of the Aquarian Sadhana mantras; used to raise the kundalini and awaken intuition

Agra (Aagraa): City in India

Ajeet: Literally "Victor"; a common Sikh name for both men and women; sometimes spelled "Ajit"

Akaal: "Timeless" or "deathless"; mantra for deathlessness, chanted after a person dies

Akal Takhat (Akaal Takhat): Literally "Undying Throne"; administrative center for Sikhism; located in Amritsar

Akhand Path (Akhand Paath): Literally, "Unbroken Recitation"; non-stop, out loud recitation of the *Siri Guru Granth Sahib* from beginning to end

Amrit: Literally "Undying Nectar"; a person who has undergone the Amrit Ceremony is said to have "taken Amrit"; also a popular Sikh first name

Amrit Ceremony: Sikh initiation or "baptism"

Amrit Kirtan (Amrit Keertan): Gurmukhi books with most standard Shabads; used as songbooks, although they contain no musical notation

Amrit Vela (Amrit Vaylaa): Literally "Ambrosial Time"; the two and a half hour period before dawn (or four to seven in the morning); optimum time for morning Sadhana

Amritdari Sikh (Amritdaaree Sikh): Practicing Sikh who has taken Amrit

Amritsar (Amritsaar): Literally "Nectar Tank"; main city in the Punjab; home of the Hari Mandir Sahib

Anand: Literally "Bliss" or "Happiness"; may be used as a Sikh name

Anand Karaj (Anand Karaaj): Literally "Bliss in the Making"; Sikh wedding ceremony

Anand Sahib (Anand Saahib): Bani by Guru Amar Das; recited in full during the Amrit Ceremony; the first part of it is sung during Gurdwara services

Anandpur Sahib (Anandpur Saahib): Literally "Respected Township of Bliss"; city in India; the setting for the birth of the Khalsa and the first ever Amrit Ceremony

Ang Sang Waa Hay Guroo: Literally, *The ecstasy of God is in all my limbs*; a mantra for experiencing the Presence of God

Aquarian Age: The two thousand year period that began on November 11, 1991

Ardas (Aardaas): Literally "Servant with Folded Hands"; prayer or supplication

Arill (Aarill): A short verse near the end of Bayntee Chaupa-ee

Asana: Posture

Ashram (Aashraam): Literally "Forest Dwelling"; a place where yogis live and/or teach; in the West, also sometimes applied to dwelling, teaching or worshipping places of 3HO Sikhs

Astapadi (Astapadee): Poem with eight (sometimes more) pauris or stanzas

Aura: Electro-magnetic field

Aurangzeb (Aurangzayb): Mughal Emperor of India from 1658 CE to 1707 CE; born in 1618 CE; much hated by Hindus and Sikhs for his bloodthirsty religious bigotry

Baba Buddha (Baabaa Buddhaa): A child follower of Guru Nanak; lived to a great age; installed Guru Angad, Guru Amar Das, Guru Ram Das, Guru Arjan Dev and Guru Hargobind; first Guru Granthi

Baba Gurditta (Baabaa Gurditaa): Son of Guru Hargobind and father of Guru Har Rai

Baisakhi (Ba-isaakhee or more correctly Va-isaakhee): Indian Spring Festival, held by Sikhs on April 13 or 14; the date of the birth of the Khalsa and the first ever Amrit Ceremony in 1699

Balwand: An author in the *Siri Guru Granth Sahib*

Bana (Baanaa): Sikh mode of dress; one of the pillars of Sikhism

Bani (Baanee): Literally, "Word"; Sikh daily prayer; Shabad or group of Shabads recited by devout Sikhs daily; one of the pillars of Sikhism

Bata (Baataa): Iron cauldron used for the Amrit Ceremony

Bayntee Chaupa-ee: Bani by Guru Gobind Singh; used in the Amrit Ceremony; sometimes recited during Sukhasan

Bein (Bay-i) River: The river in which Guru Nanak became enlightened

Bhai Gurdaas (Bhaa-ee Gurdaas): Guru Arjan Dev's secretary; author of many Shabads sung by Sikhs

Bhai Kanaiya (Bhaa-ee Kanaiyaa): Sikh follower of Guru Teg Bahadur and Guru Gobind Singh; instituted the Seva Panthi movement and the practice of tending the wounded on both sides of a battlefield

Bhai Lehna (Bhaa-ee Lehnaa): Guru Angad's original name

Bhai Mani Singh (Bhaa-ee Manee Singh): Guru Gobind Singh's secretary; compiled Guru Gobind Singh's writings

Bhai Mati Das (Bhaa-ee Matee Daas): Companion and Sikh of Guru Teg Bahadur; martyred in 1675

Bhai Nand Laal (Bhaa-ee Nand Laal): Persian poet and disciple of Guru Gobind Singh; wrote two of the lines that are sung immediately after the Ardas in a Sikh worship service

Bhog: Ending

Bhog Ceremony: Gurdwara ceremony of ending an Akhand Path; also the ending ceremony for some community Sahaj Paths

Bibi Bhani (Beebee Bhaanee): Daughter of Guru Amar Das; wife of Guru Ram Das; mother of Guru Arjan Dev; all Gurus starting with Guru Arjan Dev were her descendants

Bibi Sundari (Beebee Sundaree): A historical Sikh lady warrior; died in 1742

Bidar: Town in India

Bihaagara (Bihaagaraa): One of the Indian Raags

Bilaawal: One of the Indian Raags

Bolay So Nihaal: Literally, *Speak This Joy*; part of a jaikara in Sikh services

Brahma (Brahmaa): Hindu Creator god

Brow Point: The point on the forehead between the eyebrows; also called the Third Eye; a focal point in many meditations

Celestial Communications: Songs with specific hand motions; a mode of meditative dance used for mental relaxation; sometimes used by children in Gurdwara programs

Chakra (Chakraa): Literally "wheel" or "circle"; in some contexts, a chakra is a large steel ring that warriors once wore on their heads to deflect enemy swords; in yogic contexts, a chakra is one of eight vortices of energy in or around the body

Chandi ki Vaar (Chandee kee Vaar): Epic poem attributed to Guru Gobind Singh; its opening lines also open the Ardas

Chattar Chakkar Vartee: Literally, *In All Four Directions, Pervading*; Shabad/mantra from Jaap Sahib by Guru Gobind Singh

Chauri Sahib (Chauri Saahib or Chor Saahib): A fancy flywhisk; waved over the Guru during Sikh ceremonies for a positive vibration and as a symbol of the Guru's authority

Chauri Seva (Chauri Sayvaa or Chor Sayvaa): The service of sitting behind the Guru during a Sikh service and waving a chauri sahib

Chhant: A verse form of four or more pauris found in the *Siri Guru Granth Sahib*; often (but not always) uses bridal imagery and contains internal rhymes

Chi Gong: A Chinese martial arts form practiced for its health benefits

Chola (Cholaa): Tunic similar to a kurta

Chuni (Choonee): Extra-large scarf, usually transparent, worn by Sikh women

Churridars (Churidaars): Leggings

Dal (Daal): Lentils or other legumes; dishes made from lentils or other legumes

Darshan (Daarshan): The experience, vision or revelation one has while in the Presence of someone or something very holy

Dasam Granth: Writings of the Tenth Guru; compiled by Bhai Mani Singh after Guru Gobind Singh's death

Daya Ram (Dayaa Raam): Name of Daya Singh before he became the first of the original Panj Pi-aaray

Dhan Dhan Raam Daas Guru: *Blessed, Blessed is Guru Ram Das*; popular Shabad praising Guru Ram Das; often sung on Guru Ram Das' birthday

Dhanaasaree: One of the Indian Raags

Dhanna (Dhannaa): Hindu farmer/saint/poet whose work appears in the *Siri Guru Granth Sahib*

Dharam Das (Dharam Daas): Name of Dharam Singh before he became the second original Panj Pi-aaray

Dharma (Dharmaa): Spiritual path; Western Sikhs often refer to Sikhism as "the Dharma"

Dhir Mal (Dheer Mal): Brother of Guru Har Rai; stole the *Adi Granth* from Guru Teg Bahadur

Diaphragm Lock: Practiced on an empty stomach only by lifting the chest and pulling the diaphragm and upper abdominal area in and up on the exhale; helps to open the heart chakra and balance the emotions; also good for the intestines; not recommended for pregnant women

Dupatas (Dupaataas): Long, wide, fringeless shawls, similar to chunis, but larger and more opaque

Dwarka (Dwaarkaa): Town in India

Ek Ong Kaar, Sat Naam, Kartaa Purakh, Nirbhao, Nirvair, Akaal Moorat, Ajoonee, Saibhang, Gurprasaad, Jap, Aad Sach, Jugaad Sach, Hai Bhee Sach, Naanak Hosee Bhee Sach: *One Creator Creation. Truth Name. Being of Action. Without fear. Without vengeance. Undying. Unborn. Self-illumined. By Guru's Gift. RECITE! True in the beginning. True through all time. True even now. Nanak: Truth shall always be.*; Mool Mantra; the opening words of Japji Sahib; sung extensively by Sikhs as a mantra; one of the Aquarian Sadhana chants

Ek Ong Kaar Sat Naam Siree Waa Hay Guroo: *One Creator*

Creation. Truth Name. Incomprehensibly Great is the Light of this Wisdom.; Adi Shakti Mantra, also known as Long Chant, Morning Call, and Long Ek Ongkars; mantra for intuition and raising the kundalini; one of the Aquarian Sadhana chants

Gagan Mai Thaal: Shabad by Guru Nanak which appears in the bedtime Bani, Kirtan Sohila and at the beginning of the Aartee

Ganga (Gangaa): Wife of Guru Arjan Dev and mother of Guru Hargobind

Garam Masala (Garam Masaalaa): A variable Indian spice mix

Gauree (Gauree): One of the Indian Raags

Gauree Deepakee (Gauree Deepakee): A subsection of Raag Gauree

Gauree Maajh (Gauree Maajh): A subsection of Raag Gauree

Ghee: Clarified butter

Giani Gian Singh (Gi-aanee Gi-aan Singh): A 19th Century Sikh, four of whose lines of poetry are sung immediately after the Ardas in a Sikh worship service

Gobinday, Mukanday, Udaaray, Apaaray, Haree-ang, Karee-ang, Nirnaamay, Akaamay: *Sustainer, Liberator, Enlightener, Infinite, Destroyer, Creator, Nameless, Desireless.*; mantra used to release deep-seated blocks and balance the hemispheres of the brain; from Jaap Sahib, a Bani by Guru Gobind Singh

Gobind Rai: Guru Gobind Singh's name before he became the Tenth Sikh Guru

Goindwal (Go-indwaal): City in the Punjab with a famous Gurdwara and bathing tank

Granth Sahib (Granth Saahib): Name of the *Siri Guru Granth Sahib* before it became the Sikh Guru

Granthi (Granthee): Caretaker of the *Siri Guru Granth Sahib*; someone who sits with the *Siri Guru Granth Sahib* during a Sikh worship service

Goojaree: One of the Indian Raags

Gur ka Langar (Gur kaa Langar): Food of the Guru's kitchen

Gurdwara (Gurdwaaraa): Sikh temple and/or Sikh worship

service

Gurmukhi (Gurmukhee): Literally "from the mouth of the Guru"; the language and script used in the *Siri Guru Granth Sahib*

Guroo Guroo Waa Hay Guroo, Guroo Raam Daas Guroo: *Great is the ecstasy and wisdom of serving God.*; mantra honoring Guru Ram Das, often used for protection, healing, and humility; one of the Aquarian Sadhana chants

Gurprashaad: Literally "Gift of the Guru"; sweet made of flour, water, honey or raw sugar and ghee served to everyone at the end of a Gurdwara service as a reminder of the sweetness of God's Name

Gurpurbs: Sikh holy days

Guru: One who provides the technology to release the darkness and experience the Light

Guru Amar Das (Guru Amar Daas): Third Sikh Guru in human embodiment; wrote Anand Sahib; worked to eliminate the caste system, the immolation of widows and inequality of women; born in 1479 CE; became Guru in 1552 CE; died in 1574 CE at an advanced age

Guru Angad: Second Sikh Guru in human embodiment; born in 1504 CE; became Guru in 1539 CE; died in 1552 CE; created the Gurmukhi script as we now use it

Guru Arjan Dev (Guru Arjan Dayv): Fifth Sikh Guru in human embodiment; son of Guru Ram Das; completed the Hari Mandir Sahib; prolific poet and compiler of the *Adi Granth Sahib*; born in 1563 CE; became Guru in 1581 CE; martyred in 1606 CE

Guru Gobind Rai (Guru Gobind Raa-i): Name of Guru Gobind Singh before the first Amrit Ceremony in 1699

Guru Gobind Singh: Tenth and last Sikh Guru in human embodiment; a great Warrior-Saint and poet; founded the Khalsa and the Amrit Ceremony in 1699 CE; turned the Guruship over to the *Siri Guru Granth Sahib*; born in 1666 CE; became

Guru in 1675 CE; assassinated in 1708 CE

Guru Hargobind: Sixth Sikh Guru in human embodiment; turned Sikhs into Warrior-Saints; born in 1595 CE; became Guru in 1606 CE; died in 1645 CE

Guru Harkrishan: Eighth Sikh Guru in human embodiment; a child Guru; born in 1656 CE; became Guru at age 5 in 1661 CE; died at age eight in 1664 CE

Guru Har Rai (Guru Har Raa-i): Seventh Sikh Guru in human embodiment; born in 1630 CE; became Guru in 1645 CE; died in 1661 CE

Guru Nanak (Guru Naanak): First and founding Guru of Sikhism; born in 1469 CE; enlightened in 1496 CE; died 1539 CE; author of Japji Sahib; all succeeding Gurus in the Sikh tradition, except the last one, signed their poetry with his name

Guru Ram Das (Guru Raam Daas): Fourth Sikh Guru in human embodiment; wrote the Lavaan; founded the city of Amritsar; born in 1534 CE; became Guru in 1574 CE; died in 1581 CE

Guru Teg Bahadur (Guru Tayg Bahaadur): Ninth Sikh Guru in human embodiment; father of Guru Gobind Singh; born in 1621 CE; became Guru in 1664 CE; gave his life in 1675 CE for members of another religion

Gyan (Gi-aan): Knowledge

Gyan Mudra (Gi-aan Mudraa): Mudra for knowledge, intuition, receptivity and expanded awareness; the tip of the thumb touches the index finger

Har: The most common word for God in the *Siri Guru Granth Sahib*

Hardwar (Hardwaar): Hindu place of pilgrimage on the Ganges River

Hari Mandir Sahib (Harimandar Saahib): Literally "Great Temple of God"; main Sikh temple, now known as the Golden Temple

Harmonium: Large portable hand organ; instrument brought to India by Christian missionaries and used in Sikh services

Hatha Yoga (Haathaa Yogaa): Yoga of postures; form of yoga most commonly taught

Himmat: Name of Himmat Singh before he became the fifth (some say the fourth) original Panj Pi-aaray

Hukam: Literally "Command"; the random reading from the *Siri Guru Granth Sahib*

Jaa Kaa Hiradaa Sudh Hay Khoj Shabad Meh Layh: Literally, *Those who wish to purify their hearts should turn to the Shabad*; the correct words of the usually misquotedline in Aagi-aa Bha-ee Akaal Kee by Giani Gian Singh

Jaap Sahib (Jaap Saahib): Bani by Guru Gobind Singh; used in the Amrit Ceremony

Jaikara (Jaikaaraa): Cry of victory

Japji Sahib (Japjee Saahib): Sikh morning prayer; written by Guru Nanak, the First Sikh Guru; recited during the Amrit Ceremony

Jetha (Jaythaa): Guru Ram Das' original name; also the word for a Sikh group or troupe

Ji (Jee): Literally "Soul"; pronounced like the English "Gee"; term of affectionate respect

Kaaba: Islamic focal point of prayer in Mecca

Kaahay Ray Man Chitveh Udam: Literally, *O My Mind, Why Suffer Anxiety?*; Shabad by Guru Arjan Dev; one of several Shabads in Rehiras Sahib

Kaal Akaal, Siree Akaal, Maahaa Akaal, Akaal Moorat, Waa Hay Guroo: *Undying Death, Infinitely Great Deathlessness, Greatest Deathlessness, Undying Image, Wow! How Great is this Indescribable Understanding.*; mantra used in Sikh processions

Kabir (Kabeer): A 15th Century Indian saint and poet of both Muslim and Hindu heritage, whose poems appear in the *Siri Guru Granth Sahib*

Kacheras (Kachhairaas): Thigh length underwear; one of the 5 "k"s

Kangha (Kangaa): Wooden comb; one of the 5 "k"s

Kara (Karaa): Steel bangle; one of the 5 "k"s

Karma: Law of cause and effect

Katha (Kathaa): Spiritual talk or sermon

Kaur: Princess; gender-designator name for Sikh women

Keetaa Loree-ai Kamm: Shabad that opens the Anand Karaj; written by Guru Ram Das

Kesh (Kaysh): Uncut hair; one of the 5 "k"s

Khalsa (Khaalsaa: rhymes with Salsa): Literally "King's Own"; usually translated as "Pure Ones"; the family of all Amritdari Sikhs

Khanda (Khandaa): Double-edged sword

Khulasa (Khulasaa): "Freed Man"

Kiratpur (Keeratpur): Town in India where Guru Har Rai was born

Kirpaa: Kindness or compassion

Kirpan (Kirpaan): Short sword or knife worn by all Amritdari Sikhs; one of the 5 "k"s

Kirtan (Keertan): Sacred singing of Shabads; sometimes refers to a Gurdwara service

Kirtan Sohila (Keertan Sohilaa): Sikh bedtime Bani; a composite of five Shabads by Guru Nanak, Guru Ram Das and Guru Arjan Dev

Kitcharee: Indian dish of lentils or mung beans and rice

Krishan Kaur: Guru Har Rai's wife and Guru Harkrishan's mother

Kriya (Kriyaa): Literally "Completed Action"; In Kundalini Yoga as taught by Yogi Bhajan and some other forms of yoga, an exercise or a group of exercises leading to a specific effect

Kuja Dosha (Koojaa Doshaa) Mars: An afflicted position of Mars in Vedic Astrology that creates the tendency to pick abusive mates

Kundal (Kundal or Kundal): Coil of hair from one's beloved

Kundalini (Kundaleenee or Kundaleenee): Coil of energy; raising the kundalini develops all latent talents and positive potentials of an individual

Kundalini Yoga (Kundaleenee Yogaa): Form of Raaj Yoga that raises the kundalini, creating vitality in the body, balance in the mind and openness to spirit

Kurehits (Kuraihats): Actions that break Amrit; forbidden to Amritdari Sikhs

Kurta (Kurtaa): Tunic

Lakh Khusee-aa Paatishaahee-aa: Literally, *One Enjoys the Pleasures of Tens of Thousands of Royal Empires*; a Shabad

Langar: Communal meal eaten after (or sometimes during) a Gurdwara service; also the name of a Sikh communal dining hall

Lavaan: The Sikh wedding song; written by Guru Ram Das

Long Ek Ongkars: Ek Ong Kaar Sat Naam Siri Waa Hay Guroo; Adi Shakti Mantra

Maajh: One of the Indian Raags

Mahabandha (Maahaabandhaa): Great Lock; combination of Root Lock, Diaphragm Lock and Neck Lock

Mahan (Maahaan) Tantric: Master of White Tantric Yoga

Mala (Maalaa): Rosary

Mantra: A repeated mind-altering sound, word or phrase

Mardana (Mardaanaa): Guru Nanak's rebec player; wrote some sloks in the *Siri Guru Granth Sahib*

Mata Gujri (Maataa Gujree): Guru Teg Bahadur's wife and Guru Gobind Singh's mother

Mata Sahib Devan (Maataa Saahib Dayvan): Original name of Mata Sahib Kaur; Guru Gobind Singh's third wife

Mata Sahib Kaur (Maataa Saahib Kaur): The Mother of the Khalsa; name of Mata Sahib Devan after the birth of the Khalsa in 1699

Maya (Maayaa): The illusion that we are separate from God

Mayraa Man Lochai: Literally, *My Mind Longs*; the series of poetic letters that turned Arjan into Guru Arjan Dev; a popular Sikh Shabad, sometimes recited during Prakash or before taking the Hukam

Mihravaan Sahib Mihravaan (Mihravaan Saahib Mihravaan): Literally, *Merciful Lord Merciful*; a popular Shabad written by Guru Arjan Dev

Mohan: Eldest son of Guru Amar Das

Mohkam Chand: Name of Mohkam Singh before he became the third original Panj Pi-aaray

Moo Laalan Si-o Preet Banee: *I Have Fallen in Love with My Beloved*; a Shabad by Guru Arjan Dev

Moolbandh: See Root Lock

Mool Mantra: Literally "Root Mantra"; the opening of Japji Sahib; one of the mantras sung during Aquarian Sadhana

Moon Center: Centers of emotional energy in the body; men have just one moon center on the center of the chin, which is insulated and protected by wearing beards; women cycle between 11 different moon centers during a month

Mussoorie (Musooree): City in the Himalayan foothills of India

Mudra (Mudraa): Literally "Seal"; usually refers to a hand position in yoga

Mughal: Islamic descendants of Tamerlane who ruled much of what is now Pakistan, Afghanistan, Kashmir and Northern India from 1526-1858 CE

Naad: Sound current; subtle inner sound

Naam: Literally "Name"; in practice, the Name of God

Naam Simran (Naam Simran): Literally "Remembrance of the Name"; reciting the Name of God on the breath or during meditation

Nanak (Naanak): Literally, "No Nonsense"; the first name of Sikhism's founder

Nanaki (Naanakee): Guru Hargobind's wife and Guru Teg Bahadur's mother; also the name of Guru Nanak's elder sister

Nankana Sahib (Nankaanaa Saahib): Current name of town in Pakistan where Guru Nanak was born

Neck Lock: Pulling the chin in a bit so that the neck is in line with the rest of the spine and so that the head is held steady with the face and neck relaxed; allows energy to flow to the higher centers; always used during meditation unless otherwise specified

Nirvair: Literally "without vengeance"; a Sikh epithet for God

Nit Nem (Nit Naym): Sikh Prayer Book

Ong Naamo, Guroo Dayv Naamo: *I call upon the Creator, I call upon Divine Wisdom.*; mantra used for tuning in before any Kundalini Yoga practice

Palaa: The shawl that connects the bride and groom during the Anand Karaj

Palki Sahib (Palkee Saahib): Technically, the Guru's palanquin; a cross between a throne, an altar and a bed; used to hold the *Siri Guru Granth Sahib*

Panj: Five

Panj Pi-aaray: The Five Beloved Ones; historically the five men who gave their heads to Guru Gobind Rai; in practice, any five Amritdari Sikhs who administer Amrit or organize a Gurdwara or represent Sikhism in any way

Panj Shabad: Literally "Shabad of Five"; Saa Taa Naa Maa

Path (Paath): Recitation

Panthis (Panthees): People who read Akhand Paths professionally

Patanjali (Pataanjalee): Author of the Yoga Sutras, whose estimated dates vary widely from about 400 BCE to about 400 CE

Patashas (Pataashays): Sugar candy used in the Amrit Ceremony

Patna (Patnaa): Town in northern India where Guru Gobind Singh was born

Pauri (Pauree): Literally "Rung of a Ladder"; stanza of Sikh poetry

Pi-aara: Beloved; any single member of the Panj Pi-aaray

Prakash (Prakaash): Literally "brightening"; the ceremony of opening the *Siri Guru Granth Sahib* for the day; the Guru's open state

Prana (Praanaa): Life force energy

Pranayam (Praanaayaam): Yogic breathing exercises

Pranic Body: The subtle body of life force energy carried on the breath

Prashaad: Literally "Gift"; familiar term for Gurprashaad

Prithi Chand (Prithee Chand): Guru Arjan Dev's older brother and vehement rival

Puja: Hindu ritual prayers

Punjab (Panjaab): Birthplace of Sikhism; on both sides of the Indian/Pakistan border

Punjabi (Panjaabee): From the Punjab; also, the language spoken by Indian-born Sikhs

Puraanas: Hindu epic texts in Sanskrit

Raag: Indian melodic mode

Raag Mala (Raag Maalaa): Rosary of Raags; the controversial Shabad that concludes the *Siri Guru Granth Sahib*

Raaginis (Raageenees): "Wives" of the Raags; what some Raags are called

Raaj Yoga: One of the great branches of yoga that includes Kundalini Yoga; endows the practitioner with nobility and the ability to see the Divine everywhere

Raamkalee: One of the Raags

Ragi (Raagee): Someone who plays Raags

Raheem: "Merciful," one of the 99 attributes of God in the Islamic tradition

Rainsabhai Kirtan (Rainsabha-i Keertan): An overnight Gurdwara program

Raita (Raa-itaa): An Indian yogurt/vegetable dish with many variations

Rakhay Rakhanahaar (Rakhay Rakhanahaar): Shabad by Guru Arjan Dev; used as a mantra, especially for protection; one of the Aquarian Sadhana chants

Ram (Raam): Hindu god, an avatar of Vishnu

Ramala (Ramaalaa): Cloth of honor; placed over and under the *Siri Guru Granth Sahib*

Rebec: A lute-like stringed instrument played with a bow

Rehiras Sahib (Reharaas Saahib): Evening Bani; a composite of twenty Shabads by Guru Nanak, Guru Amar Das, Guru Ram Das, Guru Arjan Dev, and Guru Gobind Singh

Rehit (Rahit): Lifestyle; short for Rehit Maryada

Rehit Maryada (Rahit Mari-aadaa): Lifestyle for the Remembrance of Death; the Sikh code of conduct

Rehit Namas (Rahit Naamaas): Lifestyle writings by Guru Gobind Singh and his followers

Reincarnation: The movement of the soul through many lifetimes

Retroflexed Consonants: Consonant sounds made by touching the tongue to the upper palate at the place where the hard and soft palates meet

Rishi (Reeshee): A Himalayan yogi

Rishi (Reeshee) Knot: A tight hair bun worn toward the top of the head—slightly in front of center for men, slightly in back of center for women; named for Rishis who wear them; also worn by Sikhs

Root Lock: Done by pulling up on the anal sphincter muscle and sex organ and at the same time pulling in on the navel; moves excess lower chakra energy to the higher centers; stimulates creativity, inner security, empowerment and self-healing; not recommended for pregnant or menstruating women nor pre-pubescent children

Saa Taa Naa Maa: Literally, *Infinity, Form, Negation, Rebirth*; the Panj Shabad

Sadhana (Saadh'naa): Spiritual practice or discipline

Sadh Sangat (Saadh Sangat): Literally, "Disciplined Congregation"; the Company of the Holy

Sahaj (Sahaj or Sehj): Natural ease and flow

Sahaj Path (Sahaj Paath): Go-at-your-own-pace, beginning-to-end, out loud recitation of the *Siri Guru Granth Sahib* by one person or many

Sahib Chand (Saahib Chand): Name of Sahib Singh before he became the fourth (some say the fifth) original Panj Pi-aaray

Sangat: Congregation

Sat: Truth

Sat Kriya: A signature exercise of Kundalini Yoga that raises the kundalini quickly

Sat Naam: Literally, "Truth Name"; Sikh mantra frequently in Kundalini Yoga, both as an inner focus during exercise and for meditation

Sat Naam, Sat Naam, Sat Naam Jee, Waa Hay Guroo, Waa Hay Guroo, Waa Hay Guroo Jee: *Truth is our Identity, Truth is our Identity, Truth is our Identity, O Soul! Wow! What ecstasy is this Knowledge! Wow! What ecstasy is this Knowledge! Wow! What ecstasy is this Knowledge! O Soul!*; mantra used by Sikhs in meditation and for processions

Sat Sangat: Literally, "True Congregation"

Sat Siri Akaal (Sat Siree Akaal): Literally, *Truth is Great and Undying*; a standard Sikh jaikara; also used as a Sikh greeting

Sat Siree, Siree Akaal, Siree Akaal, Maahaa Akaal, Maahaa Akaal, Sat Naam, Akaal Moorat, Waa Hay Guroo: *Great Truth. Great beyond Death. Great beyond Time. Great Immortality. Great Eternality. Truth is the Identity. Deathless Divine Image. Greatest Ecstasy is this Wisdom.*; Aquarian Sadhana mantra used for deathlessness and Aquarian Age energy

Satinaam: Same as Sat Naam

Satta (Satay): Name of an author in the *Siri Guru Granth Sahib*

Seva (Savyaa): Selfless service; one of the pillars of Sikhism

Seva Panthis (Sayvaa Panthees): Those on the path of selfless service; spiritual descendants of Bhai Kanaiya

Shaastras: Sanskrit knowledge teachings

Shabad: Literally "Word that cuts the ego"; a hymn or song that functions like a mantra

Shabad Guru: That which enlightens through hymns that lock the ecstasy of consciousness into the psyche when recited or sung; the poetic writings and songs that comprise the *Siri Guru Granth Sahib*

Shabad Hazaaray: Literally "Thousand Shabads"; a composite of 7 Shabads by Guru Arjan Dev and Guru Nanak; recited as a morning Bani

Shabad Yoga (Shabad Yogaa): The technology of using Shabads to create specific changes in consciousness

Shiva (Sheevaa): Hindu Destroyer god; also the god of yoga and dance

Sikh (Sikh, but Westerners usually say "Seekh"): Literally "disciple"; follower of the Shabad Guru as embodied in the *Siri Guru Granth Sahib*

Sikh Dharma (Sikh Dharmaa): Sikhism as a spiritual path

Sikhism: The religion of Sikhs

Simran: Remembrance; one of the pillars of Sikhism

Singh: Lion; gender-designator name for Sikh men

Siree: One of the Indian Raags

Siri (Siree or Shree: Infinitely Great; beyond human comprehension

Siri Guru Granth Sahib (Siree or Shree Guroo Granth Saahib): The Sikh Guru; embodiment of the Shabad Guru; scriptures that lock the ecstasy of consciousness into the psyche when recited or sung

Siri Sahib (Siree Saahib): Long sword, usually four feet long

Siri Singh Sahib (Siree Singh Saahib): Yogi Bhajan's title as head of Sikh Dharma in the Western Hemisphere

Slok (Slok or Shlok): Short verse or epigram

Smritis: Semitic texts, including the Torah, the Bible and the Koran; also late Sanskrit texts

Solar Center: The place where we experience Inner Light; the spot that is open in a baby's head, beneath which is the pineal gland, a light-sensitive organ

Soohee: One of the Indian Raags

Sorath: One of the Indian Raags

Sternum: Breast bone

Subconscious: The filter between the conscious and unconscious minds, built of habitual thoughts and actions

Sukhasan (Sukhaasan): Literally "Posture of Peace"; the ceremony of closing the *Siri Guru Granth Sahib*; also its closed state

Sukhmani Sahib (Sukhmanee Saahib): Bani by Guru Arjan Dev; the longest composition in the *Siri Guru Granth Sahib*; often recited by the bereaved

Swaiyaa: See Swaiyay.

Swaiyay: Short verse, usually of four lines; used in songs of praise

Tablas (Taablaas): A pair of drums set in rings on the floor and played by hand

Tai Chi: A Chinese martial arts form practiced for its health benefits

Talwandi (Talwandee): Original name of town in Pakistan where Guru Nanak was born; now known as Nankana

Tav Prasaad Swaiyay: Bani by Guru Gobind Singh; used in the Amrit Ceremony

Third Eye: The point between the eyes and a bit above them; also called the Brow Point

Tune In: Chanting *Ong Naamo, Guroo Dayv Naamo* at the beginning of a Kundalini Yoga session; aligning oneself with the all the masters of Kundalini Yoga

Too Thaakur Tum Peh Ardaas (Too Ṯhaakur Tum Peh Ardaas): *You, O Master, to You I Pray*; Shabad from Sukhmani Sahib by Guru Arjan Dev; recited in Gurdwara before the Ardas

Vaar: Heroic poem, usually of considerable length

Vas Mayray Pi-aari-aa Vas Mayray Govindaa: *Dwell, O My Beloved, Dwell, O My Lord of the Universe*; title of a Shabad

Vedas (Vaydaas): Early Hindu texts

Vedic (Vaydic) Astrology: Astrological system used in India, based on a different Zodiac system than Western Astrology

Vee-aaho Hoaa Mayray Baabulaa: *My Marriage Has Been Performed, O My Father*; closing Shabad of the Anand Karaj, written by Guru Ram Das

Venus Lock: A mudra used in Kundalini Yoga to channel sexual energy, promote glandular balance and focus the mind

Vir Asana (Veer Aasana): Literally "Warrior Pose"; posture used in the Aquarian Sadhana and in the Amrit Ceremony; practiced by sitting on the left heel, with the right knee bent near the heart and the hands together in Prayer Pose

Vishnu (Vishnoo): Hindu Sustainer god

Waa Hay Guroo: Most ecstatic of the Names of God; a mantra

Waa Hay Guroo, Waa Hay Guroo, Waa Hay Guroo, Waa Hay Jeeo: An untranslatable utterance for the ecstasy of the soul in union with God; one of the mantras used in the Aquarian Sadhana

Waa Hay Guru Jee Kaa Khaalsaa, Waa Hay Guru Jee Kee Fateh: *The Pure Ones belong to God. Victory Belongs to God.*; phrase used in Sikh services and also by Amritdari Sikhs as a greeting

Waa Hay Guroo Jeeo: Short for *Waa Hay Guroo, Waa Hay Guroo, Waa Hay Guroo, Waa Hay Jeeo*

Waa Yantee, Kar Yantee, Jag Doot Patee, Aadak It Waahaa, Brahmaadeh Trayshaa Guroo, Ita Waa Hay Guroo: *Great Macroself. Creative Self. All that is creative through time. All that is the Great One. Three aspects of God: Brahma, Vishnu, Shiva. That is Waheguru.*; mantra attributed to Patanjali; an Aquarian Sadhana chant

Wadali (Wadaalee): Village outside Amritsar where Guru Hargobind was born

Waheguru (Waa Hay Guroo): Sikh Name for God; standard spelling of Waa Hay Guroo; mantra for ecstasy

Waheguru Ji Ka Khalsa, Waheguru Ji Ki Fateh (Waa Hay Guru

Jee Kaa Khaalsaa, Waa Hay Guru Jee Kee Fateh): *The Pure Ones belong to God. Victory Belongs to God.*; phrase used in Sikh services and also by Amritdari Sikhs as a greeting

White Tantric Yoga: Powerful and deeply meditative form of yoga practiced in pairs as a group under the direction of the Mahan Tantric only; beneficial for deep subconscious cleansing

Yoga (Yogaa): Union or yoke; activities that promote the experience of Oneness

Yoga Sutras (Yogaa Sutraas): Yogic writings of Patanjali

Yogi (Yogee): Someone who practices yoga

Yogi Bhajan (Yogee Bhajan): Master of Kundalini Yoga and Mahan Tantric; brought Kundalini Yoga and White Tantric Yoga to the West; born August 26, 1929, in what is now Pakistan; died October 6, 2004, in Espanola NM

Yogi Tea: Spice tea made of cloves, cinnamon, cardamom, black pepper, and ginger; also the name of a Sikh-run natural foods beverage company (see Resources), which sells yogi tea mixes in bulk and in tea bags under the name Classic India Spice Tea

Bibliography

AjitSingh, Charanjit K., compiler. (2001) *The Wisdom of Sikhism*. Oxford, England. Oneworld Publications.

Bhajan, Yogi. (2003) *The Aquarian Teacher: K.R.I. International Kundalini Yoga Teacher Training Level I*. Kundalini Research Institute.

Bhajan, Yogi. (1983) *Kundalini Yoga for Youth & Joy*. Eugene, OR. 3HO Transcripts.

Bhajan, Yogi. (1977) *Kundalini Winter Lectures 1977*. Pomona, CA. Kundalini Research Institute.

Bhajan, Yogi. (1998) *The Mind: Its Projections and Multiple Facets*. Espanola, NM. Kundalini Research Institute.

Bhajan, Yogi. (2000) *Self-Experience*. Espanola, NM. Kundalini Research Institute.

Bhajan, Yogi. (1978) *Slim & Trim: Kundalini Yoga Exercises and Meditations Especially for Women*. Pomona, CA. K.R.I. Publications.

Bhajan, Yogi. "There's More to Mantra Than Meets the Ear," *The Science of Keeping Up*, Fall/Winter 2000.

Bhajan, Yogi. (1986) *Women in Training IX 1984: The Art and Science of the Successful Woman*. Eugene, OR. 3HO Transcripts.

Contractor, Farzana. "At the Golden Temple, There's Always a Meal for the Hungry," *Upper Crust*, October-December 2001.

Crowder, Dena, M.A. "The Eighty Fourth Step," *Aquarian Times*, Spring 2002, p.44-5.

Duggal, K.S. (1993) Sikh Gurus: Their Lives & Teachings. New Delhi. UBS Publishers' Distributors Ltd.

Guru for the Aquarian Age: The Life and Teachings of Guru Nanak. (1996) Santa Cruz, NM. Yogi Ji Press.

Kaur, Bibiji Inderjit, Ph.D. "My Husband," *Aquarian Times*, Winter 2005, p.16-9.

Kaur, Bibiji Inderjit, compiler. (N.D.) *Shabad Kirtan: The Songs and Hymns of Sikh Dharma*. Los Angeles.

Kaur, Bibiji Inderjit, compiler. (N.D.) *The Psyche of the Golden Shield: Treasures of the Sikh Scriptures*. Los Angeles.

"Karsewa," *The Times of India*, August 5, 2004.

Khalsa, Atma Singh, and Khalsa, Guruprem Kaur. (2001) *Meditations for the New Millennium: 2001*. Santa Cruz, NM. Yoga Gems. This is actually a CD-Rom.

Khalsa, Bhai Sahib Guruliv Singh. (1982) *Japji of Guru Nanak: A Complete Annotated Word-by-Word Translation*. Los Angeles. G. T. International.

Khalsa, Bibiji Inderjit Kaur, Ph.D. (N.D.) *Living Reality*. Chheharta, Amritsar. Miri Piri Academy.

Khalsa, Bibiji Inderjit Kaur, Ph.D. (N.D.) *Sri Guru Granth Sahib Darshan*. Chheharta, Amritsar. Miri Piri Academy.

Khalsa, Gurudass Singh. "A Joyful Noise," *Aquarian Times*, Winter 2005, p.66-71.

Khalsa, Guru Fatha Singh. *Messenger from the Guru's House*. Unpublished biography of Yogi Bhajan.

Khalsa, Guru Singh. "My First Turban," *Aquarian Times*, Winter 2005, p.14-5.

Khalsa, Guru Terath Kaur, Ph.D. (2006) *Dying Into Life: The Yoga of Death, Loss and Transformation*. Santa Cruz, NM. Guru Ram Das Books.

Khalsa, Har Darshan Kaur. "The Marriage of the Soul Bride with Her Lord: The Passing of Amrit Kaur Khalsa, Knoxville, TN," *Prosperity Paths*, May, 1997.

Khalsa, S.S. Sant Singh, M.D., translator. (N.D.) *Sundar Gutkaa*. Tucson. Hand Made Books.

Khalsa, Sat Jiwan Singh. "A Sikh Is Judged," *Aquarian Times*, Winter 2005, p.23.

Khalsa, Sat Nam Kaur. "Facing Fear with Faith," *Aquarian Times*, Fall 2003, p.28-9.

Khalsa, S.S. Shanti Kaur. (1995) *The History of Sikh Dharma of the Western Hemisphere*. Espanola, NM. Sikh Dharma

Publications.

Khalsa, Shanti Shanti Kaur, Ph.D., "What Happens When We Die Consciously?" *Aquarian Times*, Fall 2003, p.35-7.

Khalsa, Siri Kirpal Kaur. (2002) *Yoga for Prosperity*. Santa Cruz, NM. Yogi Ji Press.

Khalsa, S. S. Snatam Kaur. March 31, 2003. "Community Sadhana for the Aquarian Age." (Unpublished.)

Kundalini Yoga Sadhana Guidelines, 2nd ed. (2007) Santa Cruz, NM. Kundalini Research Institute.

Macauliffe, Max Arthur. (1909, reprinted 2000) *The Sikh Religion*. Amritsar. Satvic Media Pvt. Ltd.

Singh, Bhai Ranjit. "A Miracle During World War II," *Prosperity Paths*, February 1999.

Singh, Gopal, Dr., translator. (1984) *Sri Guru-Granth Sahib: English Version*. New Delhi. World Sikh Centre Inc.

Singh, Jasprit and Theresa. (1998) *Style of the Lion: The Sikhs*. Ann Arbor, MI. Akal Publications.

Singh, Manmohan, translator. (1962-1969) *Sri Guru Granth Sahib (English & Punjabi Translation)*. Amritsar. Shiromani Gurdwara Parbandhak Committee.

Singh, Santokh, Dr. (2000) *The Guru's Word & Illustrated Sikh History*. Princeton, Ontario, Canada. Spiritual Awakening Studies.

Stern, Jess. (1965) *Yoga, Youth, and Reincarnation*. New York. Doubleday & Company, Inc.

Takhar, Gurkirat Singh. (1997) *The History of Sikhism (Guru Nanak Dev to Guru Gobind Singh)*. Surrey, BC, Canada. Kirpal Singh Dhaliwal.

Victory & Virtue: Ceremonies & Code of Conduct of Sikh Dharma. (1995) Espanola, New Mexico. The Office of the Bhai Sahiba of Sikh Dharma of the Western Hemisphere.

Yogananda, Paramahansa. (1946) *Autobiography of a Yogi*. Los Angeles. Self-Realization Fellowship.

Yogiji, Siri Singh Sahib Bhai Sahib Harbhajan Singh Khalsa &

Khalsa, Bhai Sahiba Sardarni Sahiba Bibiji Inderjit Kaur. (1993) *Psyche of the Soul*. Tucson. Hand Made Books.

Resources

Sources for Books, Tapes, CDs & Videos:

Ancient Healing Ways
39 Shady Lane
Espanola NM 87532
Phone (Retail Orders):1-800-359-2940
Phone (Local & International Orders): 505-747-2860
Phone (Wholesale Orders): 1-877-753-5351
Fax: (505) 747-9718
Email: customerservice@a-healing.com
www.a-healing.com
*

Sat Nam Versand
www.satnam.de
*

Spirit Voyage Music
Toll-free: 1-888-735-4800
Fax: 703-935-8297
Email: info@spiritvoyage.com
www.spiritvoyage.com
*

Yoga Technology
PO Box 443
Sunbury PA 17801
24-Hour Phone and Fax: 1-570-988-4680
Toll-free: 1-866-YOGATEC (964-2832)
www.yogatech.com
*

To Locate a KRI Certified Kundalini Yoga Teacher Near You:
International Kundalini Yoga Teachers Association
6 Narayan Ct.

Espanola NM 87532
Phone: (505) 376-1313
Fax: (505) 753-1999
Email: ikyta@3ho.org
www.kundaliniyoga.com
*

For 3HO Events and Information:
3HO Foundation
6 Narayan Ct.
Espanola NM 87532
Phone: 1-888-346-2420
Email: yogainfo@3ho.org
www.3ho.org
www.whitetantricyoga.com
www.yogafestival.org
*

To Request a Sikh Spiritual Name:
spiritualnames.3ho.org
*

Useful Sikh and 3HO Websites:
www.sikhnet.com
www.sikhseek.com
www.sikhdharma.org
www.sikhitothemax.com
www.sgpc.net
www.dasvandh.org
www.kriteachings.org
www.ourtruetales.com
www.lighttravel.org
*

Websites of People or Organizations in this Book:
www.aquariantimes.com
www.drdharma.com
www.grdcenter.org

www.gurufathasingh.com

www.gurusingh.com

www.interfaithprayer.org

www.kundaliniyogaeast.com

www.lotusproject.com

www.peaceweek.com

www.sevatheworld.com

www.sikhcoalition.org

www.snatam.com

www.unitedsikhs.org

www.uppercrustindia.com

www.yogaforyouth.org

www.yogibhajan.org

www.yogitea.com

www.yogawesteugene.com

Acknowledgements

Many people helped me with this book. My life is much richer for all the inspiration given by the greater Sikh *sangat* over the years. Many people have shared their lives and thoughts with me in ways that contributed subtly and anonymously—or very obviously—to this book.

In particular, I am grateful to S.S. Guru Fatha Singh Khalsa, Gurupurkh Kaur Khalsa, M.S.S. Guru Singh Khalsa, S.S. Har Darshan Kaur Khalsa, S.S. Krishna Singh Khalsa, Meherbani Kaur Khalsa, Ravi Singh Khalsa & Dya Kaur Khalsa, Ravitej Singh Khalsa, S.S. Sat Hanuman Singh Khalsa, S.S. Sat Jiwan Singh Khalsa, S. S. Sat Kirpal Kaur Khalsa, Sat Pavan Kaur Khalsa, Satya Kaur Khalsa, Siri Kaur Khalsa Harris, S.S. Snatam Kaur Khalsa, Sukhmani Kaur Khalsa and Viriam Kaur Khalsa for sharing their stories.

Navneet Kaur, God bless her, provided invaluable help with the glossary. My thanks to Tej Kaur Khalsa for invaluable database searches. My thanks also to Harpreet Singh of UNITED SIKHS and the humanitarian work of that organization. I am also grateful to Rev. Butterfly Wright, Harpreet Singh of Sikh Coalition, Heminder Singh, Jasmit Singh of Sikh Coalition, Pritam Rohila, S.S. Sat Jiwan Kaur Khalsa, Sat Siri Kaur Khalsa, and Sohan Singh Johal for sharing information. God bless you all!

The spirit of the late Siri Singh Sahib Bhai Sahib Harbhajan Singh Khalsa Yogiji (better known as Yogi Bhajan) informs this book more deeply and subtly than I could ever hope to convey. What a gift to have such a Teacher!

God bless the following song writers who graciously permitted the use of their lyrics: M.S.S. Livtar Singh Khalsa for permission to use the Song of the Khalsa, M.S.S. Guru Singh Khalsa for permission to use Rise Up, S.S. Gurudass Singh Khalsa for permission to use a portion of the Sikh National Anthem.

A very special thank you to John Hunt of O Books for taking the risk to publish this opus. And to Parmatma Singh Khalsa for permission to reuse material from my first book, *Yoga for Prosperity*.

I was so blessed to take the Journey to the Heart of Sikh Dharma class, which provided much inspiration for this book. S.S. Mata Mandir Kaur Khalsa and all the students and presenters provided a great deal of inspiration for this book, and helped cheer me on. My love to all of you.

I am deeply grateful for inspiration provided by Sukhmani Kaur Khalsa (Dr. Theresa Merrill).

I am also grateful to Ravitej Singh Khalsa for the photography and to Hari Rai Kaur Khalsa, Himat Singh Khalsa, Shivraj Kaur Khalsa and Siri Anand Singh Khalsa for modeling the Kundalini Yoga postures and meditations.

A big thank you to Paul De Angelis for major editorial assistance.

I am most humbly grateful to Guru Gobind Singh and Mata Sahib Kaur—the spiritual parents of all Khalsa Sikhs—for accepting my head and granting me this huge beloved spiritual family.

I am also deeply grateful for those nameless persons who helped put me on this path, then left it themselves.

My mother, Shirley Katharyne Dyer Sykes, fed me big words with my pabulum and thereby instilled in me a love of language and the Word. She also provided some editorial assistance. My love to her and to my biological brothers, Paul Frederick Sykes and Charles Arthur Sykes, and their families.

And God bless Jim Waldon, my favorite sounding board, who husbands me and provides love, support, encouragement and much tech support for the computer. All love forever.

Beyond All, God bless God for putting me on this path, for choosing to write this book through me, and for creating everyone else on this list. *Waheguru!*

B O O K S

O is a symbol of the world, of oneness and unity. In different cultures it also means the "eye," symbolizing knowledge and insight. We aim to publish books that are accessible, constructive and that challenge accepted opinion, both that of academia and the "moral majority."

Our books are available in all good English language bookstores worldwide. If you don't see the book on the shelves ask the bookstore to order it for you, quoting the ISBN number and title. Alternatively you can order online (all major online retail sites carry our titles) or contact the distributor in the relevant country, listed on the copyright page.

See our website www.o-books.net for a full list of over 500 titles, growing by 100 a year.

And tune in to myspiritradio.com for our book review radio show, hosted by June-Elleni Laine, where you can listen to the authors discussing their books.

MySpiritRadio